CUSTOMS AND CULTURES

CUSTOMS
AND CULTURES

Anthropology for Christian Missions

EUGENE A. NIDA

HARPER & BROTHERS, NEW YORK

CUSTOMS AND CULTURES

Copyright, 1954, by Harper & Brothers
Printed in the United States of America
All rights in this book are reserved.
No part of the book may be used or reproduced
in any manner whatsoever without written permission
except in the case of
brief quotations embodied in critical articles and reviews.
For information address
Harper & Brothers
49 East 33rd Street, New York 16, N. Y.

FIRST EDITION
I–D

LIBRARY OF CONGRESS CATALOG CARD NUMBER: 54-8976

To my wife

CONTENTS

Good missionaries have always been good "anthropologists." Not only have they been aware of human needs, whether stemming from the local way of life or from man's universal need of salvation, but they have recognized that the various ways of life of different peoples are the channels by which their needs take form and through which the solutions to such needs must pass. Effective missionaries have always sought to immerse themselves in a profound knowledge of the ways of life of the people to whom they have sought to minister, since only by such an understanding of the indigenous culture could they possibly communicate a new way of life. On the other hand, some missionaries have been only "children of their generation" and have carried to the field a distorted view of race and progress, culture and civilization, Christian and non-Christian ways of life. During some ten years as Secretary for Translations of the American Bible Society, I have become increasingly conscious of the tragic mistakes in cultural orientation which not only express themselves directly and indirectly in translations of the Scriptures but in the general pattern of missionary work. Accordingly, this treatment of *Anthropology for Christian Missions* is directed to those who may have been unaware of the invaluable assistance which the science of anthropology can provide or who have become desirous of knowing more of its implications in various parts of the world.

A high percentage of the data in this book comes from copious field notes collected during travel in about fifty different countries of the world. In citing praiseworthy achievements by missionaries, I have indicated the precise tribe or area, but in making adverse comments I have purposely not designated the region (though this information can be provided to those who have special reasons for inquiry), since nothing would be gained by appearing to criticize unduly the work of consecrated and well-meaning persons. Data coming from published sources have been cited in footnotes where such information is of an extensive nature or where it has seemed valuable to call the reader's attention to other literature in order to encourage further reading. In general, the literature, rather than original sources, is cited, since the literature is available in most libraries while the original sources exist only in relatively few places and they are often in foreign languages unknown to the average reader. Often repeated anthropological data, such as those concerning the Todas of South India, the Aranda of Australia, and the Polar Eskimos, have not been footnoted, since such data may be verified in several sources and they are frequently referred to in the literature.

It is generally the practice in books on anthropology to describe aboriginal societies in the present tense, as though the distinctive cultures were fully intact. We have attempted, in so far as possible, to indicate something of the breakdown of old patterns by the use of past tense forms when the cultural traits no longer exist or are only "historic relics." However, since in many societies the former dominant ways of life are in process of transition, it is very difficult to do justice to the present tempo or stage of change and to be completely accurate in all details, for obsolescence is not a uniform process. Nevertheless, it has seemed preferable to employ this type of wording, despite some slight inaccuracies not covered by qualifying adverbs or footnotes, than to commit the worse error of failing to recognize the transitory character of many of the passing traits.

In a book of this nature, which is directed to a popular audience, it has been both impossible and inadvisable to attempt to make comprehensive analyses of various culture traits, either within a single culture or in their world-wide distribution. Hence, there are a number of omissions of data well known to anthropologists. However, in the selection of the data presented here, I have endeavored to choose illustrations which would be relevant from the missionary standpoint, even though they might be less well known in anthropological literature. Because of the introductory character of this presentation of anthropology, I have purposely tried to avoid lengthy discussions of anthropological principles and procedures, hoping that the point would be adequately made by the illustrations themselves. In order not to load the text down with too many technical details or discourses on relevant but somewhat tangential themes, I have included a number of important matters in the footnotes. The reader is urged to follow the footnotes carefully during the reading of the various sections.

An Appendix has been added in order to give some elementary help to students and missionaries as to how they may most profitably proceed to acquire further background in cultural anthropology and how they may gather and classify field data, as an aid to the solving of missionary problems.

It is quite impossible to make proper acknowledgment to the scores of persons who have directly and indirectly contributed to this book, for all the many missionaries and Christian workers whom I have met in various parts of the world have provided the data and background without which such a book as this would be impossible. However, I am particularly indebted to the following persons who have read the manuscript and have offered many valuable suggestions for improvements: Ming C. Chao, Grace Gabler, Margaret T. Hills, Paul V. Leser, William and Marie (Fetzer) Reyburn, Ellen M. Ross, William A. Smalley, Robert B. Taylor, Paul Verghese, G. Henry Waterman, and William H. Wonderly.

Although the evaluation of missionary work may at times appear to be critical, we do not wish to give the impression that the missionary enterprise is basically harmful or generally unsympathetic to human needs. Despite all their limitations there has been no more genuinely altruistic endeavor in the last 150 years than Protestant foreign missions. No one needs to apologize for the selfless devotion which has not imposed itself by threat or force but has endeavored to bring to people the knowledge of redeeming love in Christ Jesus and a way of life which they may make their own if they choose to do so.

Some of the data incorporated in this book have been given in lecture series: at Princeton Theological Seminary (1950), Wheaton College, Wheaton, Illinois (1951), Summer Institute of Linguistics (1949–51, 1953), the Payton Lectures (1953) at Fuller Theological Seminary, and the Carew Lectures (1953) at the Hartford Seminary Foundation.

EUGENE A. NIDA

New York
September, 1954

SHOCKS AND SURPRISES

"But we are not going to have our wives dress like prostitutes," protested an elder in the Ngbaka church in northern Congo, as he
replied to the suggestion made by the missionary that the women
should be required to wear blouses to cover their breasts. The
church leaders were unanimous in objecting to such a requirement,
for in that part of Congo the well-dressed and fully-dressed African
women were too often prostitutes, since they alone had the money
to spend on attractive garments. Different peoples are in wide dis-
agreement as to the amount or type of clothes required by modesty.
Not long ago one of the chiefs in the Micronesian island of Yap
forbade any woman coming into the town with a blouse. However,
he insisted that all women would have to wear grass skirts reaching
almost to the ankles. To the Yapese way of thinking, bare legs are
a sign of immodesty, while the uncovered breasts are perfectly
proper.[1]

Some years ago a missionary in the Philippines was particularly
disgusted when his first guests dusted off the living-room chairs with
their handkerchiefs and spread them on the seats before sitting
down. To make matters worse they had no more than seated themselves at the dining table (after similarly dusting the chairs) when
they took the napkins and wiped off the dishes and silverware. This
missionary could scarcely contain himself. "What an affront to my
wife's housekeeping!" he thought to himself. But he soon learned
that their behavior was perfectly polite. In fact, it was the "cultured"
thing to do. The missionary's problem was that he had carried with
him the cultural patterns of his own home town and was not pre-

pared for the shock of different standards. The behavior of the Filipino guests seemed completely out of place. What was really out of place was the missionary's reaction.

Fully equipped with our own sets of values, of which we are largely unconscious, we sally forth in the world and automatically see behavior with glasses colored by our own experience. We may judge some Africans as childish because they will go hungry in order to buy squeaky shoes, which they carry on their heads to the edge of town and then proudly and loudly (the squeakier the better) march into town. However, there are perhaps an equally large number of persons in America who deprive themselves of adequate food, proper housing, and needed education in order to ride around in heavily mortgaged Cadillacs. We laugh when we see African chieftains broiling in the sun, dressed in heavy cast-off army overcoats. But I have participated in wedding parties in August in Oklahoma, where I am sure that for the sake of custom the guests were every bit as uncomfortable as any wool-clad chief in Congo. We are amused at the ostentatious manner in which some local chief may wear his badge, presented by a colonial official; but what salesman can succeed in selling a double-breasted coat to a Phi Beta Kappa member? Even the Greeks seem to us rather silly for parading home after athletic contests decorated with olive branches or parsley wreaths. We just don't do that, but we have ribbons of various shapes, sizes, and colors—not to speak of cups and trophies which are of no earthly use, except to catch dust and to provide a market for metal polish.

When some of our perfectly normal customs are transported into other parts of the world, they too appear utterly ridiculous. In one hospital in Congo, situated in an area where the women wear only a tuft of leaves in front and behind, it is the practice for the American doctor and nurse quickly to cover the patients with a sheet before examining them in the prenatal clinic. No doubt the sheet is regarded by the patients as being every bit as effective as any prenatal advice or medication. In another part of Africa, where the Negro men have their bodies smeared with red ochre but wear absolutely nothing except a string of beads around their necks, the wife of a missionary thought that her husband's shorts (regular British military shorts, reaching almost to the knees) were not quite long enough. Accordingly, she sewed on three-inch strips of pink cloth, so that his knees would be covered when he sat down. Just who would have been shocked by the exposed knees is hard to determine, but these shorts provided amusement for nearby British officialdom and utterly perplexed the Africans.

Perhaps we should contrast our own ideas about clothes with those of a Shilluk evangelist speaking to his people in the central part of the Anglo-Egyptian Sudan, "You must not think that you cannot attend church just because you have no clothes to wear. The Good News is not about clothes, and God is no respecter of persons." This does not mean that missionaries are not or should not be sensitive to the need of people being adequately clothed, but perhaps the attitude of one Mennonite missionary best expresses the sane and sensible approach. She was asked by a devout friend in a church at home, "My sister, do you teach the doctrine of the plain clothes?" To which the missionary replied, "Why, we are fortunate if they wear any clothes."

It is impossible to judge or understand the customs of others unless we appreciate their point of view. It seems very silly that in a Christian hospital in Chiengmai, Thailand, women cannot be put in second-floor rooms and men in first-floor rooms. But this simply is not done, for that would put women above men. One does not cross one's legs in Thailand and show the bottom of the foot to anyone. This would be a real insult and show very bad taste. This does not mean that the Thai people are queer—no, they are just different. Such behavior is part of the entire pattern of Thai life and has just as much validity as our habit of letting women go through doors ahead of men.

In some instances behavior may even seem to us to be bordering on insanity. Maurice Leenhardt cites the incident of a New Caledonian woman who would appear to take from her basket some invisible white rats, speak to them tenderly and caress them.[2] We would regard such a person as a fit patient for a mental institution, and yet the woman was engaging in a kind of spiritual communion with a totemic animal (the rat represented her family line). This type of incident can be paralleled by what happened to an Indian student in one of the large universities of the United States. This young man is a very devout Christian, whose family have for centuries been members of the Church of Saint Thomas in South India. As it was his practice to pray kneeling and audibly before going to bed, he did so the first evening in the dormitory. His American roommate came into the room and was startled, for he had never seen a person kneeling in prayer before. He immediately inquired if the Indian were sick and if he wanted to go to the hospital. When the Indian explained that he was praying, the American student suggested that he probably needed to consult a psychiatrist.

Even what passes in one generation for piety in our own culture may be condemned as neurotic by another generation. Certainly, some of the witch-hunting of Puritan times had a neurotic flavor to it and some aspects of the Inquisition can scarcely be classified as anything but culturally sanctioned sadism. Self-torturing complexes exhibited and cultivated by Medieval "saints" are quite out of line with our concepts of the healthy spiritual life. Future generations may find some of our pet ideas and behavior equally unjustifiable and exotic.

It is easy for us to label as "savage" a jungle Indian tribe such as the Ayore of Bolivia on the basis that they sometimes bury sick people alive. Although they are unacquainted with isolation techniques in hospitals, they have learned by sad experience how certain diseases spread with terrifying speed and destructiveness. Burying the sick alive is a kind of protection for society.[3] Some people have regarded the Chols of southern Mexico as being calloused because they laugh when they receive some tragic news, even as they broke out in riotous laughter when a missionary told them the story of the beheading of John the Baptist. They explained that they felt so sorry for John the Baptist they just had to laugh in order to keep from crying. This is quite a different viewpoint from ours, but it does have its own justification.

The Shipibos in the eastern jungles of Peru have been known to capture Cashibo children and educate them. After being taught the superior arts of the Shipibo, they are sent back to their own Cashibos, with the hope that they will help the Cashibos raise their standard of living. This kind of "missionary" work is not much different from the idea of the "White Man's Burden," a kind of self-gratifying and self-rewarding paternalism which was cited as the moral justification for colonialism by Western Europe. The Shipibos are condemned for kidnaping, while Western powers have prided themselves on "civilizing the primitive peoples."

Differences of culture can result in serious misunderstandings. There is nothing quite so aggravating as someone's failure to appreciate a gift or a kindness. Perhaps calculated lack of appreciation is nowhere further developed than in Korea. Of course, many Koreans are very thankful for gifts and expressions of kindness, but more often than not there is the well-developed concept, coming from Buddhism, that it is the giver rather than the recipient who should be thankful, since the recipient has provided a means by which the giver may gain merit through the gift or favor. This seems to reverse all the ideas of human relationships, and yet it is a real part of Oriental thinking.

Failure to understand the other person's reactions may work both ways. During World War II the bitterest pill which some prisoners of war and civilian internees in the Orient had to take was the everlasting bowing to Japanese officials. For an American, bowing implies complete subservience, almost a kind of worship. To the Japanese it was purely a matter of social respect. When, however, some enthusiastic young missionaries went to Japan after the war, they reported mass conversions of the Japanese, who readily bowed in response to rather poorly understood appeals for loyalty to Jesus Christ. It turned out that the bowing was in many instances more a response to the authority of American occupation than to any religious commitment to Christ.

Differences of culture can give rise to behavior which is inexplicable apart from the context of the people's lives. Early missionaries to the Marshall Islands in the central Pacific received their mail once a year when the sailing boat made its rounds of the South

Pacific. On one occasion the boat was one day ahead of schedule, and the missionaries were off on a neighboring island. The captain left the mail with the Marshallese people while he attended to matters of getting stores of water and provisions. At last the Marshallese were in possession of what the missionaries spoke about so often and apparently cherished so much. The people examined the mail in order to find out what was so attractive about it. They concluded that it must be good to eat, and so they proceeded to tear all the letters into tiny bits and to cook them. However, they didn't taste very good, and the Marshallese were still puzzled about the missionaries' strange interest in mail when the missionaries returned to find their year's correspondence made into mush. The Marshallese were not childish, they were just investigative in terms of the only frame of reference which made any sense to them. One missionary in Mexico was objecting strongly to an Indian's spitting on the dirt floor of the dining room by saying, "We don't do that. It is not sanitary. It's dirty." To which the Indian replied quite logically, "Yes, señorita, but the ground outside is just as dirty." How can one possibly teach people that diseases are caused by microbes that cannot be seen when the people believe that such diseases are caused by spirits and ghosts which they all declare they have seen?

It is too easy for us to regard another person's reasoning as illogical, artificial, and immature. Reasoning consists simply in judging new experiences in terms of accumulated experience. Hence, a Buddhist in Thailand was not entirely illogical in replying to a question as to what he thought about the Gospels and Acts. "Oh, they are wonderful!" he exclaimed. "Why, here is the story of a man who lived and died, then he lived and died, then he lived and died, then he lived and died, and then he arrived at Nirvana. Just think, he made it in four reincarnations. What a person!" This man had read the Gospels and Acts in order; and being quite convinced of the doctrine of reincarnations, he had interpreted the Four Gospels as being the accounts of four successive lives, not four descriptions of a single life. Then in contrast with Buddha, who is popularly thought to have gained Nirvana only after some 1,000

reincarnations, this man Jesus apparently made it in four. No
wonder the Buddhist was deeply impressed, even though he was
badly mistaken.

In considering the relationships between people and cultures,
we tend to regard ourselves as the only ones who make judgments—
or at least accurate ones. We must not forget for a moment that
other peoples make judgments of us, and that some of them are
not too complimentary. The Tarahumara people in northern Mexico
do not hesitate to classify themselves as "sons of God" and everyone else in the world as "sons of the devil." It is all very simple
for the Tarahumaras; and judging from the way foreigners behave
in their part of the world, they have some very valid reasons for
such an opinion. The tall, lanky Dinkas who stroll naked into the
Arab towns along the upper Nile are generally quite contemptuous
both of the Arabs and of the Europeans. Dinkas regard themselves
as being quite superior. As for height there is no question, for most
of the men tower head and shoulders above white men. But they
also regard their family and clan structure as superior, and they
consider themselves better behaved—at least they do not get so
violently drunk nor do they fight such devastating wars. At one
time during World War II, a delegation of Congolese in Ubangi
called on a missionary for an explanation of what they had heard,
for they had received reports of the thousands upon thousands who
had been killed. Their frank question was, "How can the people in
Europe eat so much meat?" Furthermore, they could not understand
the killing of women and children—to them an incredible act of
barbarism.

More than one person has reported the reaction of foreigners who
regard the three sacred things in America to be the turkey, the
Christmas tree, and Santa Claus—to which should probably be
added the Easter bunny. However, some Navajos have had very
good reason for misinterpreting the white man's religion. In speaking of God early missionaries insisted on using only the English
word "God," which spoken in Navajo is easily confused with the
Navajo word for "juniper bush." Since the Navajos regarded similar objects as holy and since they sometimes saw white men at

Christmas time decorating juniper bushes (where fir trees were scarce), there was good reason to think that this religion was just one dealing with juniper bushes. We can scarcely blame some Chinese who have thought that missionaries worshiped chairs, for in prayer they always knelt in front of one.

Reasoning is not solely the property of Western culture. It is true that our accumulated experience makes it possible for us in some instances to arrive at more verifiable results, but we must not be harsh with those who use the best judgment they have and who may nevertheless reach quite wrong conclusions. Two single lady missionaries were working among the Pame-Chichimec Indians in central Mexico. They were very circumspect in their behavior, but this did not impress the Indians at all. The Indians assumed that like all other young women these also had their lovers but that they succeeded in preventing pregnancy by drinking limeade every morning for breakfast. As far as the missionaries were concerned, this was for their general health, but in the eyes of the people it was to produce abortion, for lime juice is called in the Pame-Chichimec language "baby killer." The value of any object or action cannot be determined without considering the cultural context. In fact, its value or function is only in terms of such a context. Because of the teaching of some of the early missionaries, many of the Christian women on Ponape, an island in Micronesia, associate the Mother Hubbard garments only with church and religion. Hence, they carry their long, cumbersome garments to church, put them on just before arrival, and then take them off again before starting home. This is somewhat similar to our dressing up in our "Sunday best."

Judgments critical of the white man are not solely the result of failure to appreciate our way of life or our habits. For one thing, we as members of the white race often have a very obnoxious odor, in other words, B.O. It is true that other races also have characteristic odors, but in general offensiveness we are probably the greatest "stinkers." (Anyone unconvinced of this should go on a hot day into a poorly ventilated locker room in a large gymnasium.) The Thai people were utterly shocked to get hygiene books published in America saying that one should take a bath at least once a week. A Thai who does not bathe twice a day is not regarded as fit for human society. Some Oriental students in America have had to get separate rooms because they simply could not stand the offensive odor of their roommates.

White people abroad have often acted with consummate bigotry and pride, and this has not recommended either them or their kind to the people. Some missionaries have not been guiltless of overbearing paternalism, and it is not entirely without reason that some Malayalam speakers in India make a pun of the word for "missionary" and change it slightly into "poisonous tiger." One South Indian teaching in Ethiopia so incurred the displeasure of a student that the latter denounced him vehemently, finally calling him a "missionary," the worst thing he could think of. Such antimissionary outbursts are by no means the rule, but they do come as a shock to one who may have been deluded into thinking that all the "pagans" would be standing with outstretched arms to receive the newcomer to their shores.

It is the easiest thing in the world to make a superficial judgment about other people, based entirely upon one's own set of unconsciously acquired mores. One does not expect to find women sitting in church with pipes in their mouths, nor men with hats on their heads. But that is exactly what one finds in some of the churches in the San Blas Islands along the Caribbean coast of eastern Panama. Many San Blas women take up pipe smoking as they get older and the men regard the wearing of hats inside a community building as quite proper. I asked the missionary, Dr. Alcibiades Iglesias, himself a San Blas, just what all this meant, and if he ever preached against such things. "Why, no," he said, "I have so many other things more important to talk about than pipes and hats"—and he does (this attitude, in fact, is the secret of his outstanding work in the islands). On the other hand, a missionary in Congo took quite a different attitude toward a fad which spread through the congregation, namely, mixing crushed mothballs with palm oil and using the preparation as a kind of cologne or perfume. Such a practice was condemned as both "worldly" and "unbecoming," and so persons who came to church were sniffed at and then refused entrance if they smelled of mothballs. These same people had received some cheap plastic combs as a Christmas present from some churches in America. However, the combs were entirely too flimsy to be used in combing their tight kinky hair, and so naturally the only possible value that the people could see in them was as a decoration. Why not wear them to church, since they were gifts from Christians in America? But this too was forbidden as being improper, and the combs were collected at the door, or the people were turned away from church.[4]

Such strong objections to mothball cologne and colorful plastic combs are fortunately the exceptions to the rule, but they do point out the necessity of viewing customs objectively and in terms of the local situation. There is no fundamental difference between Africans using palm oil with mothballs and our employing Parisian colognes, or between their colorful combs and our fancy hats. It is not intrinsically a matter of morals that Japanese pull a saw and we push one, or that we take off our hats when we go into church while in the Near East men take off their shoes when they go into a mosque. Often what is done in one part of the world simply is not done in another, and what is a matter of respect (and reverence) in one place is regarded as both silly and meaningless in another. Such actions in themselves are nothing. What counts is the value attached to them by the particular culture.

Our difficulty is that too often we fail to understand another value system because we suffer from shortsightedness imposed upon us by familiarity with our own way of life. We would not hesitate to pass persons on the road or path, but a Shilluk of the Anglo-Egyptian Sudan would never think of doing so without coughing or in some way making his presence known, after which he would say, "I am here, I beg the road." To this the polite reply would be, "God send you on." Likewise a Shilluk would never think of offering a person anything with one hand. It must always be with two, for to offer anything to a person with one hand is to treat him as a dog. Perhaps this does not make sense to us, but it does to him. In such a little matter as pointing to something, there may be quite different techniques with very different interpretations. I committed a real *faux pas* in northern Congo because I pointed to things with my finger when I was asking for the words in a language which I was trying to analyze. I was soon told that such a gesture was lewd and vulgar. To be polite, I had to point by sticking out my lower lip. But neither a pointed finger nor an extended lower lip is polite on Ponape. On this Micronesian island one must squint with the eye at the object to which one wishes attention drawn. There are many different ways of accomplishing the same ends, and different people choose to employ different methods. Perhaps it is a little wrong to say "choose," for the individuals involved have relatively little choice in the matter; the culture in which they live has largely settled such matters for them. Nevertheless, we can speak of the particular culture as having chosen one or another method of accomplishing some end. The methods employed by other peoples seem to us to be very clumsy, while ours of course appear very efficient. Whenever a person is tempted to make such a judgment, he should stop just a moment and see whether it is possible that he is guilty of ethnocentric complacency or pride. There is much which we have learned from so-called primitive peoples, and there is still much we could learn. The remarkable ability of Marshallese sailors to cross hundreds of miles of open ocean and find tiny islands which rise only a few feet above the surface of the vast ocean is not magic, even though it seems closely related to it. These men navigate by studying the wave patterns in the open sea, the large prevailing rolls, the more recent waves of heavy storms, the lighter waves of daily breezes, and the backlash of waves which have beat upon distant islands and have been reflected over miles of open sea.[5] Such keenness of perception and careful calculation are not to be depreciated.

It is all too easy for us to view with disdain the primitive surroundings in which the Shipibos live in the jungles of Peru and to regard the condition of Spanish-speaking Peruvians in the small towns along the Ucayali as being considerably better—all because their mode of life corresponds more closely to ours. However, on the whole the Indians eat better, have better health, enjoy a more rewarding social life, and are far better adjusted to each other and to their environment than are the Spanish-speaking Peruvians.

Simplicity or primitiveness in one phase of culture is no proof that other phases may not be very complex. The fact that people appear to have a rather simple material culture, such as to live in thatched houses, ride in dugout canoes, and live primarily on bananas and coconuts, is no evidence that they are lacking in social organization or morality. The San Blas Indians of Panama are outstanding for their relatively high moral standards—in fact the non-Christian San Blas compare very favorably in sexual morality with Christian congregations in America. In matters of honesty and capacity for community living (as many as a thousand may be crowded into the space of about one city block) they far excel us.[6]

One phase of life in which we of the Western world seem to be deficient in comparison with some other peoples is our judgment of character. Perhaps we study books so much that we are deceived more easily by life situations. One missionary in central Africa was sick for a long period. Numerous doctors examined her, but none seemed to be able to tell exactly what the trouble was, though they suggested that the missionary was suffering from various physical maladies. At last, she returned to the States. She had no more than left when an old African woman remarked quite casually, "Why, it is unhappiness which makes some people sick." Later study of the missionary's case revealed that the African woman was completely right, but it took the combined efforts of several doctors and psychiatrists to arrive at the same conclusion. Africans often reveal their keen judgment of human nature in the nicknames which they give new missionaries or government officials. Such names as "Father-take-it-easy," "Mother-peace," "Mr. Talks-talks," and "Mr. Thinks-first" are all penetrating and accurate descriptions of some actual persons.

Intellectual perceptions are not the only ones in which other peoples may be superior. Their consciousness of spiritual values is sometimes both a challenging and awe-inspiring fact. The dramatic contrast between our own materialistic, sensual outlook and the spiritual awareness of other peoples is perhaps nowhere better evi-

denced than in the reported reactions of Hillary, the New Zea-
lander, and Tenzing, the Buddhist Sherpa guide, who were asked
on their return from Everest as to how they felt when once they
had reached that loftiest point in the world.[7] Hillary is cited as
saying, "Damn good," while Tenzing replied to the same question,
"I thought of God and the greatness of His work." There are differences between people, and often these differences by no means
favor the white man.

Those who do not believe as we do are too easily classified as
"pagan," with a particularly harsh ring to the word and a depreciat-
ing connotation. But we must not overlook either the intelligence
or the sincerity of those who believe differently, even though we
may not think they are right. To challenge or to suspect their sincerity is to admit our own bigotry. No Christian can escape the
challenge of a prayer of Rabi'a of Basra, an eighth-century Mohammedan mystic:

O, my Lord, the stars are shining and the eyes of men are closed, and
the kings have shut their doors, and every lover is alone with his beloved,
and here I am alone with thee. O my Lord, if I worship thee from fear
of hell, burn me in hell, and if I worship thee in hope of paradise,
exclude me thence, but if I worship thee for thine own sake, then with-
hold not from me thine eternal beauty.[8]

The wisdom of other peoples is often strikingly reflected in the
way in which they make known their Christian faith. Too often,
the missionary thinks only in terms of preaching in church or
chapels or of proclaiming the message in the open air to busy
crowds, who have neither the time nor the interest to listen. Some
Sumbanese Christians have adapted their manner of evangelizing
so as to fit the patterns of social life. It is quite in order for a person
to give a feast and then to spend most of the night telling the people
just why the feast has been given. Here in the leisure of evening
hours and at the happy occasion of a banquet, people can listen
to the plain, simple words of their host and ask questions. Furthermore, the guests are impressed that this new faith must mean something, or the host would not have spent so much in making it

possible to tell his guests about his spiritual experience. If the Good News of the Bible means anything to people, it should enter into their lives in such a way that its proclamation becomes a natural matter, rather than a foreigner's noisy propaganda.

Once we have been convinced that people all over the world are human—that they are people, just as we are, with virtues and follies, insights and limitations and that their way of life has continuity and meaning—then we will begin to look beneath the surface of actions. This does not mean that we should try to discover some hidden motive for every act, but we should assume that people are acting according to some pattern or plan. When we are shocked by the behavior of other peoples, it is usually because we erroneously assume that they have our experience and our background, or should have if they do not, or should think as we do, regardless of background. It is not that they lack a background; theirs is simply different from ours. One matter in which we seem to find ourselves quite different from the rest of the world is in the supposed degree of honesty which we claim for ourselves and disclaim for others. The fact is that the rest of the world does not regard some types of statements in the same light as we do. A missionary, himself raised in South America, returned there with his wife, who spoke terrible Spanish. She was, however, a wonderful person and loved by everyone. One day the husband overheard the maid telling his wife that she spoke perfectly "beautiful Spanish." Whereupon, he interrupted the remark, and asked the maid, "Where do people who tell such things go when they die?" Without a moment's hesitation the maid answered, "Why, to heaven, of course, for they make people happy." Most people in the world are concerned primarily with the effect of words on the hearer, rather than with the bare, bold truth. This can be exasperating to us, especially in the Orient, where the technique of replying in the desired manner is an accomplished art. In terms of our standards it can be lying of the most aggravating variety, especially when it would seem that telling the truth would be easier and even more to the advantage of the speaker. But it stems from the viewpoint of one who answers primarily what he thinks is wanted, rather than in accordance with the facts. Suppose he does tell the truth. Perhaps the truth would be irksome, and he would lose face himself, or cause someone else to lose face. Life is too full of tragedies to add another to the daily list. Furthermore, in some instances if the truth is told, anyone who is familiar with such a society will certainly not suspect it of being the truth, so in that case the truth is quite unnecessary; in fact, it may be misleading. What is more, any really intelligent person should know the answer and one who is not intelligent would probably not be able to profit from knowing the truth. And so the arguments go. They make little or no sense to us, but in their context they fit life, and strangely enough life goes on. The fascinating thing about all this is that people do understand and do .communicate. Of course, they may draw up elaborate statements or resolutions as official declarations of policy or intentions, and yet all the persons participating may understand perfectly well that no one means what he says. As one politician exclaimed, after having completed a long document on a particularly difficult social problem, "There! We have included everything and said nothing!" The only thing unusual about such a statement was its frankness. Such matters are generally left unstated, but none the less well understood. Penetrating the curtain of such patterns of behavior is most difficult for those not brought up in such an environment, and our moral indignation tends to get the better of us (rightly so for us); but for those who engage in the Oriental game of politeness and politics, such actions are not regarded as exactly immoral or dishonest. They are just part of a game which no one takes too seriously. On the other hand, we tolerate a bit of subtle deception in chess or checkers (pretending to be interested in one part of the game, while really concentrating on another), and we justify some abuses of the truth by saying, "All is fair in love and war." More than one churchgoer has thought he could cover up his having slept through the sermon by congratulating the preacher on "a most inspiring message," and many conventional expressions of greetings and thanks bear only slight resemblance to the truth. In fact, much of our politeness amounts to little more than pleasant lying.

The shock which we receive when people habitually refrain from telling the truth is sometimes matched by our surprise when people are not interested in knowing the truth. In religious matters most Kekchi Indians of Guatemala seem to be completely indifferent. They even object to someone explaining to them the basis of what they already may believe. This apparent apathy on the part of converts is not intellectual laziness or calculated obstinacy; for them religion is essentially something which cannot and should not be understood. In that very fact lies its religious value. To understand it is to secularize it, and the Kekchi seem to prefer their religion uncontaminated by detailed explanations. This does not mean that they are born mystics—far from it. They are quite earthy, but they want to keep religion a mystery, even to themselves.

Perhaps the greatest obstacle to understanding other peoples lies in failure to communicate effectively. We may speak foreign languages—even with grammatical correctness—but the thought content may be quite foreign. Some missionaries in West Africa asked for the tribal word for "grace," and they obtained what they thought was the Biblical equivalent. For years they used it, and they saw nothing wrong with it; though they did note that the people rarely if ever used the word, and if so, only in hushed tones, as if not wanting others to hear. When finally the truth was discovered, it turned out that this word was used in black magic for casting spells upon persons. No one dared to speak it too loudly, or he would be accused of casting a spell on someone else. Just how the missionaries made the original mistake in obtaining this word is hard to understand. Perhaps they asked for a word to designate what a spirit does to one. The missionaries were no doubt assuming something good and the Africans something bad. But regardless of how the error occurred, the truth of the matter was that for years the missionaries and the people had been talking about two different things.

It is possible to talk about anything in any language, but the particular words used to describe phenomena are often quite different. We normally talk about loving with the "heart." This makes no sense to the Karré people of French Equatorial Africa, for they love with the "liver." The Conobs in Guatemala insist that loving is done with the "abdomen," while the Marshallese love with the "throat." A scientific description of the psychological factors involved in love reveals that this emotion is much too complicated to be designated by any one organ of the body, or even any combination of two or three. If the Habbe people of French West Africa talk about sorrow as "My liver is sick," and their neighbors to the north, the Bambara, say that sorrow is correctly rendered as "My eye is black," who is to say which is really correct? Perhaps the Mossi people farther east are right when they say, "My heart is spoiled." On the other hand, the Uduks, living along the Ethiopian border of the Anglo-Egyptian Sudan, declare that sorrow is "having a heavy stomach." There is no way to judge nor any reason to judge which of these four expressions for sorrow is "right." There is no intrinsic merit in one of these as over against another, any more than there is in the fact that in buttoning a coat we men lap the left side over the right, while the Japanese reverse it and have the right side of the kimono lapping over the left.

If we wish to poke fun at a person, we may call him "empty headed," but in New Caledonia this expression is a high compliment.[9] Persons of great wisdom and intelligence are likened to hollow trees which are used as aqueducts to convey irrigation water over rough ground. One who is "empty headed" is as valuable to society as a hollow tree. For the average Bible reader there is no problem in the phrase "to taste death," but the Cashibo of the Peruvian jungles are too aware of the history of cannibalism in their region not to interpret this as eating human flesh.

Words are not fixed symbols which have exactly corresponding meanings in other languages. There is nothing metaphysical about the signs of one language, nothing which makes them intrinsically better or worse than those of other languages. They are all a part and parcel of the culture which they help to symbolize, and they can be understood only as an integral part of such a culture. If a person is to overcome the shock of cultural differences or reduce his surprises to intelligible happenings, he must understand a people's language, by which they carry on the complicated affairs of existence and through which they largely communicate this culture to succeeding generations.

The contrasts between cultures are especially illuminated by a consideration of the problems of Christian missions. Missionaries are not selling sewing machines, motor trucks, or refrigerators (though their possession of such objects tends to pave the way for a market). They are concerned more with the ideas by which people live. Convincing other peoples that they would profit from having some gadgets from the Western world is one thing, but inducing them to accept an entirely different orientation toward life is quite another matter. Perhaps this explains in a measure why Christian missions during the last one hundred and fifty years have been successful primarily in dealing with cultures where animistic beliefs are predominant, by which we mean that the people believe principally in spirits and have no so-called "organized religion" such as Hinduism, Buddhism, Taoism, or Mohammedanism. Christianity has had a great appeal to animists in Africa, Sumatra (where the Batak church numbers more than one-half million), Burma (among the Karens, Kachins, and Chins, but not among the Burmese, who are Buddhists), and Assam among a number of the Naga peoples), and in the South Pacific (e.g. Fiji, New Caledonia, Tonga, the Gilbert Islands, and the Marshall Islands).[10] In the small East African country of Uganda (in which missionary work began during the lives of some persons still living) there are now more than one-half million who are regarded as Christians (about 20 per cent of the total population), while in India, where Christian missionary work has been undertaken for at least 400 years, there are less than 2 per cent Christians, and many of these are so-called "Syrian Christians" whose families have lived in India for centuries. Mohammedanism has during its history been even more successful in winning converts from other world religions, including Christianity, than Christianity has been in its appeal to these same peoples. With the exception of the Philippines, there is no country in Asia which has more than 4 per cent Christians. In Thailand there is less than one-tenth of 1 per cent and in Japan less than one-half of 1 per cent.

Without a doubt a great deal of the success of Christian missions among predominantly animistic peoples is related to the lack of

security found in animistic beliefs. Ideas which animists possess
about health and disease do not stand up to the inroads of scientific
knowledge. So often the animist's religion is an integral part of a
tightly knit clan (or family) organization. When this collapses as
the result of urbanization, the religious concepts which are associated with the family unit also lose their hold. Much of the
animist's life is immersed in the fear of irresponsible actions by unpredictable evil spirits. Accordingly, it is not strange that a religion
which explains life in terms of the love of God and order in the
universe has a great appeal to him. Nevertheless, it is quite erro-
neous to think that animists will naturally gravitate toward Christianity. There is a growing recognition among some animists that
the representatives of the so-called Christian nations of Western
Europe and America are becoming less and less Christian. In fact, it
is not entirely wrong to speak of a so-called "post-Christian era" when
one realizes that neither Protestant nor Roman Catholic churches
can claim that more than 15 (or at most 20) per cent of the people
in any country of Europe are active church members and reasonably aware of the implications of the total claims of the Church and
Christ upon its members. By and large, a comparable situation
exists in the United States, though in some areas the percentages
may be higher. We do not deny that many persons retain Christian
habits of behavior, but this does not mean that such individuals
are truly Christians. They are simply habitual conformers to socially approved patterns of behavior, which can by no stretch of
the imagination be regarded as constituting their religion. The
decadence of Christianity in the Western world has led many
animists to rethink their relationship to Christian missions. It is
very unlikely that a secondhand, castoff Christianity from the West
will fully satisfy the animistic world any more than castoff clothing
from the missionary "barrels." There is, on the other hand, a very
great likelihood that the central dynamic of Christianity will pass
from the West and find a more receptive home elsewhere, among
people who have not engrossed themselves so completely in gadgets
and have not made an idol of material success.

Christian missions have not been without their problems. One mission in West Africa had the misfortune of erecting a station on a hill which was regarded as taboo, that is, too sacred to be approached. It was not strange that even after many years, the Africans hesitated—and some utterly refused—to visit the mission. Cutting off school children's hair in order to rid them of lice would be countenanced in the United States, but in some parts of South America it is regarded as an insult to older relatives, since the cutting of hair implies mourning. Some missionaries have found that it is one thing to go to a remote, isolated tribe to evangelize the people, but quite another thing to see to it that the people do not die off before they are evangelized. In one instance in South America, more than half of the tribe died off after three years' contact with the diseases of the missionary and the traders who penetrated the area to supply the missionary's need. In another instance, one-quarter of a tribe died off in about a year, once they had been induced by the missionaries to come out of the jungle.

Even at best, it is difficult for missionaries to prevent people from taking an entirely superficial attitude toward what is being taught. One Liberian chief announced his intention to become a Christian, but it was not long before it was discovered that the chief was tired of polygamy, and the only legal way he could see to divorce twenty-two of his twenty-three wives was to become a Christian. Such obvious superficiality can often be detected, but there are other varieties far more subtle and ultimately more significant. Leen-hardt [11] describes his experience with a classroom of New Caledonian young people. He wished to have them summarize for him what they had learned about "the spirit." But one of the young men replied, "Spirit? Why, we've learned nothing at all. You have not brought us knowledge about the spirit.[12] We have lived in the atmosphere of spirits. What you have brought us is the body." The result of the missionary's teaching had not been to emphasize either the spirit or the spiritual, but rather the material. The contrast is necessary, but we of the Western world are often far too pre-occupied with "things" and we fail to convey little else.

It is possible that this treatment of Christian missions and high-lighting the cultural contrasts between people will give the impression that of all white people missionaries are the most prone to make cultural blunders. This is by no means the case. Government officials and businessmen have chalked up at least an equal number of mistakes. When British officials first entered the Shilluk region of the Sudan, they were infuriated at the lack of respect which the Shilluk chiefs apparently displayed. In fact, the Shilluks refused to stand when a governor would come into their presence, and for such behavior they were sometimes beaten—that is, until the British finally discovered that the Shilluks were displaying the highest respect by remaining seated. In their society only the king may stand, and all others must be seated or approach him in a crouched position. The Shilluks paid rather dearly for their own ignorance of British customs and for British ignorance of theirs.

When the Belgians contacted the Ngombe people living in the region of Lisala, on the upper Congo, they were shocked at what seemed to be the brutal treatment of adulterers. It is reported [13] that for the first offense an ear was cut off, for the second a hand was hacked off, and if the person were caught a third time, he was driven out into the jungle. It would be unlikely that any other tribe would permit such a person to settle among them. By imposing such severe penalties a relatively high level of morality was maintained among married people. The Belgian officials objected to such "barbarous" treatment and proceeded to impose prison sentences, which to the African seemed light enough and which caused no accompanying loss of status or prestige. As a result of such light penalties and the progressive deterioration of moral standards, plus the introduction of venereal disease, it has been estimated by one medical missionary in the area that at the present rate there will scarcely be a Ngombe alive in seventy years. The premarital sexual freedom permitted young people is one important factor in the spread of venereal disease and the resultant decline in the birth rate. However, the removal of heavy sanctions against adultery has certainly had a part in speeding the disintegrating process. [14]

A missionary among the Shipibos in Peru faced a rather similar situation. All Shipibo men habitually carry on a cord around their necks a very sharp little knife, which is used primarily to lay open the back of the neck of anyone guilty of adultery. Usually such "debts" are paid off at festival occasions when everyone is a little drunk. No one is killed or really seriously injured, for the cut is made only an eighth to a quarter of an inch deep. However, a man guilty of adultery becomes a marked man by the scar which he wears, and those who are habitually guilty of such demeanor carry numerous scars. Accordingly, such persons are well known, easily recognized, and are not invited to be overnight guests without proper precautions being taken. The missionary in question first decided to preach against what he regarded as "getting revenge." However, he soon realized that this was not just a matter of revenge, but actually it served as an important social control. No doubt it would cause some important changes if it were introduced into life in the United States!

Have missionaries anything to gain from a careful consideration of the wealth of anthropological data which has been accumulated during the last two generations? If so, why have many missionaries been so critical of anthropologists and a number of anthropologists so critical of missionaries? It is true that missionaries have been impatient with the high-brow terms which anthropologists have used, with the relativistic ideas which have seemed to be a fundamental part of anthropology, and with the antipathy which anthropologists have exhibited toward changing the beliefs and lives of so-called primitive peoples. However, all good missionaries have in a sense always been good anthropologists, for they have been sensitive to the needs of the people and in a remarkable way have entered into the lives of the people, fully identifying themselves with the people. There is no fundamental conflict between the science of anthropology and Christian missions [15]—though there may be between some anthropologists and some missionaries. The accumulated experience of the science of anthropology can make important contributions to Christian missions.

No one must imagine, however, that cultural anthropology is *the* answer to the problems of Christian missions, but it can aid very materially in the process by which the missionary endeavors to communicate to others the significance of the new way of life made possible through the vicarious death of the Son of God. If a person is no longer hampered by his cultural pride and by failure to identify himself completely with those to whom he goes with the words of life, he can more fully carry out his divinely ordained mission, in which the message and the man, the Word and the witness, combine to make known the will of God. The task of Christian missions is essentially one of communication, making known in human language the nature of that life which comes from God. The message of Christian missions has three fundamental aspects: (1) it must be a message for all of life, for there is no phase which can be rightfully excluded from the all-embracing demands of the Lordship of Jesus Christ, (2) it must be understood by living men and women in terms of the only way of life which they know, namely, their own (compare St. Paul's bold use of so-called "pagan" terms in order to make the Good News clear to his listeners), and (3) it must permit the Holy Spirit to work out in the lives of the people those forms of Christian expression which are in accordance with their distinctive qualities. In the same sense that no person has attained unto the full measure of faith, but all "press on to the mark," so equally no one cultural manifestation of the Christian life (including our own) has arrived at perfection, but each has its unique contribution to make and each should be permitted to make it. This fundamental thesis as to the meaning and function of missions underlies all the following chapters, which are designed to illustrate the working out of these principles in the many aspects of human culture.

2

RHYME AND REASON

"But we want to go to hell, if it is a hot place," the Bano'o people of the French Camerouns assured the first missionaries, for the Bano'o idea of a proper place after death is one which is always hot—never subject to chilling winds with accompanying sickness and suffering. In general we do not see the rhyme and reason behind other cultural beliefs and practices because we have acquired our own beliefs and values as the result of the molding process of our own culture, of which we have been largely unaware. An anthropological understanding of culture helps us to see and comprehend more clearly not only the reasons for others' behavior but also the bases of our own.

All cultures possess some historical "hangovers," which are quite nonsensical in their outdated form. In the Western world men's coats have two or more buttons sewn on the end of the sleeves. There is, of course, no earthly purpose for such buttons—and they are certainly not very decorative. However, many years ago, when fancy lace cuffs were all the rage, these buttons served a very useful function. English spelling has many examples of outdated usefulness. Some letters no longer represent sounds as formerly pronounced, and we have changed many pronunciations without changing the spelling. In some cases we have even introduced letters which never represented sounds in English. For example, we borrowed the French word *dette* "debt," but since the Latinists of the day realized that the word was originally derived from Latin *debitus*, they insisted on inserting a *b*—a perfect illustration of the fact that too much education can make living more difficult rather than easier!

One person has been quoted as saying, "The principal advantage of an education seems to lie in the fact that one can worry about things all over the world." Nevertheless, this world awareness can prevent us from the provincialism of regarding our own behavior as the only correct one, and it may enable us to find reasons which are not always on the surface. In the early days of colonial expansion into Indonesia, Balinese women were regarded as the best mistresses and cooks for Chinese and Dutch traders. This did not mean that the Balinese women greatly excelled Javanese or Sundanese women in beauty, usually regarded as the basis for selecting mistresses. The real reason was that the Balinese were not Mohammedans and hence the women had no scruples against cooking pork. Human behavior does exhibit rhyme (patterns of related behavior) and reason, although the "reason" may not always be rational. However, behavior is not without some fundamental bases in the biological, environmental, or historical heritage of the people. Neither the rhyme nor the real reason is usually obvious, and it is the very purpose of anthropology to help us to discover these.

What Is Anthropology?

For the average person, anthropology, which means literally "the study of man," is too often taken to mean the study of men and apes; and anthropologists are regarded as eccentric people who dig up relics, try to match bones, go into ecstasy over charred bits of crude cloth, or are forever measuring somebody's skull. It is true that anthropologists do just such things, but that is certainly not all, for anthropology is essentially the science of learned human behavior, but in a much wider sense than would be understood in psychology. A more correct definition would be "the science of human culture," or as Kroeber has defined anthropology, "the science of groups of men, and their behavior and productions." [1]

This means that anthropology takes in a tremendous sphere of human knowledge and activity. In general, anthropology is divided into two main branches, physical and cultural. Under the first division comes the study of the paleontology of primates, human genetics, evolution, measurements and descriptions of the physical characteristics of different peoples, the classification of human types into races, etc. Cultural anthropology is often regarded as including the study of prehistoric cultures (archeology), ethnology (the analysis of particular human societies), folklore, social organization, linguistics, culture and personality, acculturation, and the applications of anthropology to human problems (applied anthropology). In the introduction to cultural anthropology presented in this book, we are not touching on archeology since it is a rather specialized field and somewhat beyond the limits of our immediate interest. It is, however, important in the study of human culture, for it provides a time perspective which traditional history cannot give us, since the latter is based on writing and hence a relatively late development in so many cultures.

If anthropology includes so much of human activity, it is quite legitimate to ask why anthropologists have specialized to such an extent in the study of primitive,[2] aboriginal cultures (by which we generally mean those which have not had a traditional system of writing). In the first place, such peoples have been largely neglected by the other sciences—history, political science, sociology, and psychology. But more important is the fact that cultural anthropology expects to arrive at more valid conclusions about human behavior by taking into account the greatest possible variety of ways of life. The diverse groups of people in the world have, in a sense, provided the nearest thing to a laboratory situation. It is quite impossible to subject people to controlled laboratory experiments (which would require several generations to be effective), but different cultures are in themselves laboratories of human behavior. We cannot speak in terms of control groups as a check against our conclusions, but the relatively long isolation of certain peoples living in similar environments does give us some basis for distinguishing between the importance of the geographical setting and the cultural heritage of the people. The Hopi Indians live in the same kind of country as the Navajos, and yet their cultures are very different. The former live in villages and are primarily horticulturalists, while the latter are widely scattered and are herders. The Hopis have been relatively peaceful—certainly not aggressively warlike—but the Navajos (and their close kin the Apaches) have been notorious for their fighting. It is true that the Navajos have not been in the Southwest as long as the Hopis (they obviously moved in from the north, for they are related to the Athapascan Indians of northern Canada), but the contrasts between the Navajos and the Hopis are exactly what the anthropologist wishes to study if he is to understand the variety of ways in which life may be organized and oriented.

In the analysis of the patterns of behavior in any culture, the science of cultural anthropology is concerned primarily with three questions: [3]

a. *What makes a culture click?*

What are the various features (such as food, shelter, transportation, family organization, religious beliefs, and language) and what are the dynamic drives (e.g. goals, ambitions, value systems, and prestige which provide the spark for human society)?

b. *What makes a particular member of a society act as he does?*

All persons in any society do not act alike. Why is this? What are the possibilities for diverse behavior? What is the relationship of the person to the culture? Does he have much chance for alternative behavior (such as in our Western, urban culture) or is the mold rather rigidly fixed and are people expected to conform closely to it (as in so many primitive cultures)?

c. *What are the factors involved in the culture's stability or change?*

What are the dynamics of cultural conservation and change?

As can be readily seen, we are not satisfied with describing merely the features of a culture, e.g. the types of clothing. We want to know who wears such clothing and when and why. Is some apparel reserved only for certain classes in the society? What prestige comes from wearing such clothing? How much effort will a person make in order to procure such clothing? Many people in Haiti wear shoes (they are required by law to wear them in the capital), but many others, especially in the small towns and villages, go barefooted. Is this just a matter of personal taste? By no means! Shoes are a mark of social standing. A Haitian doctor who was enjoying a little recreation in one of the small towns in the north was told that there was a patient waiting for him in a nearby building. The doctor's immediate question was, "Does he have shoes on?" If the answer were "Yes," he would be obliged to go immediately, but if "No," then the man could be expected to wait. For the anthropologist, the presence or absence of shoes is far more important than the passing tourist would imagine. What does the wearing of shoes mean in the society?

What Is Culture?

For many people, "culture" (especially when pronounced with a supersophisticated air) means music, art, and good manners. This is not, however, the anthropologist's definition of culture. For him, culture is all learned behavior which is socially acquired, that is, the material and nonmaterial traits which are passed on from one generation to another.[4] They are both transmittable and accumulative, and they are cultural in the sense that they are transmitted by the society, not by genes. This makes the transmission of culture differ from the biological heritage of humans or animals. Birds do not "learn" how to make the nests typical of their species. Their skill is entirely instinctive. Similarly, dogs raised quite apart from any other dogs will whine, growl, yelp, and bark in a manner typical of their breed, and they are not dependent upon other dogs in order to know what kind of sounds to utter in accordance with particular types of stimuli. But with humans the situation is quite reverse. A Chinese child raised entirely in an English-speaking environment will grow up knowing only English—and not a word of Chinese. Language is a feature of culture, though, of course, the capacity to make oral noises is a part of every normal human's biological equipment.

If there is to be human culture, there must be human society, which not only expresses this culture but transmits it. In other words, there is no culture apart from society, but there may be societies without culture. Ants, for instance, may engage in a kind of gardening (they raise tiny mushrooms on leaf mold which has been specially gathered), keep cattle (i.e. aphids), engage in wars, take slaves, organize marches, and exhibit a high degree of specialization of labor. However, this type of social organization is not learned, but biologically transmitted. It is not cultural, but social.

When speaking of the life of human groups (from tiny tribes to large nations), we often use the words "culture" and "society" in the same breath. There is no contradiction in terms. The first identifies the patterns of behavior; the second designates the particular aggregate of individuals who participate in the culture.

In some instances we use the word "society" to mean a very large unit, such as the people of the United States, and in other contexts we may mean a group of medicine men in some West African tribe who have banded together for professional or other reasons. The word "society" simply designates a group of mutually interacting individuals, regardless of the size of the constituency.

We should be fully aware that in a sense "culture" is an abstraction, even as the divisions of culture into material, social, religious, linguistic, and esthetic are abstractions. Culture is a way of behaving, thinking, and reacting, but we do not see culture. We see manifestations of culture in particular objects (things made or used by people) and actions (what people do or say).[5] We may see a Haitian voodoo fetish consisting of a little bottle with some reddish liquid, a small mirror backed by cardboard facing toward the bottle and all this wrapped in coarse red cloth with yards of black thread. This is the "object," but what are the actions? We can notice that the possessor of this object keeps it in the safest part of the house, that he rarely lets its presence be known to anyone else, and that the very mention of it seems to startle him. These are the immediately observable "actions." If we can induce him to talk about his fetish, he may (as in the case of the fetish here described) tell us that his father, who was a kind of voodoo priest, captured his child's soul when he was very young and put it in a bottle. As long as the bottle is preserved the person is to live, but once the bottle is broken, the soul will depart and the man must die. No wonder the man protects the bottle. But still this is not all of the Haitian culture relating to this bottle. This fetish would have no value for the man unless there were many other people who possessed similar ideas about their fetishes. This in turn is related to the whole system of religious beliefs, the majority of which are closely related to West African religion. But still this is not all the story, for the persistence of voodoo is part of the social problem of Haiti, where the masses must find release for repressed emotions. The culture of Haiti is not just the accumulated objects and actions of people. It is an abstraction from such objects and actions; it is the pattern in which such objects and actions become meaningful behavior.

In culture the whole is more than the sum total of its parts. Even as in the instance of the fetish cited above, this object is culturally more than the pieces which comprise it. Similarly, a Hopi rain dance is more than the sum total of the number of participants, their colorful costumes, the elaborate ritual dance, and the snakes held in the dancers' mouths or draped around their necks. The dance has an internal organization and an external meaning to the participants and audience it. It is neither an isolated nor an isolatable feature of the culture and cannot be rightly understood or properly evaluated except in the larger frame of reference. A family Thanksgiving dinner is not just a big meal, for people may feast on turkey at other times of the year; it has an accumulated subjective value for the participants, which is more than turkey, cranberries, stuffing, pumpkin pie, or even the presence of all the family.

In speaking of culture we so frequently shift from "primitive" (or nonliterate) societies to "civilized" ones that it may seem as though we make no distinctions at all or that we are unaware of any basic differences. Fundamentally human behavior is very similar, and in a real sense we are all "brothers under the skin." Nevertheless, there are certain differences between civilized and primitive societies.

Civilized peoples have very heterogeneous societies, with various "subcultures." There are often rather distinct patterns of behavior for different regions, classes, or occupational groups, and a number of alternative patterns of behavior for individuals, even within the same subculture. One may compare the differences in life between a Brahmin and an outcaste in India or the distinct ways of life of a Southern cotton plantation owner and a New York bus driver. In the United States a middle-class person may choose among any number of occupations; he may join any one of a number of different churches (or he can even become a Mohammedan, Buddhist, etc.); he may be highly critical of his own society, and as the result of extensive, systematic, and abstract reasoning, he may raise serious philosophical objections to it; he may marry almost anyone who is not closely related to him (except for certain states where there are racial restrictions); he may eat a wide variety of foods and spend his money (what is left after taxes) in almost any way he chooses. Such wide possibilities for different kinds of behavior do not exist in most primitive societies. In many instances, practically all the men engage in the same type of work: fishing, hunting, clearing the forest, planting, and cultivating. Some men may excel in certain activities and hence dedicate proportionately more time to them, but on the whole each man (and similarly each woman in corresponding occupations) does about the same thing. There is generally no question of difference of religion. It is taken for granted that people will espouse the beliefs of the tribe, and the people are not likely to question seriously the established patterns of behavior. When asked why they do something, the usual reply is, "We have always done it." Thinking is likely to be quite concrete and relatively unsystematic (but this is not necessarily a judgment as to its correctness). Marriage may be restricted to certain clans—a man may marry into certain families but not into others, although there may be no biological reasons for such discrimination. On the other hand, in some societies a man is expected to marry his cross-cousin (the daughter of his mother's brother or of his father's sister). In most primitive cultures the variety of foodstuffs and the things which can be purchased or bartered are strictly limited. Such societies exhibit a much greater homogeneity, and therefore are much easier to study than the complex heterogeneous civilized societies of modern times.[6]

While we are contrasting civilized and primitive peoples, we should note that on the whole such nonliterate societies tend to produce fewer psychoneurotics. That is to say, in such societies there are proportionately fewer people who "crack up." Though the fixed patterns with their strict limitations provide fewer opportunities for the fullest expression of individual interests or endowments, they nevertheless result in a relatively high percentage of satisfied individuals. When there are fewer alternatives of behavior, and accordingly fewer choices to be made, there are usually correspondingly fewer frustrations. The rewards for individual enterprise may not be so great in an aboriginal society, but the penalties for failure are generally not so severe.

Easy and Wrong Explanations

Since time immemorial men have speculated about the reasons for the differences between people. The most frequent answer is race. "People are just born to act the way they do," one often hears. The truth of the matter is that they are not so born. Of course, racial and cultural differences have been historically related, since racial distinctions have arisen and have been perpetuated during times of comparative cultural isolation. In other words, the culture of the Orient is not the culture of Africa, nor is the latter the culture of Western Europe. But history can provide too many contradictions for us to take seriously the theory of the racial basis for culture. Certainly the Indians of northern India are Caucasian (despite their dark skin), but their culture is not that of Western Europe. The Negroes of the United States do not conform to the cultures of West Africa (the region from which most of their ancestors came). It is just as hard for the average American Negro to adjust himself to African life as it is for the average white American to do the same. In fact, it is probably harder for the Negro, because his difficulties in adjusting are less easily understood by both Africans and whites.[7] The coincidence of racial and cultural differences is a historical fact, but there is no causal connection, except that cultural isolation has fortified racial characteristics and to some extent perhaps racial differences have indirectly increased cultural differences by limiting the tendency to intermarry.[8]

Having failed to explain cultural differences on the basis of race, people have attempted to explain everything on the basis of geography. But here again, though the explanation appears to be easy, it is generally quite wrong. One would certainly regard Madagascar as being geographically related to Africa, and yet it is culturally related to the Malayo-Polynesian world, and its people speak a Malayo-Polynesian language. If geography alone determined patterns of life, it is strange that New Guinea abounds in primitive Melanesian cultures while Java and Sumatra have rich cultures compounded of Buddhist, Hindu, and Islamic influences. The Ponapeans have as much water surrounding them as the Marshallese, but the latter are far better sailors. Of course, this is not to deny that geography does influence culture to some extent. In the case of New Guinea there is rugged, almost impenetrable terrain, while Java and Sumatra are more open to the outside. The Ponapeans have not been under quite the same necessity to sail to other islands as have been the Marshallese since the Ponapean cluster of volcanic islands is more self-sufficient than the Marshalls. But geography alone will not explain why a highly complex culture should have arisen in the valley of Mexico and not in the valley of California. Environment does account for Eskimos wearing skin garments and living primarily on blubber and meat while so many Central Africans wear only a loincloth or a few leaves, and eat plantains (cooking bananas) and manioc (a starchy root from which tapioca is made). However, environment does not explain why on the whole the Eskimos adapted themselves much more successfully to their environment than the nearby Athapascan tribes farther inland, nor why the Indians in frigid Tierra del Fuego eked out such a miserable existence with completely inadequate clothing and shelters. The two cultures which seem to have reveled most in human sacrifice and mass torture of captives were the Aztecs of Mexico and the Assyrians of Mesopotamia. Certainly, there are no geographical reasons which would adequately explain such facts.

Having discovered that geography and the physical environment were insufficient to account for differences in cultures, some scholars attempted to make culture accountable for everything. They contended that people simply could not do anything different. Every-

thing was supposedly conditioned by the pre-existing cultural environment, so that "mind becomes minding" and we are all set for a
completely behavioristic interpretation of life. There is far more
truth in this type of explanation than in the previous two, but still
this falls short, for if behavior were entirely conditioned by the
culture, then life would not change and cultures would not be so
drastically altered. Of course, the answer which is given is that the
changes are likewise inevitable since they are inherent within the
very pattern of cultural conditioning. This does not fully explain the
relationship of persons to culture. There are people who swim
against the stream. There are always the creative minority who exert
unforeseen and unforeseeable influences on the culture. As yet, we
do not possess enough evidence to challenge at every point a
mechanistic and deterministic interpretation of culture, but we do
see enough to warn us that such an explanation, though it provides
many insights into behavior, is certainly not the entire story.

Still a further interpretation of culture has been undertaken,
namely, the psychological, or perhaps we should say, psychoanalytic.
Freud claimed that human culture began when young males, who
had been kept from the women possessed by their father, plotted
against their father, killed him, and ate him. Because of this they
became very remorseful and expressed their feeling by sacrificing a
totemic animal, which had become for them a father substitute.
Having come into the possession of their father's wives, they developed a serious Oedipus complex and created the laws of incest.
Freud does not make it clear whether this is to be construed as a
"scientific myth," representative of what took place at various times
and in various stages with so-called primitive man, or whether this is
to be understood as a particular single event, at which time human
culture began.

Freud's theory, based on the Oedipus complex (antagonism to
one's father and sexual attraction for one's mother), has appealed to
many persons who have taken for granted that the patrilineal family
(following the father's line) with strong paternal domination, so
familiar to those of Western Europe, is characteristic of people all
over the world. The Oedipus complex does explain some psychiatric

phenomena in our culture, but it is hopelessly inadequate in a culture where one's descent is through the mother's line and the important male in the family is the mother's brother. Furthermore, it is incredible that social organization (the family and the society), religion (deification, sacrifice, and communion, i.e. eating the dead father), and law (starting with the forbidding of incest) should all be attributed to this type of situation. This myth really explains nothing. It merely shows the futility of apparently easy answers to complex problems.

"It's Just Natural"

Before we can properly appreciate culture we must see it as a particular historical development, rather than some purely "natural" development. The particular features of any culture are not "natural" in the sense that they are all biologically determined. We must admit that it is quite natural to eat, to drink, to sleep, and to make noises. It is also unnatural, because it is biologically and physically impossible, for us to jump over high mountains, swim through the air (as fish do through water), or to hibernate as cold-blooded animals do. On the other hand, in our culture we say that it is natural for a child to object to his father's having more than one wife since this would subject the child to competition with numerous half brothers for the affection of the father. From our point of view this would be true, but it is not true of most parts of Africa. Young men generally welcome half-brothers, for such brothers are bound together by strong family ties. A man with many kin is not likely to be attacked by rivals, and he can always call upon his family for support in undertakings which will promote his own and their prestige.

We assume that it is unnatural [9] for a man to wish to loan his wife to guests, but Eskimo men have been doing just this for centuries and they do not seem to suffer from jealousy. They are expected to share their wives with certain men, and they in turn have the same privilege.[10] People's feelings are not biologically, but culturally, conditioned.

We take it for granted that it is natural for people to wish to

accumulate possessions, particularly if they can be acquired without
too much effort, or at a bargain. A Bolivian rancher below Cocha-
bamba had hired an Indian to dig a hole for him, for which he
offered him a pair of pants. Just as the Indian was finishing, the
rancher decided that he needed the Indian to do a little job clearing
jungle vines and brush out of a small area. It had taken the Indian
five days to earn the pair of pants, but the Bolivian was so desperately in need of help that he offered the Indian another pair of pants
if he would work just one more day in order to clear the land. The
Indian refused, and of course was condemned for his stupidity and
completely "unnatural" behavior. It would be unnatural for us, but
what would the Indian have done with two pair of pants? He would
need only one to come into town, and the cloth of the second pair
would surely rot out in the damp weather before he could even wear
the first pair out. It is true that from the Bolivian's viewpoint the
Indian had acted unnaturally, but from the Indian's point of view
his refusal to take advantage of the "bargain" was perfectly in keeping with his own culture.

What is regarded as natural by us may be unnatural in the eyes
of others. That being the case, it is not so much a matter of nature
as of culture. Because of our emphasis upon individualism and outstanding personalities we take a certain pride in our differences, but
not to the point of appearing queer. Accordingly, photographers
have learned to appeal to the vanity of their customers by accentuat-
ing the attractive features of their appearance, so as to give them
"personality." But the situation is quite different in Japan, where
the emphasis is far more on rigid conformity. There the photographers touch up a picture so that the person will correspond more
closely to the proper Japanese type. Accordingly, when a Japanese
exclaims over a picture of a Japanese girl, "How lovely, she looks
just like anyone!" this is not an insult; in fact, it is quite a compliment—a perfectly "natural" one.

Why People Act As They Do

Having pointed out that race, geographical environment, social
environment, and the Oedipus complex are not adequate reasons in

themselves for explaining culture, we must not, however, discard such factors entirely; for though they are inadequate when considered alone, nevertheless, they do combine to give us the fundamental bases of culture. We may describe culture as being determined fundamentally by (1) the antecedent culture,[11] (2) the situation, and (3) the biological capacities of the individuals involved. Primarily, people act as they do because of the fact that earlier members of the culture acted in a particular way. We in America drive on the right side of the road because in earlier times wagons passed on the right side. People in Australia, however, drive on the left side, because in England, from which most of them came, people drive on the left. But the tendency to follow the antecedent culture does not mean that cultures can never change. Formerly, people in Argentina drove on the left as they do in England, but Argentinians started importing more and more U. S. cars. Gradually the situation became such as to demand a change, and in one night everything did change (with considerable confusion for all). People do adapt themselves to new situations, even as the Plains Indians took over the horse from the Spanish, and in one generation the horse became one of the primary features of their seminomadic life.

The biological heritage of the human race is amazingly similar, as we shall have reason to note in the following chapter; but no doubt there are some specialties which, because of the biological heritage, are more highly developed in one culture than in another. Biological superiority in physical stature and strength would seem to be part of the reason why the Bantu were successful in overcoming the pygmies, who were once far more widely scattered in Africa than they are now; but biology does not explain why these same Bantu peoples are primarily horticulturalists while the pygmies are often the hunters, who exchange game for grain.

What Makes People Click?

Life does not go on simply because it has always gone on. There are certain dynamic drives which provide the powerful motivation for existence. Fundamentally these are of two types: (1) biological and (2) psychological.[12] The principal biological drives are for food (including drink) and sex. Where the physical environment is harsh, there is the added drive for shelter and protection. Individual persons cannot continue to exist without nourishment, and human societies cannot be perpetuated without sex. With some persons the sexual desire may be sublimated or diverted into other channels of creativity or self-expression, but in general sex is regarded by most societies as being quite as natural as eating and drinking.

The primary psychological drives are (1) the sense of belonging and (2) a desire for recognition.[13] Though these psychological drives are not so elemental as food and sex, they may manifest themselves in more complex and numerous ways. Man does not remain a part of a society just because he finds it economically more profitable or because he is assured of greater physical security. Sometimes neither is the case. People live in association with others because they desire to have a sense of belonging. They sometimes define it as a sense of security; but it is not primarily physical, but emotional security, a sense of "being at home" or "fitting" in a particular group. Where this emotional drive is not properly satisfied, people often attempt to compensate by becoming "joiners," that is to say, they attempt to join all kinds of organizations as a means of making up for some fundamental deficiency in the home or family unit. Others, frustrated in their desire to belong, seek compensation in an exaggerated desire for recognition. If they can be greeted with approval, so much the better, but if not, they will seek notoriety rather than fame, because recognition they must have. In fact, they will often sacrifice the proper fulfillment of biological drives in order to attain psychological ones. What is natural about human behavior is precisely the existence of these drives. The particular form which they assume in any culture is determined by the already established patterns, but the drives are functioning constantly. In America the drive for recognition and approval culminates in the ideal of the successful businessman; in traditional China, the ideal was the scholar (just an "egg-head" in the contemporary United States); in the India of only a few years back it was the philosopher ascetic (our idea of a "queer duck").

These basic biological and psychological drives are curbed or fortified, as the case may be, by the mores of a people. These are not the formal laws, but the unwritten sanctions, folkways, and customs which have emotional coloring and which enforce any particular way of life by controlling approval or disapproval. Such mores are, in a sense, abstractions, but they are none the less real in directing and channeling the basic drives of life.

Fried or Scrambled?

Some people like eggs fried, others prefer them scrambled, while there are many who do not care (they like them either way), and some people do not want eggs in any form. People are very "selective" about what they do, and so it is with cultures. The physical limitations of the environment and human capacities do place restrictions on activities. For example, the Chukchi of Siberia do not live on bananas and painters do not stand on their hands while they paint with their feet. However, there are no cultures which are so isolated and restricted by their environment that the people could not do something different from what they are doing. That is to say, all cultures select certain features out of the total range of possibilities. In the United States we could choose to eat rice as our staple food rather than potatoes (rice is preferred in some parts of the South), but yet as a nation we do not. This is not because the United States is incapable of raising enough rice. It is just that our culture has selected potatoes. There are certain historical reasons why the Irish potato (which originally came from the Andean highlands and was introduced to North America by way of Europe) was chosen instead of rice; but nevertheless, the culture has been selective. If we so desired, we could adopt as a national delicacy the *balot* of the Philippines (an egg, boiled after being incubated under a hen for ten days), but most people are disgusted at the very thought of eating a half-formed baby chick. Rather than selecting to emphasize social responsibility and community living, we have laid stress on "rugged individualism" and a pattern of dog-eat-dog economic competition, which is no doubt efficient in bringing people more gadgets at less expense, but also brings incomparably more suffering at incalculably greater cost.

Selectivity operates not only for a culture as a whole but also for parts of the culture. We may describe certain features as universals (everyone does it) or alternatives (the same people may or may not do it), or specialties (only some people do it). A universal in any culture is eating, but whether a person eats raw fish or cooked fish may be an alternative. The eating of fish eggs may, however, be reserved for only the rich who can afford them. For us, drinking milk is an alternative, for it depends on whether we want to or not. For the Shilluk in the Anglo-Egyptian Sudan drinking milk is a specialty of children and men only, since the drinking of milk by a menstruating woman is believed to cause a cow to dry up. (Some Shilluk women have blamed the men for imposing such an idea, but if so, it was a long time ago, for the belief is quite widespread in Africa.)

Selectivity within a culture becomes a very important matter of conduct. When should one offer to shake hands and when not? When is a compliment acceptable, and when does it appear to be "soft soap"? When should one use standard English and when not? *It is I* can be exceedingly pedantic in some situations. In answer to the question "What do you want out of an education?" one high-school boy summarized the entire matter by saying, "I want to learn when to use good English and when not to."

How Many Parts Make the Whole?

The features of culture may be classified in a number of different ways, but perhaps the most satisfactory, and certainly the most common, is the primary division into material, social, and religious culture.[14] At the same time one must recognize that language is an integral part of the entire cultural process and a system of symbolization for its explicit parts. Esthetics, in a somewhat similar manner, may enter into every phase of culture: the exquisite decoration of paddles (as in Polynesia), elaboration of games and dances (the latter, especially in Africa), and the beautifying of religious ritual (as in Thailand).[15]

The Part of Culture We Take for Granted

In every culture there are features which practically everyone takes for granted. In a very self-conscious society such as our own,

implicit features are perhaps fewer; but still such aspects of culture
do exist with us. The average person certainly does not question the
grammatical categories of the English language. He is generally not
aware that in the English language only six words: *him, her, me, us,
them, whom,* show special forms when they are used as objects of
verbs. It does not strike such a person as queer that we should make
distinctions between the singular and plural of nouns, that is, to
have one form for single items and another form for objects ranging
in number from two to infinity. Nor do people become concerned
that only one verb in the English language (i.e. *to be*) has three
forms in the present, namely, *am, are,* and *is,* while all other verbs
have only two forms (or, as in the case of auxiliary verbs, only one
form). All such facts are simply taken for granted.

We also take for granted the idea that we have a practically classless society in the United States, while in reality there are classes,
and some of them rather impenetrable, even in the smaller towns of
the Middle West. Most people just assume that there must be an
afterlife. A contrary belief strikes them as not only heretical but
unnatural. Our implicit belief in optimism is summarized in the
saying, "Every cloud has a silver lining." And we are convinced that
the common people can be relied on to show sound judgment in
political matters and we base our political system on that principle.
But all these ideas are largely assumptions which we take for granted
but which we justify by arguing about the qualities of human
nature.

Other peoples in the world do not take the same things for
granted. One of our basic philosophical assumptions is that something may exist or may not exist, but that one and the same thing
cannot both exist and not exist at the same time. However, simultaneous existence and nonexistence is not an uncommon feature of
Oriental philosophy. We take it for granted that women should go
first, but Japanese men generally assume that women should follow.
We take for granted that morals and sex are related, while this is
quite a strange idea for many peoples. It is implicit with us that a
religious man should be a good man, but for most of the predominantly animistic religions of the world there is no essential

connection. Such a religion is primarily a technique for dealing with supernatural phenomena, and it makes few or no moral demands on anyone. For the most part the deities are occupied with more practical affairs: fertility of the crops, sending rain, increasing the number of game animals, warding off illness, and giving victory in war. We assume that anyone who has violated socially sanctioned customs will have a sense of guilt, but this is not true in many parts of the world. Such a man may be afraid of apprehension or feel shame at having been seen, but a genuine sense of guilt (as we understand the word) is by no means as widespread in the world as we would imagine.

Things and Ideas

The features of culture may be either material or nonmaterial. A swanky yacht is a very material feature of upper-class society, but by some it may be less coveted than the nonmaterial membership in a very exclusive club. Canoes, huts, clothing, weapons, domesticated animals and farm crops are all material parts of culture; but equally important—and usually much more prized—are titles, rank, prestige, family connections, and religious beliefs. The features of a culture which tend to give it a distinctive quality, or ethos, are far more likely to be the nonmaterial than the material. There are thousands of objects and gadgets, but the value which a culture places on these may be more important than the objects themselves.

How Much Is It Worth?

Because people have gold is no sign that they value it highly. In fact, it was the relatively low value set on gold which in part prompted the Incas of South America to give in to Pizzarro's demands. If he had demanded turquoise, it is doubtful if he or his men would have conquered the Inca Empire. The Palauans living in the Eastern Caroline Islands in Micronesia place great value on beads and tiny cylinders of glass and porcelain, some of which are very old and may even date from around the time of Christ. There are numerous classes of this money and all important pieces (there are hundreds of them) have individual names. The value depends not only on the size, shape, and perfection of form but also on the history of the piece, that is to say, who owned it and how much it was valued in some transaction. Some of these small beads were so valuable that they served to redeem whole villages which were taken in war. On the other hand, the Yapese who live in the very next set of islands have no interest in such "money." They have specialized in huge stone disks, which they quarried out of the ground in Palau and shaped and then transported across more than a hundred miles of open sea in order to bring them to their own island. The Palauans could certainly have had such stone money, but they put no value upon it.

The Western cowboy is generally regarded as entirely dedicated to his cattle, and so are the Dinkas of the Anglo-Egyptian Sudan. But if an American cowboy has to make a choice between the life of his wife or sweetheart and the life of a favorite cow, he will certainly choose to defend his woman. However, that is not so true of Dinkas, who would in many instances choose to defend a favorite cow. Dinkas simply do not have the same value system.

Both the Germans and the Japanese have had emperors, but the Germans were able to dispense with their emperor much more easily than the Japanese, for the latter had deified their ruler. He was not only the symbol of their national unity but their link with the divine. Kaiser Wilhelm may have used the phrase *Gott und ich* "God and I," but the Germans attached no such value to the person of their emperor as did the Japanese, since the historical associations were quite different.

The Liberty Bell has very little intrinsic value—it is just an old cracked bell, and yet it is "priceless," that is to say, it cannot be purchased, for it is a symbol which is highly valued by the American people.

It is hard for us to appreciate fully the value which other people attach to objects. Australian officials found it almost incomprehensible that the Australian aborigines of that country refused to leave some of their practically worthless land to take up residence elsewhere. Only when the religious value of such land became known was the aborigines' reluctance to leave fully appreciated.

Certain religious rites could be celebrated only in these sacred places. The Zionist Jews' love for Jerusalem, the Mohammedans' adoration of Mecca, and the Japanese reverence for the shrine of Ise all reflect the same process of giving to objects a value beyond their strictly utilitarian function.

How Does It Work?

It is not enough to know the form of a cultural feature or even its value (i.e. its meaning to the people); we must also know its function. We know the form of a wedding ring in our culture, and we can appreciate the fact that it is supposed to have deep sentimental meaning to the one who wears it (somewhat dependent upon the happiness of the marriage). But what is its actual function, apart from serving as a part of the wedding ceremony? For one thing, it marks married persons (Private Property, No Trespassing), and as such it tends to promote the stability of marriage.

In Africa a quite different feature of marriage, namely, the payment of cattle as a kind of "bride price" (it might better be called an equilibrium or compensation payment, for it compensates a clan for the loss of a member) has a meaning of legalizing the marriage and legitimatizing the offspring. The function of such a bride price is very similar to the ring in our culture, for it also increases the stability of marriage.[16]

In some instances identical forms may have utterly different functions. The Navajos cannot operate stores successfully because the social patterns of sharing are such that they would have to give extended credit to all their relatives and friends, and they would find it almost impossible to collect. Some Navajos have tried to run stores, and almost invariably they have failed because of the social patterns. Somewhat similar patterns of sharing exist in the Philippines, where anyone who has much money or foodstuffs is expected to help all the members of his extended family. However, a number of Filipinos have purposely set up small stores in order that they may not have to give away their surplus produce to needy and demanding relatives. In this case the fact that one has a store means that the relatives are expected to pay, rather than to receive a dole.

All the Pieces Fit Together

Culture is not a mere accumulation of traits, but an arrangement of parts in such a way that there is a systematic functioning of the society. There may be some serious maladjustments, such as the breakdown of clan life in urbanized Africa and the distintegration of homelife in the United States; but despite all this there is a pattern, and the pieces fit together, even though the results may not always be advantageous to the participants.

If we study the significance of beer in the Tarahumara culture of northern Mexico, we soon realize that the entire economic system is involved. If a man has plenty of beer, he can invite many friends and neighbors to come and help him cut down trees to clear land for planting more corn. The number of people who flock in to help him will be almost directly proportionate to the amount of beer which is known to be on hand. If more people help, more ground will be cleared for planting, and accordingly, the next year more corn can be harvested, and from this more beer can be made. There is another economic cycle which meshes with the one just cited. It begins with corn, which can be used to obtain more cattle, which in turn produce more fertilizer (cattle are kept very largely for their fertilizer), and this in turn means more corn. These two integrating systems may be diagrammed as follows:

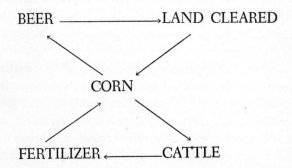

Patterns of culture are exceedingly complex in some societies by virtue of the very multiplicity of activities and organizations. Within a radius of about two hundred yards in the town of Chiengmai in northern Thailand one finds a Buddhist temple, a government liquor factory (despite the fact that Buddhists are not supposed to drink intoxicating liquors), a British teakwood company, a Jehovah's Witness Kingdom Hall, an American Presbyterian school, and a Chinese Protestant church. It is true that to some extent these institutions function on different levels; and yet they are interrelated, despite the contradictions which are inherent in them. The same Thai government which condemns the production and sale of opium still reaps huge profits indirectly from its sale. But this is scarcely different from what we have in America where all city governments are publicly on record as being opposed to vice and yet prostitution is one of the major sources of revenue for financing the political machines in large cities.

Not only are the patterns of culture complex, but they reveal interpenetration and interdependence of the various divisions of culture. During the Middle Ages in Europe esthetics and religion were closely bound together. In British Columbia an Indian's decision as to becoming a warrior, hunter, or shaman was largely determined by a religious vision. In New Caledonia religion and economics become almost inseparable in the process of raising sweet potatoes. Religious beliefs in totems dictate social organizations in many parts of the world, while religious beliefs in America may largely determine whether one marries a Roman Catholic, Protestant, or Jew. One's economic status is a very determining factor for social position in American life, but it has little to do with Zuni social ranking, which is primarily a religious affair and largely inherited.

Though we shall be speaking of material, social, religious, esthetic, and linguistic culture in chapters three to seven respectively, we should not lose sight of their interdependence and interrelatedness. No part of life exists in and of itself. It is all a part of the larger whole and is only understandable in terms of that wider frame of reference.

Is There Purpose in Culture?

In trying to answer the question as to whether or not culture reflects purpose, we are not talking about the particular action of a man buying a pair of shoes because his old pair has worn out. We are here concerned with the broader aspects of the culture as a whole. Does culture express purpose, in the sense that it responds to biological and psychological needs? In general it does, but the purposes which it serves may be "imaginary" as well as "real." Some tribes in South America believe that after the birth of a child the father must rest for several days or weeks and take very special precautions for his own health if the child is to be well and strong. This observance, known as the couvade, rests on no "real" need, but it does satisfy an imaginary [17] need. Likewise in some cultures one cannot marry a person who is even distantly related. There is no biological justification for this, any more than there are biological reasons why a person should not marry his father's second wife (i.e. not the man's own mother) or his sister-in-law or godmother; but all of these types of marriages are condemned by one or more groups in our own culture. In some cultures, however, marriage with a sister-in-law is not only encouraged; it is almost obligatory. The so-called levirate marriage of the Old Testament in which a man was required to marry his brother's widow is an example.

Purpose in culture may be easily perceived in the practice of female infanticide and the suicide of old people in Eskimo culture. In many instances there simply was not enough food, and hence the killing of female babies (who were primarily consumers rather than procurers of food) was a kind of protection for the society as a whole. Similarly, when men got beyond the age when they were able to be active hunters or women were no longer able to chew the hides and thus prepare them, they were usually expected to commit suicide or to induce friends or relatives to kill them. All this may seem inhuman, but it was purposeful. It is not quite so easy to see how an Indian farmer among the Guambiano Indians of southern Colombia can gain prestige as a good farmer by going on a prolonged binge. We would assume that a successful farmer would want to fix up his home, buy more cattle, extend his holdings, or in some way or other better his condition—and certainly the Guambianos have a very miserable existence. However, as one Guambiano told me, "We cannot improve our homes or farms, for if we do, the Spanish-speaking neighbors will find some way (by legal trickery or force) to take away from us what we have. But if we have had a good crop, we can be drunk for several weeks, and then everyone will know that we have been successful farmers." There is no doubt an element of escapism involved in the drunkenness. Nevertheless, prestige is to be gained by drunkenness, while the techniques of our culture would very likely result in the Indian's total ruin.

Coca chewing among the Indians in South America is in the long run quite harmful, for it destroys their health, and yet it does serve a purpose in alleviating the pain and utter fatigue which comes to those who must toil so hard in the harsh climate of the Andes. Not all purposes are valid in that they correspond to real needs; nor are all purposes justifiable by their end results. Most human behavior, however, does respond to either real or imaginary needs, and to this extent it is purposeful.

"If Other People Do It, Why Can't We?"

Because anthropologists have pointed out that the morals of other peoples are different from our own and that such differences are not entirely without reason, they have been widely accused of preaching the doctrine of complete relativity of behavior and morality. Toward the end of the last century there was great interest in this subject, for people were reacting strongly to some of the stuffy Victorian concepts and false ideas about modesty. They reasoned that if Eskimos could kill old people who were no longer economically profitable, what was wrong with our doing so? If the Africans engaged in orgiastic sex practices as a part of religious fertility rites, what was to prevent us from doing the same and regarding them as altogether proper? Lurking behind such reasoning was the romanticizing of "primitive man" and false deductions from the popular theory of evolution that the actions of primitive peoples represented a kind of "natural behavior."

Such reasoning about relativity of behavior involved two basic errors: (1) the assumption that primitive man does behave "naturally," and (2) that one can transpose into one's own society all the factors in so-called primitive society which would in any measure justify such deeds. Primitive man is the result of just as long a

process of cultural development as is civilized man. Most evolution-
ists no longer claim that present-day primitive people are a true
picture of the social culture of primeval times. In fact, social evolu-
tionists are not concerned with justifying the morals of any group,
and the naïve assumption that actions can be isolated from the total
context of behavior has long since convinced any thoughtful analyst
that cultural justification for civilized man cannot be based on the
actions of primitives.

There is a sense, however, in which relativism does have a point
and a very valid one, namely, that actions in different societies have
different values, depending upon the mores of the people. Certainly,
to kill one's father in our society would be morally much more
reprehensible than for an Eskimo to do the same thing in his society.
Similarly, wife exchange among the Eskimos is not to be regarded
in the same light as in our culture. But this does not justify our
doing what the Eskimos do, nor their taking over some of our vices,
such as, excessive individualism, selfishness, and a mean disposition,
which are less condemned by our culture than by theirs.

The cultural relativism of modern science has been essentially an
absolute relativism. Redfield [18] describes this position as follows:

> Cultural relativism means that the values expressed in any culture are
> to be both understood and themselves valued only according to the way
> the people who carry that culture see things.

He goes on to point out, however, that this type of cultural relativism "is in for some difficult times." [19] Such a relativism is not only
impossible as a practical basis for anthropological investigation [20]
but it is also invalid in terms of an historical perspective.[21] Even if a
person insists on adopting the position of ethical neutralism, he is
still not justified in being ethically indifferent; in fact no one can
be, for we are all human beings, and not only the students of culture
but the results of a cultural process. All of this, however, does not
mean that we should be any less objective in our analyses or judgments, but we must reject emphatically the assumption that in order
to be objective about cultural facts one must wholeheartedly adopt
the dogma of absolute cultural relativity.

In contrast with the absolute relativity of some contemporary social scientists, the Biblical position may be described as a "relative relativism," for the Bible clearly recognizes that different cultures have different standards and that these differences are recognized by God as having different values. The relativism of the Bible is relative to three principal factors: (1) the endowment and opportunities of people, (2) the extent of revelation, and (3) the cultural patterns of the society in question.

The Parable of the Talents (Matthew 25:14-30) must mean that rewards and judgment are relative to people's endowments, for the one who receives five talents and gains five additional talents receives not only the commendation of his master, but an additional talent. (Compare also the Parable of the Pounds, Luke 19:12-27.) The Biblical position is clearly stated in Luke 12:48, "For unto whomsoever much is given, of him shall much be required."

Biblical relativism is also relative to the extent of revelation. The Apostle Paul indicates that the extent of revelation which men have received will be a factor in the final judgment: "For when the Gentiles, which have not the law, do by nature the things contained in the law, these, having not the law, are a law unto themselves" (Romans 2:14). Jesus himself did not hesitate to point out the distinction between the former revelation (e.g. Leviticus 24:20 and Deuteronomy 23:6) and his own declarations by saying, "Ye have heard . . . but I say unto you . . ." (Matthew 5:38, 39, 44.) The old standard of "an eye for an eye and a tooth for a tooth" was no longer valid by virtue of Christ's declaration that we must "love our enemies."

Jesus further explains the relationship of revelation to responsibility by saying, "That servant, which knew his lord's will, and prepared not himself, neither did according to his will, shall be beaten with many stripes. But he that knew not, and did commit things worthy of stripes, shall be beaten with few stripes" (Luke 12:47-48a).

Biblical relativism is also relative to the cultural patterns of the society. The Old Testament sanctioned the slavery of Gentiles by Jews (Leviticus 25:39-46), made provision for trial of jealousy by

ordeal involving the use of a curse (Numbers 5), sanctioned polygamy (not only by tacit consent but by such declarations as "Thus
saith the Lord God of Israel, I anointed thee king . . . and I gave
thee . . . thy master's wives into thy bosom . . ." [2 Samuel 12:7–
8]), and provided for relatively easy divorce (Deuteronomy 24:1–4).
These patterns of culture which were permitted or explicitly sanctioned in Old Testament times were not endorsed in the New Testament. In challenging the custom of easy divorce, by which a man
simply wrote out a letter and the wife was without recourse to
justice, Jesus said, "It hath been said, 'Whosoever shall put away
his wife, let him give her a writing of divorcement': but I say unto
you, That whosoever shall put away his wife, saving for the cause
of fornication, causeth her to commit adultery . . ." (Matthew 5:
31–32). In Mark 10:2–12 Jesus further elaborated on this problem
by pointing out that "for the hardness of your heart he [Moses]
wrote you this precept." Jesus makes it clear that this was not the
original plan and purpose of God.

Not only is there a relative relativism in the contrast between the
Old and New Testament standards, but even within the New
Testament this same principle is unmistakably enunciated. The
Apostle Paul attempted to be "all things to all men" that he
might win some. Paul lays down his principle in the following
manner:

And unto the Jews I became as a Jew, that I might gain the Jews; to
them that are under the law, as under the law, that I might gain them
that are under the law; to them that are without law, as without law
(being not without law to God, but under the law to Christ,) that I
might gain them that are without law. [1 Corinthians 9:20–21.]

This meant that Paul could conscientiously and vigorously object
to Peter's yielding to pressure from the Judaizers (Galatians 2:11–
16), while later Paul himself underwent rites of purification in the
temple, at the suggestion of the elders in Jerusalem who urged him
to show to all that "thou thyself also walkest orderly, and keepest the
law" (Acts 21:24). On the one hand, Timothy, whose father was
a Greek, was circumcised by Paul "because of the Jews which were

in those quarters" (Acts 16:3), but in Galatians 2:3 Paul makes a strong point of the fact that "neither Titus, who was with me, being a Greek, was compelled to be circumcised."

Biblical relativism [22] is not a matter of inconsistency, but a recognition of the different cultural factors which influence standards and actions. While the Koran attempts to fix for all time the behavior of Muslims, the Bible clearly establishes the principle of relative relativism, which permits growth, adaptation, and freedom, under the Lordship of Jesus Christ. The Bible presents realistically the facts of culture and the plan of God, by which He continues to work in the hearts of men "till we all come in the unity of the faith, and of the knowledge of the Son of God, unto a perfect man, unto the measure of the stature of the fulness of Christ" (Ephesians 4:13). The Christian position is not one of static conformance to dead rules, but of dynamic obedience to a living God.

What Does Anthropology Show Us?

Anthropology has made a number of contributions to our knowledge of ourselves and others, but we can summarize the most outstanding insights under three statements:

   a. *The behavior of people is not haphazard, but conforms to a pattern.* The fact that Aymara Indians have customarily let their comrades drown in Lake Titicaca rather than doing anything to rescue them is not to be attributed to inhuman, calloused disregard for human life. It results from a belief that the spirit of the lake is requiring a sacrificial victim, and that if the drowning man is rescued, his rescuer will be the next victim.

   b. *The parts of the pattern of behavior are interrelated.* The fact that San Blas fishermen do not sell fish but will sell coconuts, does not reflect any lack of commercial interest in life. These Indians are quite good businessmen, but fish are smoked and kept for fiestas, and a man's prestige and the acceptance of his daughter in society (in the case of puberty-rite festivals) are at least partially dependent upon his ability to have enough fish to serve the guests. Coconuts are not, however, related to social activities and hence are readily sold to anyone who offers a good price.

c. *The life of a people may be oriented in many different directions.* Americans have glorified strong individualism, the will to power, the accumulation of wealth, and the prestige which comes from being well known, whether as a gangster like Al Capone, or as an actress like Marilyn Monroe. The Zuni culture is oriented around religious ceremonialism, something which our culture appreciated more in the Middle Ages. The Shipibos of Peru have as their ideal "the one who has a heart," by which they describe a person who is entirely socially integrated. He does not talk too much or too little, he is helpful to others but does not neglect his own responsibilities; in short, he is an ideal member of the social unit of the village. On the other hand, the Dobus in Melanesia would regard the Shipibo ideal as being a fool, for their life is oriented around intrigue, treachery, and black magic, with extreme self-interest and anticommunity social motives.

3

RACE AND RANTING

The proud Batusi in Ruanda-Urundi (lying just to the east of the Belgian Congo proper) look down their long noses with utter contempt for the Bahutu, the *hoi polloi* of the land, who constitute more than 90 per cent of its population. Not for a moment do these tall, arrogant Batusi forget that their Nilotic, cattle-herding ancestors came down from the north and conquered the Bantu-speaking Bahutu. Even now, in an overpopulated land where terraced gardens hoard so much of the fertile soil, the Batusi lords let their long-horned cattle wander in what seems to be almost total disregard for the Bahutu's rights. These Batusi are not only conscious of their superior social status but of the racial differences which separate them from the smaller, chunkier Bahutu. Social status has been interpreted in terms of racial distinctions, and the Batusi feel that their racial characteristics account for their cultural superiority and for the fact that they are now masters of the land.

The despised Bahutu, on the other hand, satisfy their racial pride by looking down on the Batwa, pygmies who live in small groups and in more or less isolated areas. The Bahutu would never think of associating closely with a pygmy; in fact, they regard such a person as little better than an animal. It is true that the Bahutu carry on business with the Batwa, for the latter make rather crude pottery which they sell in exchange for grain, and in places where wild game still exists, the Batwa are professional hunters. If a pygmy wishes to buy a pitcher of beer to drink, the Bahutu will go and place it on the ground, then stand off at least ten feet while the pygmy drinks, and only after the pygmy has retired a culturally safe distance, will the Bahutu go and pick up the pitcher. Of course, if it is not quite empty, the Bahutu does not hesitate to drain it dry (good to the last drop!), but the Bahutu would not want to be closer than ten feet to the despised Batwa.

It was not without some severe emotional strains that some Batusi ever agreed to sit in the same church with the Bahutu, and the Bahutu were even more reluctant to admit Batwa converts. The Batwa, on the other hand, have erected a wall of relative cultural isolation behind which they defend their way of life by exclusiveness and an appearance of complete self-satisfaction.

Prejudice Is Universal

Everywhere in the world people recognize the in-group (the one with which they identify themselves) and the out-group (meaning all others). The establishing of an in-group consciousness is part of the psychological drive for a sense of belonging. The hostility which is so frequently a part of the out-group consciousness is in a measure a fortification of the in-group solidarity by sentiments of superiority; but in more instances than not, it is simply the poultry-yard complex, that is to say, each chicken knows what other chicken can be pecked at with reasonable guarantee of getting by with it. In other words, the out-group is a kind of scapegoat for one's hate satisfaction. Of course, there may be varying degrees of in-groups and out-groups, units with which one is more and more intimately associated and those which are more and more remote from one's own society. On one level a Protestant in the United States may feel that both Jews and Catholics constitute an out-group, but all these groups may identify themselves as an in-group in conflict with some foreign enemy, which now becomes the out-group.

Though we state that "prejudice is universal," that does not mean necessarily that racial prejudice as we know it today is universal in the world or has been universal throughout recorded history. Racial prejudice with its present-day type of rationalization has been primarily the development of the last two hundred years. It scarcely existed in classical times—certainly not in its present proportions— and it is relatively less acute in the Orient than it is in the West.

In the past certain peoples have regarded themselves as superior, and for a number of alleged reasons: divine descent (the Japanese), specially chosen of God (the Jews), or numerous cultural accomplishments (the ancient Greeks, who, however, were not infected with the virus of racial hostility). It is only within the last two or three centuries that cultural contrasts and antagonisms have been identified with racial differences. This social disease of racial prejudice, which began principally among the Anglo-Saxons and still exists there in its most accentuated form, has gradually spread to other parts of the world, thus constituting one of the gravest threats to "One World."

The Myth of Racial Superiority

By the beginning of the nineteenth century colonialism, imperialism, and slavery were in dire need of some social and moral justification. The fact that missionaries were being sent out to raise the moral level of the "benighted peoples" scarcely sufficed to warrant the unabashed exploitation of so many millions of people. Some persons were ready to employ the supposed Biblical doctrine of damnation to the Negroes by citing Genesis 9:25 in which Canaan as a son of Ham was cursed. However, even this was not the kind of "scientific" basis which seemed necessary for the nineteenth century. Such a basis was found, however, in the ethnocentric appeal of the evolutionary hypothesis. The theory of biological evolution provided the basis for ideas about social evolution. These related concepts were popularly accepted, and Western Europe soon had a "scientific" basis for its superiority, founded so largely on gunpowder (which was invented in China), on navigation (which was improved, but not invented, by Europeans), and on a desire for wealth (scarcely a unique cultural contribution).

On the basis of the evolutionary hypothesis, social scientists of the day rated the Negroes as the least evolved and, of course, the white race (especially the people of Western Europe) as the most evolved. Races such as the Chinese and the American Indians were some place in between. Scientists looked for correlations in languages, and they soon found what they regarded as the most primitive languages (in all instances these were spoken by culturally retarded peoples). They then contrasted these with the Indo-European languages, which include most of the languages of Europe. Matters of social organization, economic life, and religious concepts were all scaled from the "lowest" to the "highest." Invariably the victims of colonial exploitation were in the lowest categories and the imperialists' culture rated the highest. Perhaps never in the history of the world have those who claimed to speak in the name of science been so infected with the plague of racial egotism.

It is to the credit of present-day scientists that they have thoroughly discredited such ideas of racial superiority; but for the average man there lingers the idea that his contempt for other people is scientifically justified. It will take a long time to erase such cherished prejudices.

What Is Race?

Race is a very valid biological concept, but it is not a valid socio-cultural concept. There are biologically different specimens of humanity, and part of the task of anthropology is to describe and classify these types.

There are a number of methods for classifying races, none of which is totally satisfactory, by virtue of the very complexity of the subject matter.[1] The various races of mankind just do not neatly fit into any classification, but perhaps the most generally accepted formulation is the following:[2]

Caucasian
  Hindu (north India)
  Nordic (northern Europe)
  Alpine (central Europe)
  Mediterranean (Mediterranean region)
Mongoloid
  Mongolian (including Chinese, Vietnamese, Thai, Tibetan, etc.)
  Malaysian (including Malay and most of Indonesia)
  American Indian (often called Amerindian)

> Negroid
>> Negro
>> Melanesian (the black woolly-haired people of New Guinea, Solomons, New Britain and New Caledonia, and parts of the nearby South Pacific)
>> • Negritos, including pygmies in Africa, and similar small-statured, woolly-haired people in the Andaman Islands, Malay peninsula, and the Philippines.
>> Bushman and Hottentot (South Africa; these people have pepper-corn tufts of kinky hair and eyes somewhat resembling Mongoloids)
> Doubtful classification
>> Australoid (the aborigines of Australia, with dark skin, heavy eyebrow ridges and long wavy hair)
>> Veddoid (the Veddas of Ceylon, who have some of the same characteristics as the Australoid peoples)
>> Polynesian
>> Ainu (the very hairy, non-Mongoloid appearing people in Northern Japan)

Anthropologists employ numerous characteristics in determining race, including relative length of different parts of the body, size and shape of the head, amount of body hair, texture of body hair, blood types, shape of fleshy portions (nose, lips, epicanthic fold of the eye, etc.), and color of the skin. By giving greater or less priority to various features one comes out with a somewhat different classification of racial types. Actually, it is impossible to draw a line at any point and neatly separate peoples into their proper racial groups. One must think in terms of a continuum with *many* borderline cases. A "typical" person of any race is a kind of abstraction based on averages, and within any one race there are differences equally as great as between the respective averages of the races.[3]

It is not without some irony that skin color, the criterion most employed by the average man in determining race, has been found by anthropologists to be among the least satisfactory determinants.[4] Hindus, who certainly belong to the Caucasian race, may have skin which is darker than that of some Negroes. Similarly, some Amerindians have skin which is darker than some African Negroes; but this does not disqualify them from being predominantly Mongoloid. In East Africa there are such borderline cases as many Ethiopians, who in terms of general body form are Caucasian, but who possess dark skin and kinky hair. The classification of Ethiopians depends entirely upon the relative importance which is attached to certain criteria.[5]

Within particular racial groups (as determined by some classifications) we find some of the greatest variations. The tall, excessively slender Nilotics and the very short Bushmen and pygmies have all been classified as belonging to the Negroid race. Caucasians include narrow-headed, medium-headed, and broad-headed types, and the same is also true of American Indians. This type of criteria accordingly does not mean much when it comes to making the broader racial classifications.

It was once supposed that physical characteristics were more or less fixed, but Boas pointed out that the stature and head shape of children born of immigrant parents who had come to the United States tended to be successively more like the U.S. average depending upon the length of time the parents had been in this country.[6] This type of fact is difficult to explain, but it is true.

In judging some presumed racial differences one must always take the environment into consideration. The fact that in the United States the death rate from malaria is eight times higher among Negroes than among whites does not mean that the Negroes as a race are more susceptible to malaria than whites. Negroes in Africa have appreciably more immunity than whites, but in the United States Negroes, in comparison with whites, live in poorer homes, have less general resistance to such diseases because of poorer nutrition, and can afford much less medical attention. The fact that Negroes have a greater malaria death rate is thus primarily a matter of environment, not race.

Negroes in the United States also show more of a tendency to high blood pressure than do whites. This can be attributed in a measure to the cultural frustrations and resultant nervous tensions.

In our attempt to point out some of the anomalous features of racial distinctions we must not lose sight of the fact that there are differences and that these differences are biologically significant. That is to say, they are part of the biological heredity of each race. Some groups of people have developed certain biological specialties: the Nilotics are tall and thin, and Bushmen and Hottentot women during times of abundance of food develop excessively fatty buttocks, technically called steatopygia.

It is very easy to assume that a particular cultural group represents a race. Jews have been regarded as a "race" by many persons, but the truth is that they tend to approximate the local Gentile type wherever they have lived for any long period of time. This is conspicuously true of Jews from such diverse areas as Germany, Spain, and the Near East. Some observers have noted a little accentuation of the curl of the nostril where it joins the face,[7] but Jewish persons are much more marked by their manners, gestures, intonation of speech, and dress than they are because of their physical appearance.[8] If Jews had been an obvious racial element in Nazi Germany, Hitler would not have required them to wear the star of David so that they might be readily identified.

Racial differences do exist, but the types are not easily classified, and there is no correspondence between race and culture.

Are Some Races More Intelligent than Others?

Behind much of the average man's interest in racial differences is a haunting desire to find some basis for his own superiority. Some people reason that since intelligence is related to the brain, the greater the skull capacity the greater the intelligence. At one time this seemed to be a satisfactory theory, until it was realized that European females averaged about 10 per cent less in skull capacity than European males, and the ladies objected to being rated as 10 per cent less intelligent. Furthermore, the average skull capacity of the "primitive aborigines" of Australia was approximately that of European women. European men did not object too much to such a comparison, but the discovery that Hindu men had a conspicuously greater skull capacity than modern Europeans led to the complete abandonment of theories which tied physical form to intellectual capacity.

Another attack on the problem of the relative intelligence of the races was by means of intelligence tests. During World War I the U. S. Army gave the Alpha and Beta tests to hundreds of thousands of men. In the Alpha tests literate Negroes from some northern states were superior to illiterate whites from certain southern states. Negroes from Ohio and Indiana averaged higher in both the Alpha and Beta tests than whites from Kentucky and Mississippi. In other words, on the basis of such tests, one would conclude that the I.Q. of literate Negroes was better than that of illiterate whites. This of course points out the lack of validity of the tests to indicate accurately the intrinsic intellectual capacity. They did give a rough estimate of acquired knowledge and some general data on mental ability, since the latter can be trained and stimulated by education. Kluckhohn [9] cites tests of Negro children who had come from the South to New York City. These showed progressive improvement in I.Q. tests depending upon the number of years they had been in the North:

Years in New York City	Average I.Q.
1 or 2	72
3 or 4	76
5 or 6	84
7, 8, or 9	92

Some tests conducted with Hopi children in Arizona [10] indicate that these exceed the white American average about 10 per cent. On the other hand, it is very difficult to obtain satisfactory tests which are not dependent upon the cultural background of the people. Too often the tests reveal different cultural attitudes and training rather than different intellectual capacities. Even the manner in which we classify people is open to serious question. Why should persons be classified as Negro when they may have only a small percentage of Negro blood? Why should not, as in Brazil, a Negro who has a small amount of white blood be considered as a white? The reason is to be found in the structure of U. S. society, and not in any set of biological facts. It is sometimes argued that racial superiority shows up readily because mulattoes are consistently superior to Negroes who have no white blood. This is likewise a false judgment of inherent racial capacities. In the first place, in slave days those slaves who showed most individual capacity and were the readiest to learn were often selected as household servants and given considerable responsibility. Interbreeding of white masters with such superior Negroes naturally tended to produce superior children, who in turn were raised in or about the manor house and thus had additional cultural advantages. Such advantages have been maintained among mulattoes by a degree of social stratification in Negro society. Hence, the superiority of present-day mulattoes is no evidence that such qualities as they may exhibit are directly related to the addition of white blood.

Many persons have argued that cultural accomplishments are sure indications of racial capacities; and since Negroid peoples have not developed any large enduring empires or established any world civilizations, they conclude that the Negro is racially inferior. Sometimes people forget that the University of Timbuctu in the twelfth century compared quite favorably with contemporary universities in Europe. But quite apart from such isolated features of conspicuous accomplishments, it must be remembered that Negroid peoples have encountered heavy environmental liabilities: generally enervating climates, debilitating tropical diseases, and relative cultural isolation. For the most part they have lacked the cultural stimuli which the Greeks gave the Romans and which the classical world provided Western Europe. Furthermore, recorded history is still very short and world events certainly point to a shift of power from the white to the nonwhite races.

The fact that some primitive peoples of the world have not produced outstanding "geniuses" is scarcely evidence that such people are basically inferior. There may have been numerous geniuses of whom we have heard nothing or who, because of the limitations of their own culture, may have had little or no opportunity to express themselves in dramatic, creative ways. If a genius should arise among the Hopi people, he would have little chance for recognition, for Hopi life is not oriented so as to encourage individuals to be outstanding. In fact, Hopis try not to be conspicuous. Schoolteachers among them have found that it is fatal to praise one child above another or to select one child for special rewards. This is contrary to the Hopi pattern of an integrated social structure where the individual should be a functioning part but not a conspicuous leader of the social unit.[11]

Not only do we fail to find any correlation between race and intelligence; there is no correspondence between race and national characteristics. We usually regard the African Negro as relaxed, talkative, friendly, and decidedly extrovert. Even under the social strains of an inferior status in America he continues to have much the same outlook. However, many of the Negroid peoples of Melanesia are quiet, sensitive introverts, given to worrying and scheming. These differences in the Negroid race are the result of cultural distinctions and are not a part of their biological heredity.[12]

Mixed Races

The manner in which nationalist demagogues shout the praises of "purity of race" has brought the entire matter of racial purity into sharper focus. Only by the most colossal distortions of facts could Nazi "scientists" come out with the theory of "the pure Aryan race," of blond-haired, blue-eyed supermen who were to rule the world.

It is quite naïve to talk about any pure race at this stage in the world's history. Of course, there may be, as in the jungles of South America, some relatively small tribes who have inbred for such a long time that there is a high degree of resemblance among all the members of the tribe. But all the large aggregations of people have undergone considerable mixture. The peoples of Egypt, Mesopotamia, Greece, India, and China all reflect racial mixtures. From the biological standpoint hybrid races are more vigorous than inbred races. Fundamentally, therefore, there is no biological basis for objecting to such "hybrid races" or for classifying them as inherently inferior.[13]

Scapegoats and Scapelions

Racial prejudice is essentially scapegoatism. In some periods and societies such scapegoats have been witches, infidels, anabaptists, or Jews—minority groups who became a target for hate satisfaction. Of course, hate satisfaction is never given as a reason, for that would ruin the psychological basis of scapegoatism. Always there are other reasons: threats to national security, threats to national solidarity, affront to deities, or international conspiracy. The dominant social group always pictures itself as being threatened, and thus takes out its revenge on some minority group which cannot strike back. An interesting feature of such developments is that those classes which are the closest in the social structure reveal the greatest prejudice. The poor southern whites are on the whole much more racially prejudiced than the more wealthy ones. The poor have been struck from above, and hence they satisfy their frustrations by striking more fiercely at those below.

There is no doubt that economic and social competition contributes greatly to racial prejudice, but the economic and social antagonisms are primarily stimulants to, not causes of, racial hatred.

It must not be thought that every person who exhibits racial hatred is equally the victim of a desire for hate satisfaction. Once such a pattern becomes established for a particular social and economic group, the feeling of in-group and out-group consciousness fortifies the position of the entire group; and members who may not themselves have special reason to seek social revenge are caught up in the pattern.

Racial prejudice is complicated to a considerable degree by contextual setting. For instance, some missionaries from the southern part of the United States work in Brazil, where there is relatively little racial prejudice.[14] These missionaries have confessed that in Brazil they think nothing of associating with Negro people, staying in their homes, and having them as guests in their own homes. But back in the United States these same missionaries react strongly to a Negro sitting down beside them in a train or bus, and they would not think of having them as members of the same church.

Though Anglo-Saxons for the most part exhibit the most intense degrees of racial consciousness and prejudice, this same tendency exists throughout the world, wherever classes and racial groups are parallel. In Indo-China there is quite a hierarchy of racial classes, which, however, do not possess what we would call racial hatred, but rather racial antagonism, reflected in attitudes of competition and degrees of superiority. Because of political and economic advantages the French have been at the top. These are followed by the Chinese, who dominate much of the economic life. The next in rank are the Vietnamese, who in turn have a status superior to the Indians. Such people as the Laotians and Cambodians are generally next in the scale, while the primitive mountain tribes occupy the lowest rung of the socio-economic ladder. In South Africa the picture is exceedingly complex.[15] The British and Dutch are the top rivals, struggling for supremacy, and they tend to compensate for some of this frustration by racial conflicts with the rest of the population. The large numbers of Indians brought into the country for indentured labor have found a place as petty merchants and tradesmen, and their interests conflict with those of the whites as well as of the Negroes. Africans will in some instances strike back at Indians when they do not as yet dare to fight so openly with whites. Still another factor in the South African situation is the number of European Jews who have entered the country, especially during the last few years. More and more non-Semitic whites tend to find in the Jews a scapegoat for their frustrations. Even the Africans are divided by old tribal jealousies, but they constitute the vast majority of the population and are growing rapidly in numbers. With such a complex array of racial antagonisms and the balance between opposing parties so delicate, it is no wonder that people fear that scapegoats will turn into scapelions. Hatred is man's most dangerous emotion, for it breeds its own kind and paralyzes its victims with fear.

Back Doors and Bogeymen

In order to understand racial prejudice better, especially as it may affect the work of Christian missions, we need to examine it more closely, for racial prejudice infects and affects our churches and missionary work. It can probably be said that of all large national institutions (with the possible exception of some types of fraternal lodges) the Protestant church, especially in its more theologically conservative branches, is the most racially prejudiced institution in American life. Certainly, political parties, labor unions, civic clubs, and philanthropic societies have a much broader racial base than does the average Protestant church. Some commendable attempts are being made to correct this situation, but the tempo needs to be increased if the Protestant church is to speak with effectiveness to the contemporary world, which is growing more and more impatient with the racial intolerance of some of our churches.

The racial prejudice among church members and missionaries [16] is frequently only a kind of standoffish paternalism, which consists of patting oneself on the back for all that is being done to reach the poor benighted heathen. Audiences seem to be charmed by the most gruesome pictures of conditions in foreign countries, and any attempt to picture "natives" as just people of different cultures rather than half-savage brutes, is too often met with sheer indifference. A number of African students who have been trained in Christian mission institutions in their own countries find that when they attend churches in the United States they are often either shunned or effusively paternalized. As one student described his experience,

I had the feeling that I was regarded as exhibit A of their philanthropy. They would ask me to speak, not for what I had to say (for I know I am not a good speaker), but for the fact that I was a kind of freak—something which they had not seen before. I was to them a "native" and they frequently asked me to dress in my native costume.

Not a few missionaries in Africa make it the rule that all Africans must come to the back door. Dr. Lorenzo Turner, the distinguished professor from Roosevelt College, related [17] an experience which he had in West Africa. Since his small electric generator had broken down, he wished to ask an American missionary for the use of the mission's electrical current in order to record some folk music. The

African porter who met him at the gate was very perturbed as to what to do. Here was an American—of the same nation as the missionary—but a Negro. Should he take the guest to the front door or the back door? As a safety precaution the porter escorted Dr. Turner to the back door. However, the missionary, on learning that the recordings were to be African folk songs and dance music, refused the request anyway.

Some missionaries make it a practice not to shake hands with "natives" if there are any whites around, and they object seriously to having "natives" in for tea or refreshments. The feeling is that the indigenous peoples will not know their place if they are given too many privileges. As one missionary expressed it, "We once invited one young fellow in for tea, and from then on he thought he ran the mission." The obvious mistake was that only one person was invited and that it happened only once.

In one region of the Congo some missionaries tried to discipline their children by threatening them with such words as "You had better behave or the black men will get you." To their amazement they discovered that African mothers were using a similar technique by threatening their children, "You had better be good or the missionary will catch you."

It would be unfair to the vast majority of missionaries if one were to leave the impression that missionaries in general exhibit racial prejudice and that they engage in the kind of paternalism which talks about "your natives" and "our natives." Fortunately such missionaries are in the minority. When one missionary was returning from his last term in South Africa an African leader declared, "We loved this man because we knew we could always go to his front door and that he would shake hands with us wherever he saw us." Of another outstanding missionary in Africa it was said, "Our brother's skin may be white, but his heart is as black as any of ours"—a compliment of the highest order, for he was a brother under the skin.

On the whole, missionaries have tended to be far more sympathetic and less obviously racially prejudiced than the average colonial officials or businessmen. The missionary's problem has been

somewhat more subtle, for his contacts have been more prolonged
and intimate, and his goals have been more all-inclusive. The missionary's belief in the superiority of his message has too often
influenced him to think the same about his own culture, and this
danger of identifying Western culture with the Christian message
has been all too evident. Such real barriers as standards of living,
which the missionary either has refused to give up or has found
necessary to maintain for the sake of health, have added other causes
for misunderstanding. The use of such weighted words as "savage,"
"pagan," "heathen," and "native" has also contributed to the social
tensions. As a result one finds that back of many problems of the
indigenous church is the specter of race. Racial antagonisms are at
work even within the church itself.

Frustrations and Resentments

Racial prejudice inevitably breeds frustration and resentment in
the lower groups. This certainly has something to do with the high
rate of violent crimes within many of these groups.[18] Often these
resentments are blind and the hatred may be satisfied on members
of the same group.

People seem to be largely indifferent to the fact that color bars
are economically inefficient or socially disastrous. In South Africa
the African's ceiling is generally the European's floor as far as salary
and advancement are concerned. As a result of low income, there
is widespread inefficiency, lack of incentive and productivity, malnutrition resulting in bad health, demoralizing housing, and a fear
psychosis.

One very inadequate answer to the problem of racial discrimination is the creation of a "native elite." The French have done this
in Africa by officially recognizing the évolués (literally, "evolved
ones"), who receive French citizenship. The Portuguese have created a similar class of assimilados ("assimilated persons") in their
African colonies. Such groups are not, however, the ultimate solution, for they tend, as a natural reaction to their own position of
inferiority, to put as much distance as they can between themselves
and the rest of the indigenous population. They become a kind of
second-class elite, and as a defense mechanism they not infrequently

become more contemptuous of the lower class than the upper class is of the second class. Such groups in Africa have in some instances been the gullible adherents to theories which have tried to explain practically all of Negro culture as coming from Egypt. It is not without reason that Africans have thought that Europeans would respect Egyptian culture, and indirectly the Africans' status would be raised.

The degree of frustration in groups which suffer the results of racial prejudice can be seen in the experience of some Negro church leaders. One well-trained Cuban of Negro ancestry has attempted to work primarily among Negroes in Cuba—in fact, he was specially trained for this work and delegated to undertake it. However, he has not been successful with the Cuban Negro population, but has built up fine churches among people who are predominantly whites. It may seem strange, but the problem in Cuba is not uncommon. Negroes prefer to go to a church where a non-Negro is pastor, for this gives them more prestige. Furthermore, if the majority of the congregation is Negro, the church likewise has less appeal to other Negroes, for it is regarded as having less social standing. Accordingly, a Negro pastor has difficulty in developing a distinctly Negro congregation. It is no doubt better to have churches of mixed racial groups, but it is none the less a significant fact that the feelings of racial antagonism dictate such a situation.

Negro pastors in the United States are not infrequently accused of being racketeers since they receive so many "gifts" from their people. However, a popular Negro preacher finds it difficult not to be put in a position of accepting rewards beyond what would be a normal salary. The people in his congregation realize that as individuals they cannot attain the social status which comes from the possession of Cadillacs, furs, good clothing, and a nice home, but by giving their pastor such benefits they vicariously acquire some of his glory and social prestige.

Not Problems but People

A proper frontal attack on the question of race will not treat it primarily as a "problem," but in terms of people. As long as we insist on generalities we become confused by social pressures and historical precedents. Once the difficulty is grasped in terms of people, it is much more likely to be solved. Racial prejudice is largely a matter of culturally acquired personal prejudice. It must ultimately be dealt with on the individual, personal level.

If Christian missions (and Western civilization itself, for that matter) are to have any important voice in the world of tomorrow, the difficulties which arise from racial antagonisms and misunderstandings must be faced and resolved. It is not without some reason that Mohammedans are credited with being several times more effective in their missionary work in Nigeria than are Christian missionaries. A few years ago it was reported that in Tanganyika considerably more converts were won to Islam than to Christianity.[19] It is true that Mohammedanism offers the African status in a world religion and requires relatively little change in his present life— he continues with his same wives, fetishes, and most of his animistic practices. However, it cannot be denied that a very major element in the appeal of Mohammedanism to animist Africans is that Islam recognizes no racial barriers. The African knows that he is welcome in any mosque, and he also is aware that there are Christian churches which he cannot enter—simply because of his color.

Communism likewise has an effective appeal to indigenous populations who smart under the lash of racial discrimination. Soviet communism is not without its class distinctions, but in its revolutionary phases in various countries it is particularly careful to avoid any sign of racial discrimination. Furthermore, Africans and Orientals who have studied in Moscow generally return to their own countries with little or no resentment while many who have studied in the United States and Great Britain carry away deep antagonisms against Anglo-Saxons.

It would be unfair to suggest that nothing is being done to correct racial injustices and wrongs both at home and abroad. In a number of countries missionaries are working under the direction of local church leaders. In many instances missionaries and nationals receive identical salaries for the same experience and responsibility. In a number of institutions missionaries and nationals live in identical types of houses and share all the same social advantages and opportunities.[20]

Those who object to facing up to the racial problem often argue that we should wait until people are ready. However, the U. S. Army found that the best thing was to put people together and let them work out their problems. Similarly, housing authorities have not waited for people to adjust themselves to an "idea," but by being housed in the same apartment houses people of different races have adjusted themselves to each other. It is scarcely feasible to say, "Let the Negro prove himself first, and then we will accept him," when in the State of Mississippi during the school year 1935–36 about $30 was spent on each white child and only $9 was spent on each Negro child. (Compare this with $115 spent during the same year in California on each child—irrespective of racial background.)[21]

The fundamental rule for dealing with racial problems is to treat people as people. They do not care for paternalistic pampering— sometimes more deeply resented than outright slurs—nor do they wish to be subjected to galling restrictions. If only people were accepted for what they are or could be, there would be no problem; but to know that something over which one has no control—namely, one's biologically inherited appearance—is forever a bar to the realization of an ideal, this is what hurts and hurts deeply.

The following suggested "rules" may help to see beneath the surface of some of our own unanalyzed habits and attitudes and to aid us in our dealings with people of other races. One should:

a. *Adapt oneself to local customs of etiquette.*
   If, for example, people offer things with two hands, rather than one, it is important to follow the local custom, for there may be much more implied in such actions than meets the eye.[22]

b. *Show a vital interest in the beliefs of others.*
   It is not enough to avoid contemptuous attitudes toward another person's ideas. One should be vitally and sympathetically concerned with what other people think. This, of course, does

not necessitate compromising one's own ideas; it is simply the basis for effective communication.

✓ c. *Seek ways to heal tender susceptibilities and feelings.*

The disabilities and discriminations resulting from racial differences have often worn the personality raw. Only by appreciating this fact and by seeking not only to avoid slurs but to repair the wrong done by others can one possibly enter effectively into the understanding of others.

✓ d. *Seek to find matters of essential agreement and identity of attitudes between people of different cultural backgrounds.* Too often we are satisfied just to avoid pointing out differences between ourselves and others. We must go one step further and seek to find and encourage those points of contact in which we have similar outlooks. It is not enough that we should understand others (this can be a subtle form of patronizing); they must also understand us.

4

HOES AND HEADACHES

Our typical mental picture of a "primitive" farmer is too often that of a Neanderthal-looking savage carrying a short, heavy hoe through dense jungle on his way to a clearing, where he will scratch the surface of the earth so that it will sprout forth in all its splendor and leave our primitive friend plenty of time to sit in the shade of his favorite fruit tree. However, man's task of fulfilling his basic physical needs of food, shelter, clothing, and transportation is not accomplished so easily. There are some who seem to take the easy way and engage primarily in hunting, fishing, and gathering. Such people as the Motilones, living along the frontier between Colombia and Venezuela, may do a little planting, provided some huge tree in the forest crashes, smashing smaller trees and brush as it falls and in this way letting some light into the heavily forested region. But for the most part the Motilones are the hunters and scavengers of the region, eating practically anything, including some kinds of animal dung and mineral-rich clays. Their material culture is, however, considerably more complicated than that of the aborigines of Australia and Tasmania who hunted with spears and lived largely on wild roots and seeds, but whose life was anything but easy.

Provided that one's physical wants are not too great or varied, it is possible to live in some parts of the world without very much exertion. Many of the islands in the Central South Pacific abound in coconuts, breadfruit, pandanus, arrowroot, shellfish, and fish. If one is willing to eat such food and is not too much concerned about snails, landcrabs, ants, and mosquitos, one can live and live well.

But the tropics, in which so many nonliterate peoples live, are not the paradise that some have pictured. Fast-growing weeds, torrential rains, which leach the mineral content out of the soil, and hordes of insects make the problems of sustenance far more difficult than we are likely to imagine.

Not So Dumb

Since our own society has specialized in mechanical devices, it is sometimes difficult for us to conceive of life without cars, refrigerators, automatic washing machines, and running hot and cold water. Accordingly, we tend to look down our noses at other people because they have not invented or copied us in inventing and using such machines. However, other people in the world have also shown ingenuity and initiative in material developments.

In the United States we are only now coming to appreciate the value of terracing the farm land, but this has been practiced for generations in China, Ruanda-Urundi, Peru, Arabia and the northern Philippines. In fact, the irrigation systems which were developed by the Inca Empire in Peru are extraordinary feats of engineering. Steep mountainsides were skillfully terraced, and the irrigation canals were engineered in such a way that every terrace received its proportionate amount of water without causing heavy erosion or flooding. Present-day irrigation engineers have produced nothing more ingenious than the Incas devised centuries ago.

Windowless huts of mud and thatch strike us as being quite "impossible," but there is no type of construction in Central Africa which is cooler. Furthermore, a dark interior is not hospitable to flies, which means that one can stay inside during the day with comfort.

Eskimos discovered, no doubt by accident, that one way to keep cold air out of their igloos was to trap it in a tunnel leading into the igloo. The tunnel is constructed with a dip, so that the cold air, which is heavier, is caught in a natural trap, thus permitting the interior of the house to be heated much more economically.

The Dinkas' custom of sleeping in the ashes of a dung fire and smearing themselves with such ashes is not just a method of making themselves look ghastly. These ashes, in combination with perspiration or water used for bathing, produce a kind of lye and serve to provide the Dinkas with a mild antiseptic, and as a result they suffer from conspicuously fewer skin diseases.

The Motilones, as well as many other Indians of South America, demonstrate remarkable manual skill in making excellent blow guns. The Tarahumaras in northern Mexico are exceptionally adroit in constructing granaries out of hand-hewn logs, which fit so tightly that a knife blade can be rarely forced between them. Remarkable engineering skills were shown by the Indians in the region of Cuzco, Peru, who built walls of huge irregular blocks of stone, some of them weighing many tons, but all joined together with incredible accuracy. One stone of eleven sides fits so snugly into a wall that there is no point at which even the thinnest object can be inserted between this and the adjoining stones. The Shipibos make exceedingly thin pottery without the aid of a potter's wheel, but it is remarkably well formed and fired so evenly that it rings like a bell.

In the sciences, Western civilization now has the lead, but it cannot take credit for everything. Zero, one of the most important concepts in mathematics, was invented by the Hindus and also by the Mayans in Yucatan. These same Mayans could predict eclipses and had worked out an amazingly accurate calendar. It is to the credit of South American Indians that we have quinine as an antimalarial drug, and "primitive" agriculturalists have given to the world such foods as corn (maize), white potatoes, chile, tomatoes, and chocolate (from the Western Hemisphere), and coffee (which still grows wild in some parts of Abyssinia), wheat, rye, rice, and bananas (from the Eastern Hemisphere). They also domesticated most animals used for food or work. As far as the development of foodstuffs is concerned, modern civilized man is very much a debtor to the so-called uncivilized peoples.

It would not be correct to imply that indigenous peoples have always been highly intelligent or farseeing in their practices. The Paez Indians of southern Colombia have engaged in slash-and-burn agriculture for generations. They cut down the forests and brush at the beginning of the dry season; and then just before the heavy rains set in, they burn the fields, including the grasslands. This is the easiest way to lay bare the soil for planting and to enrich it with chemically valuable ash, but it also exposes the soil to heavy erosion. In times past, when there were always plenty of other mountain slopes on which to cut and burn, this was not too ruinous to the Paez economy; but because of the ever-encroaching private lands of Spanish-speaking farmers such disastrous practices will have to be stopped. Nevertheless, it is not easy for people to learn new practices overnight, especially when they do not have the tools to clear the land and to plow the soil. On the other hand, many Indian farmers permit their fields to be littered with debris of sticks, dead grass, weeds, and clumps of dead roots. This may be untidy, but it is a very important deterrent to erosion. Though the man with a hoe may only scratch the soil, his work results in less disastrous erosion than would occur if the soil were plowed with turning plows.[1]

Shell Axes and Sewn Planks

People must adapt themselves to their physical environments. People do not wear parkas in southern Florida nor dress in sun suits at Point Barrow, Alaska. As Malayo-Polynesian people spread through the islands of the South Pacific they came to coral atolls which had no stones for making stone axes. The only equivalent substance was the relatively hard part of huge mollusk shells. Accordingly, shell axes came into use. The constant wet, damp climate of the Pacific Northwest resulted in most of the Indians of that area going barefooted, for the climate tends to rot leather, and there is very little spiny vegetation.

On large volcanic islands of the South Pacific where there are huge trees the method of making a canoe is to hollow out large logs. However, there are no such trees in the low coral atolls of the Marshalls. Nevertheless, the people make large boats for themselves, using planks from irregularly shaped breadfruit trees. These planks are carefully shaped and ingeniously laced together, and the prow of the boat is slightly curved to one side so as to compensate for the lateral drag of the outrigger.

In a number of instances people have attempted to carry with them features of their culture which simply do not fit in the new environment. The Batusi in Ruanda-Urundi insist on having their cattle; and the Onas in Tierra del Fuego seemed content to erect very inadequate shelters, which were perfectly all right in the warmer regions to the north, but not in the inclement region of Antarctic storms. The Japanese, as they pushed north in Japan and drove out the Ainus, continued to construct thin wooden houses with paper-screen partitions. These houses are admirably designed for lands farther south and are delightful for summer weather in Japan, but they can be insufferably cold in winter. On the other hand, Americans, whose ideas of houses originated largely in northern Europe, are only now beginning in the southern states to build the kinds of houses which are more open to the outdoors.

Sour Mush and Sauerkraut

Nowhere is the principle of selectivity in culture more striking than in the matter of foods. Though there is an almost infinite variety of things which people can and do eat, it does not mean that all eat the same things. One missionary in Congo used to make fun of her cook for eating a kind of sour mush made of manioc root which was permitted to sour. Actually, the sour food was better for the people since some of the starch was changed to sugar by the souring process, and the fermentation resulted in some vitamin B. When the missionary was leaving for a furlough, she gave her cook a few cans of food which were left over. But before she had left, the cook came back to the house, holding his nose and carrying at arm's length a can of sauerkraut. Jokingly but emphatically he said, "Don't ever talk to us about eating sour mush." (One wonders what the cook would have thought about limburger cheese.)

Termites are regarded as a great delicacy in Congo, and I can testify that they are good, both raw and fried. Eating a live termite may seem a terribly uncouth thing to do, but we eat live oysters, while most Africans would regard oysters as completely unfit for human food. Some people of Western Europe and America have strong scruples against eating blood, but the Masai of Kenya consider warm blood a great delicacy. They draw it from the veins of a cow through hollow arrows and often mix it with fresh milk (their equivalent of our strawberry soda).

Even if people have cattle it does not mean that they will use them as we do. The Nilotic men drink milk, but they make no cheese. The Chinese, on the other hand, will have practically nothing to do with milk products, but are passionately fond of pork. Orthodox Jews and Mohammedans will not touch pork, but they use dairy products abundantly. Some people of Africa make butter, but only to smear on their bodies for decorative purposes, and the inhabitants of the island of Ukara in Lake Victoria in East Africa keep cattle primarily for producing fertilizer.

The variety of material objects of a culture may be almost numberless, depending upon the complexity and the degree to which such a culture has borrowed from others. We have not the space to consider many of the fascinating features of housing, clothing, food, agriculture, transportation, domesticated animals, tools, arms, and decorations—all of which go to make up the material culture of a people. We are more concerned here with the importance which is attached to material possessions and with the ways in which certain material features of culture affect other areas of life, e.g. the social, religious, and esthetic, and how these in turn affect the material culture.

"Not by Bread Alone"

Since the time when theories of economic determinism became popular, there has been a tendency to exaggerate the importance of the economic aspects of life. There is no doubt about the fact that economic factors were present in the Crusades of the Middle Ages, the Inquisition, the Reformation, and the Civil War in the United States. However, economics does not tell the whole story. In the Crusades, the Inquisition, and the Reformation, people were convinced that they were struggling primarily for religious reasons, and during the Civil War in the United States people were deeply concerned with the humanitarian attitude toward slavery. "The Battle Hymn of the Republic" echoes the deep religious sentiment which existed at the time. Economic factors contribute very extensively to cultural patterns, but they do not in themselves explain culture. In fact, many people engage in activities which are economically quite unprofitable. For example, community labor enterprises in aboriginal societies are rarely economical in terms of time and energy expended and results accomplished. The common practice among most Aztec Indians in Mexico is to invite all the neighbors to help in building a house. The future owner may have already cut most of the important poles and obtained most of the thatch, but the actual construction is a community enterprise. In order to obtain his neighbors' help the future owner has to provide a great deal of food and liquor for the guests. It would be more economical for him to build the house slowly by himself, or to hire professional builders by the day. But this is just not done if one wishes to be an accepted member of the village. The community activity is a time of merriment and social exchange; and though it is not economical, it is perpetuated.

The economic patterns of a culture do not necessarily determine whether inheritance is to be reckoned through the mother's or the father's line (there are contiguous matrilineal and patrilineal tribes in Africa which have almost identical economic systems). Wealth may have nothing to do with religious privileges, as in the Zuni culture; and the complexity of the material culture has no special effect on languages, except that people always have words to talk about all the things they have or wish they had, and their vocabulary may be accordingly greater depending upon the variety of items in the material culture. It would be wrong, however, to underestimate the effect of the material culture on the other phases of culture. In a region such as the arid plateaus of Nevada the Indians did not develop a professional priesthood. The fact that the subsistence level was so low that it took practically the entire population to procure enough food to exist may in part explain the lack of specialized activities. Such a region did not provide the material resources for high specialization of work or nonproductive elaboration of culture.

One does not find complex cultures in the jungles of South

America, where economic units are necessarily small due to the relative scarcity of game, difficulties of land transportation, and the impossibility of storing food over long periods of time. Where only a small number of people can exist together and where they have to change location frequently because of the shortage of game or the changing course of rivers, it is quite understandable that one does not find elaboration of culture resulting from extensive specialization of activities. It is therefore a very valid principle that the margin of subsistence does provide for the specialization of work and the multiplication of cultural features. Nevertheless, even in such a very primitive material culture as that possessed by the aborigines of Australia, one finds surprisingly complex social structures. One cannot establish a simple one-to-one correspondence between the advantages of the physical environment and the complexity of any and all phases of the culture.

Share, Give, Barter, or Buy

There are four principal methods by which material possessions pass from one person to another. In some small village and tribal units there is a high degree of sharing. A hunter may kill a wild pig, but the meat belongs almost equally to all members of the village. However, complete economic communism probably nowhere exists. A hunter may be required to share his game, but his corn crop may be regarded as his, for the use of himself and his family.

Some societies in the South Pacific have worked out an elaborate system of "gifts." One village may make a gift of fish to another village, and in return this second village is expected to reciprocate with a gift of sweet potatoes, sometimes left at a remote spot and with no direct communication between the parties concerned. There is a tacit, traditional agreement as to the corresponding values, and failure to conform can bring on dire consequences.

Where there has been no system of money or credit, people may barter their goods, but this is usually awkward. Accordingly money systems developed in various parts of the world: cocoa beans among the Aztecs, cowrie shells in the Malayo-Polynesian areas (as well as elsewhere), glass and porcelain beads in Palau, metal coins in the Near East and Asia, and paper money in the Orient.

Even a relatively simple culture may have quite a complex pattern of economic life. We may make an overly simplified diagram of the two major economic cycles in the Shilluk economy:

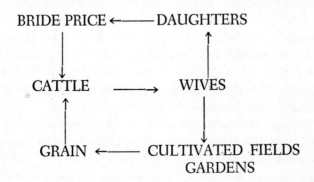

There are two interlocking cycles. If one has plenty of cattle, then he can have several wives. By having more wives, one can have more cultivated fields, since the women do most of the farming. With more fields one can harvest more grain, which in turn makes it possible to acquire more cattle. However, some of the cattle go for wives of one's sons, but this is just extending the family unit. By having more wives, one presumably has more daughters, and thus more cattle come back as part of the bride price. In general, sons and daughters more or less cancel each other out as far as acquiring more cattle is concerned, but the larger the family, the greater the economic resources. The Shilluk economy (even in its simplest outline) is by no means simple. What appears to be a hand-to-mouth existence may be relatively complex.

Modern civilized man is not the only one who has been caught up in the highly competitive economic struggle for prestige and power. The Indians of the Northwest Pacific coast developed a truly dog-eat-dog kind of economy with interest rates of about 100 per cent a year, great show of possessions, arrogant destruction of one's wealth in order to force one's competitor to destroy an equal amount, and even the slaying of slaves in order to demonstrate one's prowess in the vicious game of unrestricted economic competition. Every child began this life-consuming game at a very young age, when he received from his relatives some blankets, which he in turn distributed and then waited for them to be returned with interest. Not only was his livelihood dependent upon his success in this venture of trading, but his future rank in society and his reputation for being a "success" were determined primarily by his business acumen and capacity to bring public ridicule upon his competitors by outbluffing or outsmarting them. With the change of only a few details in this picture we would not be too far from contemporary Western civilization.

Planned economies are not solely the development of contemporary man. The Incas worked out an exceedingly well-controlled and regulated economy. The entire country was divided into districts and each district subdivided into units of 1,000, 100, and finally 10 heads of families. People were expected to marry at a certain age, engage in work assigned by a bureaucracy with headquarters in Cuzco, produce established quotas of various products, consume a specified amount, and store the rest for the use of the military and civil government officials or for transportation to parts of the empire which might have suffered crop failures. All of this was managed without writing but by means of an intricate system of bookkeeping made possible by the use of *quipus*, various colored strings which could be tied in different kinds and numbers of knots in order to record significant information.[2]

How Much Is He Worth?

The question, "How much is he worth?" is not easy to answer unless one fully understands the culture and the context. He may be the wealthiest person in Palau, in that he possesses the finest and historically more famous glass and porcelain beads, but these beads are not immediately convertible into U. S. dollars in order to buy cars, boats, and other foreign merchandise. One may own part of the largest piece of Yap money ever quarried, a piece which broke the tackle and sank to the bottom of a shallow harbor in Palau, where it can still be seen and on the basis of which people still do business. This is, however, a kind of "credit" no more queer nor less valid than floating loans on the basis of gold in Fort Knox or of stocks and bonds carefully stored away in the subterranean vault of a city bank.

Possessions are not just accumulations of things. Copyrights, patents, caste in India and union cards in America (both of which mean permission to work at a particular occupation), the privilege of conducting certain religious ceremonies (much prized by the Zunis), and membership in certain clubs and lodges are all non-material possessions which may be even more valuable. Poets in the Andaman Islands are very jealous of their songs. In fact, no one else can sing them without paying a handsome fee. Among the Hidatsa Indians of the Middle West, membership and high position in one of the warrior societies was regarded as the most prized possession, and this could only be acquired through buying the membership and the rank. In some societies high distinction comes to one who possesses some symbol of authority. In Great Britain the keeper of the Privy Seal is a person of great distinction, but in Uganda it is the keeper of the king's umbilical cord (carefully preserved at the time of birth) who has status and prestige.

Our concepts of property must undergo radical changes when we come into contact with some cultures. In northeast Congo one may buy land, but that does not mean one owns the termite hills which are on the land. Such hills are passed on from one generation to another and may be owned by persons living several miles away. On the night after the first heavy downpour of the rainy season, the people in the villages scatter in every direction to gather termites at their own hills, situated more frequently than not on other people's land. In the Philippines squatters are permitted to build on almost any unfenced, unimproved land. The owner of the land must usually recompense such squatters if at a later time he wishes to use the land himself. In a Maya village in Yucatan the farm land surrounding the village belongs to all the people collectively. A man may choose any piece he wishes to cut, burn, and plant, and for as long as he uses the field (usually about three years) the land is his. However, when it is finally left to grow back to jungle in order to kill out the grass which makes continuous planting unprofitable, it is again the property of any person in the village who wishes to use it. The aborigines in Australia regard the land as a perpetual inheritance of the residents. Warring bands may fight and kill one another, but they would not think of expropriating the land, for they regard the original residents as having a spiritual connection with the land. It would be both improper and unwise for someone else to try to live there, for he would lack the protection of the local spirits.

Wealth means more than accumulated possessions. It is fundamentally a symbol and a means of prestige, aggression, or security. Money cannot be eaten and usually it is not worn for decoration. Generally it is not loved purely for its own sake. It stands for prestige, especially in our Western culture, and it is one of the most effective means of aggression, since it provides a technique for controlling other persons. It likewise signifies security, but usually this aspect is exaggerated beyond what is really involved. What is meant when one talks of security is not generally in relation to the basic physical needs but the security of position, status, prestige, and a feeling of power.

Material and Social Culture [3]

It is inevitable that features of material culture affect the social patterns of society. In the desertlike interior of Australia, where the indigenous population has not exceeded five persons per hundred square miles, one inevitably finds a different type of social life from what exists in Java, where the population is around 90,000 persons per hundred square miles. Where people are primarily hunters and gatherers, living in relatively isolated bands, there is not the same chance for a highly centralized type of government, an integrated economic life, or full and frequent exchange of ideas. Through the years dialects gradually differ more and more, and finally there are scores of mutually unintelligible languages. Isolated peoples are generally characterized by considerable independence of action and thinking. They are largely self-reliant and do not take easily to the introduction of new ideas or techniques. Herding peoples are quite similar, for they likewise roam over large tracts of land and cannot live in restricted areas. However, they tend to come together more frequently than hunters and gatherers, since seasonal differences in climate often involve moving animals from one area to another.

Among stock-raising peoples, women often hold a rather inferior position, while in a hoe culture, where women frequently do much of the work, there are more opportunities for them to influence decisions. However, there are some exceptions to this, for among the Hottentots, who have been pastoral, women have a relatively higher position than among the Bantus, most of whom engage in hoe horticulture.

In some instances the change of an economic factor in the culture has modified the social structure. Before the introduction of firearms, some of the Athapascan Indians of northern Canada not infrequently practiced polyandry; that is to say, two or three men would share a single wife. The rigors of the climate were hard on women, and the absence of game made it difficult for each man to support a wife and family. However, after the introduction of firearms and the almost insatiable demand for fur pelts, which the women prepared for the trading companies, it became not only possible but profitable for a man to have more than one wife. Accordingly, there was a tendency to shift to a degree of polygyny. Here the material culture feature of guns and the economic demand for furs seriously affected the social pattern of marriage.

The introduction of turning plows into Angola has upset the division of labor between men and women. In the hoe culture women did most of the field work—as well as most of the domestic work—but with the coming of the plow, men have had to take over, for it is considered highly improper for a woman to touch a cow or ox. For this reason men must do the plowing and cultivating, and there has been a corresponding shift in the social structure.

At the present time the great mining centers of Africa are upsetting many of the social patterns of tribal life.[4] Men are off working in the mines for many months at a time. Marital fidelity is neither required nor expected, and accordingly marriage bonds are relatively brittle. Villages often lack the leadership of a high percentage of the most active men, and persons who are guilty of crimes against the local society can always escape to the mines, from which they may return with money and prestige. For the most part whites are either unaware of or unconcerned about the incalculable damage to human life and the immense amount of human suffering and frustration which such "material and economic progress" has introduced into African society.

The relationship between the material and social aspects of culture is by no means a one-way influence. The social patterns also affect the material features. Among the Ifugao of northern Luzon, in the Philippines, the acquisition of material possessions is the one thing which counts. A man may be industrious and brave—both are valued qualities among the Ifugao—but if he is not wealthy, all his bravery and industry count for very little. Since the social structure places so much emphasis upon the acquisition of wealth, it is no wonder that this provides a very powerful incentive for a highly competitive economic life, involving the development of some of the most ingeniously terraced rice fields in the world.

Socio-religious features of culture may cause considerable hardship in the material aspects. The Yapese insist that each person should eat food from his own inherited gardens and that such food should be cooked in individual pots so that it will not be contaminated by the food of others. This means that Yapese cooking is no easy task—but fortunately for the women it is not very fancy.

The evaluation of certain types of jobs in terms of the prestige of those who engage in such work certainly influences a person's choice of occupation. We grant considerable prestige to a college professor (even though he may be thought of as a kind of fuddy-duddy) in contrast with a plumber, who, if he is any good at all, makes considerably more money than the professor. Some women would much prefer to be hostesses in a restaurant rather than waitresses, even though the latter are often better paid. At one time the white-collar worker was the object of social envy, but his poor pay in proportion to his training is tending to change all this; and now mechanics, who are more important to our mechanized life, receive more of the material benefits. When as in some instances college janitors—

now called "building engineers"—make more money than many teachers in the same institutions, it is a sign that our systems of social (i.e. prestige) and material (i.e. money) rewards are not synchronized.

Societies generally find some means of restricting the heavy concentration of material possessions in too few hands. Such concentrations of wealth may be liquidated by such legal means as income and inheritance taxes or by the cultural pressures of demanding gifts to be made to the people. The ancient Greeks required the rich to undertake such tasks as the building of shrines and the equipping of warships, and the Aztecs insist that the rich take their turn in providing fiestas for the villagers. Where cultural pressures do not yield "voluntary" contributions the have-nots may, on occasion, shoot the rich and confiscate their wealth. Some of the Dakota Indians in Canada have a more subtle way of discouraging the accumulation and display of wealth and prestige. If on some important occasion a Dakota warrior wants to show off his military honors by wearing his war regalia (our equivalent to pinning on ribbons and medals), he is required to give away some valuable possession, such as a horse or a wagon. This kind of deterrent is both effective and socially beneficial. Some Shilluks take great precautions against one of their number becoming too wealthy. One young man near Malakal had obtained some small mango trees, which he carefully tended for several years. They were just getting to the point where they might become productive (there is a considerable demand for such fruit in the city of Malakal) when he went out one morning to discover that they had been cut off right at the root. Since they were so near his home, only a member of the family or one in the same small social unit could have destroyed the trees. Nothing was ever said and no complaints brought, but it was clearly understood that the other Shilluks were opposed to this young man's innovation and potential economic advantage.

Material and Religious Culture

We must not presume that religion is primarily associated with a sense of economic insecurity and that such fears and apprehensions are the stuff out of which religious culture grows. No doubt there is some relationship between material insecurity and certain types of religious experiences, and yet religious fervor is not directly proportionate to material insecurity. The people of West Africa are not on the whole economically insecure, but they have developed some very elaborate religious rites and ceremonies. Life in China has been anything but secure for many hundreds of years, for the very dense population in proportion to the material resources of the country has resulted in a rather short life expectancy for the average peasant. Nevertheless, one cannot accuse the Chinese of being a highly religious people. Except for a carryover of some aspects of animism in the philosophical cloak of Taoism the Chinese are very materialistic and earthy. It will be argued by some that this results from intellectual enlightenment and is paralleled by the recent antireligious developments in Western Europe. To an extent this is true, and yet it equally well substantiates the fact that material insecurity alone does not induce religion.

One missionary working among some Indians in Latin America complained to me that the Indians among whom he worked were "just too well-to-do to become converts." These Indians did not respond very enthusiastically to the opportunity to buy sugar and kerosene from the missionary at a reduced price, but the principal reason for the failure of this work was the utter incapacity of the missionary to understand the people. Their severe frustrations, combined with the desire for prestige and with certain religious concepts which encouraged drunkenness, resulted in weekly debaucheries of whole communities. It was not the possession of money which made them unresponsive to the Christian message. They had never understood that it was in any vital way related to their lives.

In one area of Angola it was considered to be a grievous religious offense against the spirits to farm the rich alluvial soil in some of the valleys. An agriculturally trained missionary, himself a Negro from the United States, defied the taboos and planted in the forbidden territory. The bumper crop which he harvested and the fact that he suffered no evil consequences induced the less timid people nearby to do the same. Soon the valleys were producing great quantities of food and thus meeting a critical need of the people.

Material and Esthetic Culture

Material culture provides some of the raw materials for esthetic expression, and the esthetic tastes of the people dictate the form which the artistic production takes. South American Indians do not carve elephant ivory, nor do Central Africans weave intricate designs with llama wool. Each area is dependent upon its material objects. Micronesians make exquisite necklaces and headdresses of beautiful shells and finely woven pandanus fiber. Many Indonesians, especially the Balinese, are masterful carvers of beautiful hardwoods. The Eskimos have shown remarkable talent with walrus ivory; the Indians of the Northwest Pacific coast produced massive totem poles and delicate stone carvings, while Navajos developed sand painting into a remarkable art.

One must not forget, however, that even the simplest objects may have unsuspected esthetic value. A Navajo, who was helping a white man build a house, could not refrain from voicing his objection to putting interior walls and partitions in the house. This, he claimed, would destroy the unity of the family. He insisted that the round Navajo *hogan* without interior partitions was much more meaningful and appropriate for the family, which should live together without the imposition of such artificial barriers as interior partitions.

Clothing is often thought to be primarily for protection, but it is more often than not a means of decoration. Style magazines such as *Vogue, Charm,* and *Mademoiselle* do not waste time in pointing out that a particular new dress design will "cover one up." Rather, the advertisements try to indicate how such a model will expose one in the culturally accepted way. Western clothes tend to do just that, namely, to reveal the body contours in the most culturally approved or desired manner. On the other hand, the typical Japanese kimono, with heavy girdle in front and padding in the back, succeeds in disguising or "leveling out" almost all the body contours.

It is taken for granted by most people that those primitive tribes who wear little or no clothing must feel some hidden shame. So far as can be determined, they have no such sense of shame, but on the other hand, regard the wearing of clothes as being exceedingly peculiar. It is true that when such people become Christian converts, they do put on clothing, often in an indescribably ludicrous way; but that does not necessarily mean that they had any inherent shame formerly nor that they regard clothes as a necessary part of Christianity, though they are often told that such is the case. For them the wearing of certain types of clothing is just a matter of conformance to other standards. Clothing provides social acceptance and a feeling of identification with the prestige-laden foreign culture, but it may or may not be a response to spiritual convictions.

On the basis of very wide observation and study, it can be said that there is no correlation between the amount of clothing which people wear and their standards of morality. However, in any one society those who are "modest"—in terms of the local system of etiquette—are more likely to be moral than those who do not so conform. Nevertheless, a person may be modest in terms of the amount or kind of clothing and yet be a sexual exhibitionist.

Material Culture and Christian Missions

It has been entirely too easy to divorce the message of Christianity from the material culture by concentrating on heaven and leaving the earth to take care of itself. This error has arisen because of the fatal division into the sacred and secular elements of life, and it has been reinforced by a reaction against the diluted humanitarianism of an exclusively social gospel. The truth is that if God is left out of anything He is not entirely in anything. Life is not so neatly compartmentalized as our easy consciences would lead us to think.

The missionary who begins to preach is soon confronted with the acute need of sick human bodies. But he discovers not only that medicine is indispensable, but that many diseases are the direct result of malnutrition. Accordingly, he realizes that agricultural work is vital to a message of life. To meet such needs some missionaries in Angola have introduced new wheat, improved sweet potatoes, and better breeds of pigs; in the Lake Titicaca region of

Bolivia missionaries brought in eucalyptus trees and better strains of wheat and onions. A co-operative ranch of Christian farmers has been formed in eastern Cuba, and a highly organized fishing and industrial village of Christians has been established under African leadership near the mouth of the Niger. The agricultural Institute of Allahabad, India, is world famous for its far-reaching effects. This does not mean that Christian missions are simply religious philanthropy.[5] They are not; but if the message of Christian missions is to reach living people, it must show them how they can make the Christian message a reality in every area of life, and this must include material culture as well as all other aspects.

One of the major contrasts between Western secularized culture (in which religion is only for Sunday) and most primitive cultures is the high degree to which in primitive societies religion pervades all phases of life. These cultures are now undergoing drastic upheavals, in which the religious and spiritual values are being violently denied or indifferently cast aside. The Christian missionary can potentially be one of the greatest integrating forces in the present cultural turmoil and change, if in the conflict produced by the new technologies he can show the complete relevance of his life-embracing message.

5

FRIENDS AND FRUSTRATIONS

People live together in groups, but not simply because of the physical necessities of life or for the nurture of the young. People associate with one another primarily in order to satisfy the basic psychological needs of belonging and recognition.[1] Such needs are fundamentally egocentric, and yet they depend upon associations for fulfillment. Here lies the basic reason for the numerous frustrations which accompany social culture. When man is dealing with things, he feels a sense of mastery or challenge. When he is dealing with what seem to be supernatural phenomena, he is more inclined to be overwhelmed or resigned. But in association and competition with other people his successes and failures, rewards and penalties, elation and dejection, have heavy emotional content. For man to find his place in the social structure is one of his most urgent and frustrating tasks.[2]

One reason why the study of social structure provides so many problems for the investigator is the unpredictability of social patterns. We do not find it hard to understand the Ifugao insistence on revenge for murder, nor even the feuds which continue sometimes for generations. What is more incredible to us is the attitude of some Eskimos who may take a murderer into the family as a kind of compensation for the loss of the member. If in the consideration of material culture we have found that selectivity is very great, we should be prepared to recognize even greater diversities in the different social structures in the world.

From a Single Family to One World [3]

The associations of humans start with the smallest functional unit, the biological family, and by ever larger and more varied types of groupings include all of mankind. Despite some of the weaknesses of such organizations as the League of Nations and the United Nations, they nevertheless symbolize the fact that whether we like it or not, practically all humans (with the exception of such isolated tribes as exist in some regions of Amazonia and the interior of New Guinea) are interdependent. Though relationships are not formalized on every level, yet there are so many interlocking associations of people that the social structure of the entire world has become highly integrated.

Associations may result from a number of reasons. There are groupings based on (1) the biological family: clans,[4] phratries, (2) sex: women's clubs, men's clubs, boys' puberty classes, girls' puberty classes, (3) age: age groups (as among the Masai of East Africa), (4) profession: unions, guilds, professional fraternities, army clubs, chambers of commerce, business companies, (5) politics: parties, caucuses, councils, (6) religion: churches, denominations, religious orders, (7) honor and prestige: honorary fraternities, legions of merit, (8) geography: neighborhood gatherings, socially significant geographical divisions of a village, (9) language: language and dialect groups, (10) education: alumni organizations, public schools of England (these are actually expensive private schools which turn out a rather distinct, socially recognized class of Englishmen), (11) socio-economic: Rotary, Lions, Exchange, (12) recreation: country clubs, sporting clubs, bridge clubs.

We could go on at some length listing various types of associations and indicating how one and the same individual in modern society is directly or indirectly associated with millions of other persons through numerous organizations. Such associations may be well defined and intimately related to one's life, as in the case of the family, or highly intangible and remote, as in the case of a distant corporation in a foreign country which may, however, vitally affect one's life by purchasing the products of the factory which is the principal economic support of one's home community. Whether or not such purchases are made may be determined by the foreign policy of one's own country, and this in turn reflects the force of political associations. But we are not primarily concerned with the multiplicity of human associations; we are more interested in just how people come to be associated and the function of that association in the society.

In many cultures, one's role in society is largely determined by birth. This is true of most of the social relationships among the aborigines of Australia. The status one has in society, one's close friendships, one's comrades in religious activities, the narrow choice of one's wife—even where one is to sit at some of the religious ceremonies and what part one is to have in some of the dances—all this, and much more, is determined almost completely by one's birth. Among the Zunis in New Mexico inheritance by birth is likewise the controlling factor in having certain religious privileges and honors. However, a Zuni infant is allotted to the lodge of the husband of the midwife who first touches him at the time of birth. This man—not the child's father—sponsors the boy in the lodge.

In many societies, the distinction of certain associations can be purchased. This is true not only of our society, where money is one of the prime features in getting into some exclusive clubs and can even be employed to buy honorary degrees from some educational institutions, but it is particularly true of some of the societies in Melanesia, such as the Banks Islands.

Education may be a significant factor, as among the elite in Haiti, where education is closely linked with wealth to form a small ruling class. Education was a highly important feature of ancient Chinese society. Even though the classical education, involving memorization of whole books of poetry and philosophy, was relatively impracticable, in terms of one's learning administration techniques, nevertheless, it was the indispensable requirement for membership in the ruling class.

Some of the Plains Indians emphasized bravery as the basis for membership in some societies while the Trobriand Islanders recognize success in raising large sweet potatoes (reputedly through the use of magic) as the principal factor in acquiring social status. Still other groups have put great stock in religious visions. Among the Kwakiutl, for example, one's profession and some socio-religious associations were determined by the vision which one saw during puberty initiation rites.

Not only do cultures differ as to the basis of membership in the various associations, but the individual cultures may have quite distinct social qualities. The Eskimo society is what could be called distinctly individualistic, for the primary reliance is on the individual, and he is relatively free to work out his own problems either on a small family basis or in voluntary groupings. However, the Eskimo society is not competitive as is the Kwakiutl, where the entire social structure tends to pit people against each other in a merciless struggle for economic power through trading. The Zuni society, consisting of a highly integrated community with a considerable degree of friendly helpfulness among its members, could be called co-operative, in contrast with the Eskimo and the Kwakiutl. The Tarahumaras in northern Mexico have both individualistic and co-operative tendencies, and our own U. S. culture could probably be described most accurately as being individualistic and competitive. However, it is not possible to classify neatly each society as individualistic, competitive, or co-operative (or even as having certain well-defined combinations of these qualities). On one level a society may be co-operative and on another quite competitive. The more highly complex societies of our modern world even have many contradictory features.

The Family—Small and Large

For us, the family consists of a father, a mother, and their children. We may talk about cousins, aunts, uncles, nephews, nieces, grandfathers, grandmothers as well as the in-laws as being part of the "family," but in general our concept of family is strictly limited. Even in the case of in-laws, we scarcely know how to classify them, for we say, "He married into the family," and some persons make jokes about the in-laws being the family "out-laws." Such a restricted concept of the family seems quite strange to many societies, where the immediate biological family and close relatives are immersed in the clan, which includes all the persons who are regarded as having descended from the same ancestor. Even though the clan may include thousands of persons, as in some cases in West Africa, yet each person is regarded as being closely related to all others. In some societies a person calls all women of the same clan and of the immediately preceding generation by the same word which he applies to his mother. All women of the same clan and belonging to still an earlier generation receive the title of "grandmother," while all women of his clan and of his own generation are "sisters." One important characteristic of most clans is that they are exogamous,[5] that is to say, one does not marry within the clan. That would be interpreted as marrying a close relative, or in other words, incest.

Many clans trace their lineage back to a mythological ancestor, who becomes the totem of the clan. Beliefs in totemic ancestors are very widespread, occurring as they do in Australia, Melanesia, Africa, Asia, and the Americas. Such totems may be animals, plants, or objects such as the sun, a star, or the moon. In many societies one would not think of killing and eating one's totemic animal. That would be tantamount to murder and cannibalism combined. Some clans not only respect their totems but they expect reciprocal benefits. Members of the scorpion clan among the Shilluks in the Anglo-Egyptian Sudan demonstrate how they can pick up scorpions without being stung by them. Missionaries, as well as Shilluks of other clans, who have tried to do the same, have been severely stung. It is claimed by members of the crocodile clan that no member of the crocodile clan has ever been eaten by a crocodile; and as evidence they cite the instance of a member of the crocodile clan who was seized by a crocodile but later released. However, one does not see members of the crocodile clan intentionally exposing themselves to crocodiles in order to prove their family connections.

Family lineage may be reckoned on the basis of either the mother's line (called matrilineal) or the father's line (called patrilineal). Sometimes both are recognized, but for different purposes.

In some parts of Melanesia one inherits land on the mother's side and fruit trees on the father's side. We are relatively familiar with patrilineal reckoning, for that is the way Western Europe describes family trees. Each child belongs primarily to the family of his father and from that family receives his surname (only in Spain and in areas of Hispanic colonization is the mother's family name added to that of the father's and that usually as a final initial). Economically, however, our society is primarily bilateral and a child inherits both through his father and his mother. In matrilineal societies the father is usually quite unimportant, for it is the mother's older brother to whom the child generally looks for sponsorship in the society and for ultimate inheritance of property. In New Caledonia, as in many other matrilineal societies, it is the maternal uncle who performs the ceremony of breathing life into the newborn child and who decides on the marriage partners for his nephews and nieces. This does not mean that in a matrilineal society fathers are completely uninterested in their own children. They may love them very much and do many things for them, but in matrilineal societies the strong family "tie" is with the mother and her family.[6]

Clan relationships, whether patrilineal or matrilineal, often serve a very important function in the society. They give members a sense of security and belonging, even though one's own parents may be dead or divorced. They may also provide protection from abuse. Ifugao clansmen will spare no pains to avenge the death of one of their members. This means a considerable measure of security for the members—since no one is going to start an interclan conflict without carefully weighing all the consequences. Social controls often operate effectively through clans, which in many societies are counted as responsible for the behavior of their members. Among the Kipsigis of East Africa each clan is responsible for the conduct of its members, and in lawsuits it is the clan which must pay for any misbehavior or damage if the guilty party cannot pay for himself. This means that a Kipsigis clan brings all its social pressure to bear upon expensive culprits, and in desperation a person's own clansmen may disclaim him by judging him and casting leaves upon him. In this way they indicate to the members of other clans that the person in question may be killed without fear of retaliation. In other words, one's own clan passes the death sentence.

The Daughters of the American Revolution are not unique among the devotees of family trees. The aristocratic Polynesians put great stock in being bluebloods of the bluebloods; the Chinese are world famous for their devotion to family connections; and many members of the Church of St. Thomas in South India take considerable pride in tracing their family connections back four and five hundred years.

Sex before Marriage

In most of the world premarital sex relationships are not regarded as wrong; in fact, the persons who do not engage in such affairs are not infrequently considered as queer and abnormal.[7] It is hard for people like the Palauans to imagine healthy, emotionally balanced individuals as not profiting from such escapades. Accordingly, they traditionally arranged for young women to go for a period of a year to the men's lodge of a neighboring community where they served as lovers and prostitutes. What compensation they received was turned over to the chiefs of their own village. The Masai of East Africa also institutionalize premarital relations by organizing warrior groups of young men who undergo circumcision rites at the same time (these are held each four years) and by encouraging these men to live out in kraals with their mistresses, with whom they have sexual freedom, except that they are not to cause pregnancy. A man's own fiancee is always in another kraal. The Kipsigis in East Africa also encourage love affairs among young people, and if the woman becomes pregnant that is no special deterrent to marriage, since it is a proof of fertility and the future husband obtains title to the child and is regarded as fortunate.

The Zulu have generally tried to restrict premarital relationships to those couples intending to marry, while other tribes have imposed ritual avoidances upon engaged couples. At one time the Kgatla[8] had very severe restrictions against premarital sex relationships. If a woman became pregnant she was publicly humiliated, shunned, mocked in songs, and her child was usually killed. But at the present time most of these rules are unenforced and 23 per cent of the unmarried women have had children. The Korango and Mesakin of the Nuba Hills are quoted [9] as commenting on their almost complete premarital sexual license, "We are like goats."

In some societies there is a good deal of trial marriage before formal marriage. Among the Ngombe of Congo it is expected that for several years a young man will live first with one woman and then with another, in order to find the person with whom he wishes to live permanently. This practice is regarded as perfectly normal and carries no social stigma. In fact, it has been almost impossible to get Christian converts among the Ngombe to take a stand against this practice, even though they will admit the moral wrong and can see some of the disastrous results in the spread of venereal disease.[10]

On the other hand, the Andaman Islanders have traditionally separated unmarried men and women and have made them live at opposite ends of the village. In this way they have tried to discourage premarital relations.

In some instances the particular status of a person influences matters of sex. Among the Shilluk the daughters of kings cannot marry. They are permitted to have lovers, but must not become pregnant—not primarily because of any moral implications, but simply because this would indicate that the king's person (as reflected in his daughter) had been defiled by sexual familiarity.

The attitude toward premarital sex relations may correspond to differences between matrilineal and patrilineal social structures, although it often does not. The Marshallese and the Gilbertese live on contiguous groups of coral islands in the central South Pacific. The Marshallese permit great freedom in premarital relations, and pregnancy outside of wedlock is not considered as too serious a matter, but the Gilbertese are—or at least pretend to be—very strict about the virginity of brides. The reason for this difference is that the Marshallese, who are matrilineal, reckon the heredity of the child in terms of the mother's line and the identity of the child's father is not so important. On the other hand, the Gilbertese, being patrilineal, attach great significance to the role of the father in procreation.

It would not be right to give the impression that all primitive peoples are highly promiscuous in premarital relations. This is not true. But it is also not true that present-day Western civilization as a whole is very different from the rest of the world. Institutionalized prostitution (whether legal or illegal) and increasingly ineffective social restrictions against premarital license mean that our own society is not far from the average, though it is certainly not as promiscuous as some societies where sexual freedom is definitely encouraged. Where the real difference lies between the behavior in our own society and that of many others is that such sex practices are generally regarded by the majority in our own culture as being "immoral." Such actions are said to be contrary to established moral "standards," which, though they often reflect ideal rather than real behavior, nevertheless, are standards, even though they are undergoing rather rapid change. In many other societies, premarital relationships are not regarded as immoral, for they do not violate any recognized moral codes. They are simply amoral, since the people do not associate such behavior with actions which they think of as reprehensible or contrary to the mores of the people. On the other hand, adultery, which is extramarital, may be regarded as very bad. It is practically impossible for such people as the Marshallese to see any connection or resemblance between premarital and extramarital relations.[11]

Who Marries Whom?

The popular idea is that primitive man just grabs a woman by the hair and carries her off. But the picture is far more complicated than that. In fact, getting married in most aboriginal societies involves far more people, proportionately more wealth, and many more negotiations than are characteristic of our marriage arrangements.

In the first place marriage in primitive societies is predominantly the affair of the group, and the bride and groom have much less choice in making arrangements than they have in our society. Generally, a man marries outside of his family and group. However, in the case of the kings of Hawaii, the Inca emperors of Peru, and the

Pharaohs of Egypt, brother-sister marriage was practiced as a means of preserving the purity of the lineage and the inheritance within the same family. Among the Todas of South India the clans are exogamous, but the tribe is divided into two halves, called moieties, and these divisions are endogamous, i.e. one must marry within his own half of the tribe. In some instances classes determine whom one should marry. Among the Loanga of Africa a king is required to marry a commoner, and his children become commoners. A princess likewise marries a commoner, but her children become nobles. The socio-religious castes of India are generally endogamous, in the sense that persons must marry within their own caste. The royal families of Europe have formed a kind of endogamous society and severe limitations have been imposed on the rights of sovereigns to marry whom they wish—witness the famous case of Edward VIII (who could, however, have married an undivorced commoner).

One curious restriction on marriage is "cross-cousin" marriage, meaning that a man marries the daughter of his mother's brother or of his father's sister. Among people who exchange bride prices (or equilibrium payments), it is quite natural that such cross-cousin arrangements would be welcomed. Among the Lovedu [12] it is regarded as ideal for every man to marry a daughter of the actual woman with whose cattle (i.e. the cattle which had originally been given for her) his father obtained a wife. Likewise, the sister in question has the right to demand a son of her brother to be her daughter's husband. This kind of arrangement greatly restricts the possibilities as to whom one is to marry.[13] However, such restrictions do not upset marriage, as we might suppose, for marriage in aboriginal societies is fundamentally an arrangement between groups, and there is generally not the same personal romantic element which we assume to be a fundamental prerequisite for any type of even halfway successful marriage.[14]

Economic and social factors can so affect the institution of marriage as to seem to pervert its entire structure. For example, in some instances among the Kiroba people of Tanganyika, older women, who, as widowed first wives receive their share of the inheritance, may marry other women. They do so by formally paying the bride price, and they permit certain men to live with the "wife," so that she may have children. These children then belong to the older woman, who has the social and economic status of a husband.

One special development regarding the choice of mates involves the tendency for women to marry brothers-in-law and for men to marry sisters-in-law. The Old Testament practice of the levirate marriage is rather widespread in the world, especially in Africa. If a man dies, it is quite natural for a brother to take the widow, for she has already been "paid for" by equilibrium payments from the husband's group. Among the Xhosa of South Africa the woman is not actually married to a brother-in-law, but the practice of the levirate exists to the extent that she is to "raise seed" to her dead husband by intercourse with strangers.[15]

The Shasta Indians of California carried out a sororate practice, in that if the first wife died or proved unsatisfactory because of sterility, the wife's family must provide a sister. Such levirate and sororate marriages tend to run into conflict with ecclesiastical law maintained by some missions. For example, the Church of England has regarded in-laws as close kindred, even though there is no biological relationship. Such conflicts only add difficult frustrations, for in terms of the indigenous patterns such marriages to in-laws may be regarded not only as moral, but also as socially obligatory.[16]

"Here Comes the Bride!"

In most aboriginal societies it takes far more than a two-dollar license to obtain a bride. It may be a long and arduous process, in which the principal characters—the bride and groom—may have little or nothing to say. With the exception of some modern San Blas young people who have broken with the dictates of tradition, it has been the practice for parents in that society to make all the decisions with regard to who should marry whom and when. Neither the young man nor the young woman is consulted, but on a day agreed on by the parents the two are seized by their age-mates and thrown into a large hammock together. For a few minutes they are rocked back and forth, and a fire brand is waved beneath them. Then they are lectured for several hours on their matrimonial duties to one another, whereupon the young man goes to sleep in his wife's home, but each night for several nights he leaves during the night and goes to his own home. At last his mother-in-law comes after him, and from then on he lives with his wife's family in a large thatched house containing as many as twenty of the extended family.

There are three fundamental characteristics of marriage in most primitive societies: (1) the marriage is regarded as an obligation between groups, (2) there is a payment made from the man's group to the woman's, or in some instances an exchange of gifts (a bride price and a dowry), and (3) the woman has a status of legal inferiority.

In some societies, as among the Koryak of Siberia, a man cannot marry until he has proven his worth by working for his future father-in-law and suffering considerable privation and humiliating treatment. This is similar to the treatment which Jacob suffered at the hands of Laban (Genesis 29:15–30). Among the Arawak of British Guiana a man must prove his worth by clearing a field, building a house, and showing his skill with the bow and arrow. Among the Kai people of Papua [17] not only must payments be made to the girl's maternal uncles, but the man must work for her clan as much as she does for his.

The bride price, which is not the purchase price of the woman but rather a compensation to her group (especially for the loss of her labor), has the advantage of creating a certain stability in marriage. That is, the young bride is not going to run home to mother at the first small provocation, for she would be sent right back, considering the fact that the group has received a sizeable payment for her in goods such as cattle, goats, hoes, or even in money. This wealth may already have been exchanged with another group in order to procure a wife for the young bride's brother. The bride price establishes the legality of the relationship between the man and woman, and it guarantees the acceptance of the children by the group. On the other hand, the bride price tends to put the bride under the legal jurisdiction of her husband's group, and often her own family is unwilling to rescue her from a bitter situation by returning the bride price. In modern times when the bride price is earned by the groom and paid in cash, there is not the same feeling of group responsibility. This leads to the commercialization of a profoundly personal, emotionally charged experience and tends to facilitate the dissolution of the marriage relationship.

In many areas of the world Western ideas of monogamy, personal choice of mates, and the use of such superficial features as veils, white dresses, and flower girls are increasing. At the same time one must also reckon with an increase of concubinage (instead of plural wives), prostitution, divorce, and child delinquency.

Multiple Mates

A man having more than one wife (a type of marriage called polygyny) is not too uncommon in the world, but a woman with several husbands (polyandry) [18] is much more of a rarity. This latter situation has occurred among some Eskimos (where extensive female infanticide, i.e. killing girl babies, was practiced), among some of the peoples of Tibet (where the climate is particularly hard on women), and among the Todas in South India (who practiced female infanticide, but apparently not for any economic reasons). Among the Todas the polyandry was of a special type in which several brothers shared the same wife. In some instances, however, several brothers have shared several wives, a combination of polyandry and polygyny. A special type of polyandry occurs among the Lele of Africa,[19] who designate certain women (some of whom are captured in raiding parties or have fled from other villages) as "wives of the village." About one woman in ten is such a village wife, and she may have relations with all except members of her own clan. However, she gradually has fewer husbands, as the men become formally married to other women. The children of a village wife belong to the village as a whole, and such a woman is regarded as having a very honorable position. She is certainly not in the corresponding position of a prostitute in Western culture.[20]

The average person seriously overestimates the extent of polygyny in such areas of the world as Africa. Reports about African kings with scores of wives tend to reinforce one's mental image of Solomon with his 700 wives and 300 concubines. However, with the birth rate of boy and girl babies being substantially equal, one is not likely to find excessive polygyny without serious social consequences and revolution. No society is going to tolerate the hoarding of too many women by too few men. In a study of polygyny among five tribes in East Africa, including a total of 17,000 men, the percentage of men who had only one wife ranged from 93 per cent in one tribe to 37 per cent in another. The percentage of those who had two or more wives ranged from 7 per cent in one to 29 per cent in another (in one tribe 34 per cent of the men were not married).[21] In Basutoland in 1912 one man in 5.5 had more than one wife, and one man in 27 had more than two. However, in 1936 only one man in 9 had more than one wife and only one in 64 had more than two. Similar shifts away from polygyny have occurred throughout Africa, but such changes are due to several factors, of which the most important is economic. Polygyny is only economically profitable for a man when the women support the household in a rural, agricultural economy; but in an urban, money economy (based on unskilled manual labor in mines and factories) the average man cannot afford several wives, nor can he support a great many children.

If people overestimate the extent of polygyny, they even more seriously misconstrue the reasons for it. They attribute plurality of wives almost exclusively to a man's sexual appetite. It is quite true that men are usually more concerned with and interested in sex than are women, but sexual factors are by no means the only reason for polygyny. The economic factors are very important. Frequently a man cannot hire workers, but he can marry more wives. In a hoe economy such women are great economic assets. Not only do they bring in more profits, but the children are valuable in terms of cultural prestige and the rank of one's family. The fact that in most polygynous societies the first wife bosses the second, and so on down the line, means that a first wife will often induce her husband to take another in order that the latter may share in the work of the household and be subservient to the first. Similar pressure may be exerted by the second wife for obtaining a third one, and so it goes. The fact that there may be more women than men in the society, perhaps as the result of men's occupations (especially war) being somewhat more dangerous, only adds to the pressures for assimilating all women into the society in a productive manner.

An additional aspect of polygyny closely related to sex is the existence in many societies of strong social disapproval of marital relations between the time of conception (or of birth) and weaning (often at the age of two or three years). Of course, pregnancy before weaning would result in incapacity to nurse the baby and without other sources of milk for babies (such food does not exist in most aboriginal parts of the world), the baby is doomed to die. In other words such a pregnancy kills the child who has already been born. It is no wonder that in many parts of Africa sexual relations between a man and wife during the relatively long period from conception (or birth) [22] to weaning are so vigorously condemned. However, during this same period extramarital relations are not generally denounced. In view of the biological problem involved in providing nourishment for the newborn child,[23] it is very understandable why polygyny should be regarded by the people in a somewhat different light than it is by us who have no such problem.[24]

Sex and Procreation

Procreation is almost universally regarded by aboriginal peoples as being highly mysterious and full of religious significance. Some peoples seem to understand the relationship of sex to procreation, but others do not. The New Caledonians [25] regard the husband's function as preparing the wife but believe that she actually becomes pregnant when she crosses a sacred place in the forest where the germs of life exist. It is then the husband's task to strengthen the child through sexual relations with his wife. The Trobriand Islanders [26] have a slightly different version of this. The child is supposed to be inserted into the womb by the spirit of a deceased kinswoman of the mother's clan. The Tswana of Bechuanaland [27] regard the male sperm and the menstrual blood as being the essential factors in the growth of the child while in the womb.

The popular impression is that primitive peoples are very highly sexed, especially those who live in tropical lands. Perhaps some of this idea arises from what may be ritually sanctioned extramarital relations. Among the Yoruba there are special rites for women who have no children. Such rites involve music, dancing, and purposeful sexual promiscuity, as a kind of magic force which will guarantee fertility. The Ila people of Africa engage in orgiastic sex rites at the time of feasts for the dead, but such activities are highly religious and involve a kind of symbolization of the perpetuation of clan life. On some socio-religious occasions the aborigines of Australia include relatively promiscuous sex relations as an integral part of the tribal life. Such extramarital relations are not only expected, but required. The Eskimos and the Chukchi of Siberia are well known for reciprocal hospitality in loaning wives to travelers, and among some groups of Eskimos there are occasions of almost uninhibited sex license. However, despite such socially sanctioned sexual practices, it is doubtful whether primitive man can be regarded as being any more highly sexed than civilized man. Of course, individuals differ greatly, both in capacity and interest; and the social sanctions in any one society may act as deterrents for certain kinds of sexual practices. But there is no evidence that primitive peoples differ appreciably from nonprimitives in the potentiality of sex expression.

The fact that primitive and civilized peoples do not differ appreciably in the degree of sex potentiality does not mean that they express sex in the same manner. The Mossi people of West Africa are relatively tolerant of wives having lovers, while the Nkundo of the Belgian Congo have traditionally imposed heavy sanctions against such women, including torture, public exposure, being bitten by ants, and magical washing and purification by red pepper mixed with water. But even as in our society, there is generally a double standard between men and women. In many nonliterate societies adultery is classified as a kind of stealing, or appropriating rights which are not one's own, and accordingly the guilty person must pay a fine to the husband.

Sexual perversions such as homosexuality and masturbation also exist in many primitive societies, though in general they are less common since women are much more readily available. Homosexuality in our culture is generally condemned, despite its rather wide occurrence. In ancient Greece the practice was not only very common, but was idealized by persons like Plato and Sappho (the famous poetess of Lesbos). Among the Marshallese homosexuals in the form of transvestites (men or women who dress and behave as do those of the opposite sex) were almost unknown. However, homosexuals among American troops during World War II introduced among the Marshallese, at least for the time being, some homosexuality in areas near military bases.

Universal Wrongs

So far as is known, there are only two universally recognized wrongs—that is, actions which are disapproved in all societies. These are murder and incest. Note that we do not say killing and extramarital relations, for killing of an enemy is generally praised, and the killing of a person of a different group may be regarded as an act of bravery. By murder we mean the killing of someone whom the particular society regards as being a member of the in-group composed of mutually responsible individuals. Incest, meaning sexual relations between close relatives, is very differently defined in various cultures. The Nuer, a Nilotic tribe of the Anglo-Egyptian Sudan, regard sexual relations with any person of the same clan as being incest—hence to be definitely avoided. Throughout most of Melanesia and Polynesia, there is a very strong brother-sister avoidance pattern. From the time young children begin to wear clothes, brothers and sisters must refrain from all physical contact; in some regions they cannot even so much as speak to each other, and they must not sleep in the same house. The Ifugao seem to have an almost pathological fear of brother-sister incest, and even the mention of genital organs in the presence of near kin of the opposite sex is regarded as practically equivalent to incest. It is claimed that in former times a person would be killed on the spot for using such language.

There is no necessary connection, however, between prudery and morality. The Dobus of Melanesia are very prudish about any mention of sex,[28] and they are exceedingly circumspect about exposure of themselves in undressing, and yet by our standards they are quite immoral. On the other hand, the Puritans were also quite prudish, but had rather rigid moral standards.

As in the case of extramarital sex relations, there are some instances in which incest is socially sanctioned. The Tonga of Mozambique permit father-daughter relations before a man goes to hunt hippos,[29] and incest is expected of members of certain secret societies among the Nyamwezi as a part of the initiation ceremony.[30]

Grounds for Divorce

In our society the one generally unchallenged ground for divorce is marital infidelity. However, in many parts of the world adultery is not a basis for divorce, but only for proper compensation to the husband. On the other hand, a wife's sterility is regarded in many places as being quite sufficient to justify a divorce, for if a woman cannot produce children, then the principal purpose of marriage, as viewed by such persons, is thwarted. In other places, laziness or foolishness may merit a divorce. A contagious disease such as leprosy is grounds for divorce in some parts of Africa.

Sterility may be regarded as not only depriving the husband of his right to have children (as among the Ganda), but even as causing the unproductivity of the fields in which the woman works. If a Ganda woman has twins, that is a sure sign that her fields will produce a plentiful harvest.[31]

The technique of obtaining a divorce may involve a complicated court case and settlement, as with us, or only a threefold declaration of "I divorce you," as among some Mohammedans. The ancient Jews simply provided the estranged woman with a letter of divorce, but the Navajo women just put their husbands' clothes outside of the house, since in the Navajo matrilineal society the home belongs to the women.

Family Life

There are two important differences between our ideal of family life and the type of family relationship which exists in many parts of the world.[32] One involves the partnership of mates and the other the love for children. We regard the intimate partnership of man and wife in all aspects of life as being essential to a happy marriage. We cannot help being somewhat shocked to discover that in many parts of Oceania husbands and wives have traditionally lived in separate establishments (men's and women's clubs or lodges). Even where such relative isolation does not occur, the diversity of interests often means that husbands and wives have little in common. In numerous African villages men spend most of their time with men and women with women. The attitude of the Plateau Tonga is quite different from that of most societies in that they say, "Your wife is the best friend you have." [33]

On the other hand, most of the so-called primitive world is extremely desirous of having children.[34] In fact, as we have noted, one of the principal causes for divorce is supposed sterility. Children may be wanted not only for the immediate satisfaction of having offspring, but to guarantee perpetuation of the group and to assure oneself a proper place in the afterworld. Religious beliefs may reinforce the social patterns at this point and result in an intense concern for and interest in having children.

There may be religious objections to certain types of reproduction, as in the case of twins. For example, the Akha people of eastern Burma slay the twins and drive the parents out of the village for one year. Their house is burned, their fields are left untilled, and they cannot speak with anyone in the village until the year is past. Then they may return as regular participants in community life.

Birth control by certain sexual practices or by abortion is not too common in aboriginal societies, since in most instances there is no overpopulation. On the one hand, a high infant mortality keeps the population limited, and on the other hand religious and social motives encourage people to have as many children as possible. However, in some of the very dense populations, such as in India and Japan, birth control is an important social factor, particularly as economic difficulties become increasingly more acute. The traditional pattern in Africa has been for the people to desire children, but the change in clan life and the new economic patterns which make large families economically burdensome rather than profitable mean that many urban parents are now saying that they do not want as many children as formerly.[35]

The grandparent generation in a family may be very highly venerated (as in China), given a comfortable place of respect (as in most parts of Latin America), just tolerated (as in many instances in our society), or expected to eliminate themselves when they become a burden to society (as has been the case among the Eskimos).

What Shall We Name Him?

The naming of children not only reveals how diverse such cultural practices may be, but also indicates a number of fundamental social attitudes, which need to be known if one is to understand the people.

One of the strangest developments in names is the practice in some parts of the world of using vile names for children in order that the evil spirits may not be inclined to harm the offspring. The Moni people of New Guinea use such names as "dog-dung" and "pig-dung," but it does make a difference which name is used. One missionary mistakenly called a child by the name of "dog-dung" when he should have said "pig-dung." His mistake was a grave insult, for among the Moni people pigs have much greater "social standing" than do dogs. The Mazatec people of Mexico do not give their children repulsive names, but they habitually speak of a child as being ugly so as to fool the malicious spirits, whom they always refer to as "good spirits." Euphemisms are not uncommon among us. At a funeral we rarely speak of "dying," but use such circumlocutions as "passing away," "departing from this life," and "entering beyond the veil"; but we do not use depreciatory language in order to distract evil spirits.

Eskimos have traditionally had an old woman recite the names of the child's dead ancestors during the time that the mother is in labor. The one which is uttered at the time when the child first becomes visible is regarded as the appropriate name. It is not uncommon for some societies to employ a number of names for a person, some of which are known to strangers, others only to the family, and there may be one special name which a person reserves almost entirely for communion with himself. Should this name become known, his enemies could do him great harm through black magic. The Aranda of Australia customarily gave two names to each person, one known to everyone and another which was secret and sacred and only used on very solemn occasions. In fact, so secret was the name that women never learned what their own sacred names were. The old men kept this knowledge to themselves.

In some societies children do not receive names when they are very young. This is true of the San Blas, and the children are designated simply as the first, second, third, etc. child of so-and-so. On the other hand, the Ayore of Bolivia call the parents by the names of the children, referring to them as "the mother of so-and-so," or "the father of so-and-so," a custom which is also widespread in Southeast Asia.

There may be certain restrictions on the use of names. An Akha man in eastern Burma cannot mention the name of his own wife. She must be addressed as "woman," "you," or "mother of so-and-so" (naming her oldest child).

Education, Formal and Informal

For us, the word "education" means the classroom, probably the most artificial technique ever devised for conveying instruction. It is entirely too easy for us to lose sight of the fact that other societies educate their children even though they do not have formal schools. Children are taught fishing, hunting, housebuilding, tribal lore—all in the natural surroundings of meaningful activity. Little African children are not paraded up and down with bundles of sticks on their heads in order to teach them how to balance such objects. Rather, when they are old enough to walk home from the fields, they are given a stick to carry, and they quite naturally attempt to carry it as their parents do, namely, on their heads. This type of training is meaningful, since the child is actually doing something that counts. It has social and economic value, even though it is a very small contribution. In many primitive cultures children participate much more in the activities of the community than they do in ours, and their presence at evening palavers around the camp-fire is not only tolerated but encouraged. Children generally have much more of a sense of being wanted and of belonging. Accordingly, disciplinary problems are often fewer than they are in our own society.

A further distinction between fundamental characteristics of education in primitive and our Western cultures is that we emphasize so much the competition between children. We constantly compare children with each other and make such statements as "Johnny can do that and he is younger than you are. Why can't you do as well?" This may be a means of getting children conditioned to some of the fierce competition of adult life, but it may play havoc with the child's own personality.

Primitive societies differ radically from us in the purposes and function of education. They employ educational methods in order to produce continuity in society so that the younger generation may follow the same traditions as their elders. We regard education as a means of achieving discontinuity, by which we hope to produce a succeeding generation which will be different from and superior to their parents. Education is one of the principal ingredients in the concept of progress, and progress necessitates change, reform, and discontinuity. It is not difficult for a primitive society to determine what they should teach their children, but for us the content and goals of education are difficult, if not impossible, to formulate, for we have not defined our cultural objectives.

It would be wrong to give the impression that all primitive societies employ the very best methods in raising children. Often they do not. In Palau, for example, there are serious personality problems among children because they are severely thrust away from their mothers at weaning time. At about five years of age there is another emotional wrenching of the child from his mother, for at that time he is told that he is not wanted around the house any longer. His compensation is in playing almost exclusively with other boys and finally being incorporated into the lodge for men. The structure of Palau society, in which the men's life centers almost entirely in their lodge, makes some drastic change necessary for the young boy, but the transition certainly could be made easier and with fewer emotional maladjustments.

Most primitive societies have little use for co-education. It would seem that they object to it because they think that men and women should be trained to do different kinds of work and because they regard their being together as inviting moral difficulties. Of course, many societies in which there is a good deal of premarital license go through the show of erecting artificial barriers, which are not expected to be effectual. Many missionaries—and not without good reason—have insisted that men and women must have more in common if they are to build Christian homes, and hence they have established co-educational institutions. These have not been without their problems, but they have been justified by the total results. In some parts of Micronesia many Christian parents have objected rather strenuously to co-educational schools. To their way of thinking the earlier schools, established by German missionaries with strict rules and severe discipline, were much better. Nevertheless, these early schools failed in large measure to inculcate proper attitudes toward the opposite sex or moral life in general. They were more like prisons than life situations. One missionary said, "I know that we shall have some problems, but under the old system there were about 99 per cent failures. Even if only a small percentage learn to live constructively and meaningfully and can establish truly Christian homes, we will be further ahead than before. Christian missions must prepare people for life by learning to live together, not by being isolated from one another." [36]

The capacity which all cultures possess for molding individuals to fit the cultural pattern is truly remarkable. With little formal regimentation and often without any corporal punishment, societies not only teach necessary skills but inculcate concepts of loyalty, responsibility, and for the most part complete agreement with the moral order of the culture in question. Actual crime and delinquency rarely become serious problems in primitive societies until Western cultural influences break down the traditional sanctions.

Coming of Age

Puberty marks a very important time in many cultures. So significant is the physical and emotional change which occurs that it is endowed with great religious significance. The Ila people of Rhodesia separate menstruating girls entirely. It is thought that a man will lose his virility if he so much as eats with such a person. However, among the Pueblo Indians of the Southwest such a girl is regarded as a source of rich spiritual blessing, and in some elaborate religious ceremonies these girls may bless the priests by virtue of their condition.

African societies in general make much of this puberty period by means of initiation schools where tribal traditions and skills are taught and where young people are subjected to physical tests and ordeals. In many societies boys undergo circumcision and girls are subjected to a corresponding operation called excision. However, since these operations are so closely related to important religious concepts, they are treated in the following chapter.[37]

Who Does What?

In all societies there is some division of labor between men and women. However, there are no universal patterns of distinction. The Navajo women do the spinning and weaving in their society, but among the neighboring Hopis it is the men who spin and weave. Among the Quechuas of northern Ecuador women spin and men weave. However, in some localities men also spin, but women never weave.

We picture women as working in the home and men in the fields, but in many parts of Africa there are some striking contradictions to this practice. If a missionary wishes to hire someone in the home to cook, wash, clean house, or tend the baby, it is the men who are available, not the women. The reasons for this are that in most of African societies the women are responsible for their own gardens and homes. Formerly, the men were much more occupied than at present since they had to do the hunting, fighting, housebuilding, and some clearing of the forest. However, hunting is greatly diminished in most areas and fighting is prohibited by colonial govern-ments. This means that men are available to take outside employ-ment, and they do.

Division of labor may be culturally a very important matter. Among the Mayas of Yucatan, Mexico, only women draw water. When a missionary attempted to teach some of the Mayan men a lesson by drawing water for his wife, he was severely admonished not to repeat such an act, for his example might disturb the division of labor in favor of the women.

The Weaker Sex?

It is not uncommon for American men to complain of living in a matriarchy (a rule by women). An honest-to-goodness matriarchy, a society formally and actually controlled by women, has never been found, but that does not mean that the so-called weaker sex has not exerted tremendous influence. Among the Iroquois the women pos-sessed the land and the houses. They nominated for vacancies in the council of the chiefs, but strangely enough no woman could be a member of the supreme council of the Iroquois league. Neverthe-less, from behind the scenes they did a good deal of controlling of the society.

In order to evaluate the position of women in a society, one must consider four factors: (1) treatment, (2) legal status and rights, (3) public activity, and (4) type and extent of work. These are not necessarily related. For example, the Ifugao women are legally equal to men, but they also have an equal amount of the hard agricultural work to do. In traditional Jewish society women have been highly regarded and well treated, but they have not had any-thing like comparable legal status with men nor have they enjoyed privileges of public activity. In general, however, it can be said that in primitive societies women engage in just about as much physical work as men, have fewer legal rights (the Ifugao are a notable exception), are often excluded from certain social situations, such as men's secret societies (which are more numerous than women's secret societies), suffer religious disabilities, and receive fewer edu-cational opportunities.

As an antidote to our own much vaunted pride in the rights which women have in our society, it might be well for us to look at some of the features of Ifugao life. Women can enter any and all professions, including the priesthood and politics. They are respected by warriors and are not carried off as hostages. A man who slaps his wife may be killed by her relatives for such a vile deed of cowardice. If a man's wife dies, he cannot remarry without paying an indemnity to her family; if he insists on a divorce, all the property goes to the wife to be kept till the children are married, at which time they inherit it. Considering the fact that only within recent years have women in the United States had the right to vote, it ill-behooves us to be too proud of the status of women in our culture.

Death, Inheritance, and Retaliation

Death and burial are so closely related to religious concepts that we shall be considering many of these matters in the following chapter. However, what a society does with a dead man's possessions and the social attitudes which people have toward death and inheritance constitute problems of social culture. Among the Maidu of the West Coast a dead person's possessions may be almost totally destroyed; while the Tarahumara of northern Mexico destroy practically nothing. In fact, there is no coffin (except among some of those who have adopted the practice from neighboring Mexicans), and the body is put in a shallow grave, where it is not infrequently dug up by coyotes. The Navajos abandon any house in which a person has died, and they will not so much as touch the wood of such a house. This has caused many Navajos to be desperately fearful of hospitals, in which they know people have died. They often bury along with a person a good deal of his jewelry. In former times the graves were quite safe from molestation, for most people were very much afraid of the spirits of the dead. However, some Navajos are no longer fearful and consequently grave robbery is no longer uncommon.

The Ifugaos divide the property of the parents equally among the first three children, while the Maori of New Zealand give all the property to the firstborn, but each successive brother is to receive the property before the sons of the firstborn. In a few areas of the world, as in South India, the youngest child may take precedence over the others in the inheritance of property.

Headhunting, which is so common in parts of Indonesia and Melanesia, is prompted primarily by the concept of retaliation deeply embedded in their animistic beliefs. Death cannot be regarded as completely natural, and hence someone somewhere must have caused it. Moreover, if one society has lost a member, an enemy group should also lose a member, and so the religiously and socially sanctioned ceremonial headhunting is carried on. The prospects of going out to get a head in order to pay off one's obligation to a dead relative are generally not greeted with joy. In fact, a number of Indonesian folk songs are laments for having to embark on such an expedition. In the megalomaniac society of the North-west Pacific Coast a chief who had lost a son might go out to kill someone else of comparable rank in order, as it were, to transfer his grief. Death had attacked his pride, and therefore to fight back he felt obliged to find a victim for his perverted sorrow. This is quite different from the headhunting of Indonesia and Melanesia.

Suicide

Regardless of what people have believed about the joys of the afterlife, few people have attempted to hasten their arrival by taking their own lives. In fact, most societies—as a matter of self-preservation—have strong sanctions against suicide. Nevertheless, there are certain socially sanctioned types of suicide which reveal interesting phases of culture. We have already spoken of the Eskimo approval of suicide by old, economically useless persons. The hara-kiri suicide of Japanese military persons in the face of defeat or disgrace is based upon the concept that in such dire circumstances they have ceased to be socially acceptable. Their only chance of obtaining social acceptance is through suicide. Even in Western Europe army officers have traditionally been given the privilege of disposing of themselves rather than being brought to trial for disgrace. Part of the German people's reaction to Hermann Goering's famous suicide was the vindication of this old military tradition. In India widow-burn-

ing has had great social approval, and even severe repressive measures have not been successful in stamping it out.

Governments

As long as societies are small, consisting of a few hundred or
even a few thousand people, government can be quite an informal
affair. Sometimes there are no chiefs whatsoever and all government
in these instances is based on informal social interaction. More
frequently there are chiefs or headmen (one or several) who are
either formally elected or take their place by common consent as
the result of their demonstrated abilities. Larger societies are organized around one of two principles: (1) the kinship system or
(2) the modern state system. Under the kinship system the functions of state such as taxes, military levies, and justice are carried
out through clan leaders. Clan chiefs are responsible for the conduct of their clan members, and the loyalty of the members is
primarily to their own chief and then to the tribal unit. This in
general was characteristic of the Yoruba and Ashanti kingdoms.
However, kinship systems tend to break down with the numerical
growth of societies. Ancient Athens changed from a kinship organization to one in which people were organized according to geographical units. This is fundamentally the basis of modern "national" states, in which clans may still exist, but the principal
governmental functions are conducted on the basis of geographical
not family divisions. The Hausa kingdom of northern Nigeria is a
state of this type.

There is still another way in which we may classify governments,
namely, as to whether they are episcopal, presbyterian, or congregational.[38] An episcopal type of government can be described as one
which has a self-perpetuating "hierarchy." A monarchy is such a
system. Presbyterian government is one in which the elders—heads
of clans or prominent persons—have the primary authority. They
may set up individual rulers, but such rulers are primarily figure-
heads, for the real power exists with the elders. In a congregational
type of government there is a good deal of participation by the
people as a whole—a kind of democracy.

The church of the first few centuries had an episcopal type of government patterned after the social structure of that day. At the time of the Reformation, when feudal concepts were still rather strong and clan structure (especially in Scotland) was important, a presbyterian type of church government was widely employed. Congregational organization became popular in small minority groups who were in revolt against authoritarianism and who had imbibed many ideas of government from the Age of Enlightenment. It is interesting to note that all of these seek and claim to find in the New Testament the justification for their organizational setup.

It is difficult to classify societies neatly as episcopal, presbyterian, or congregational since there may be important conflicts within the society. In Oceania there have been traditional struggles between the "kings" and the "noblemen," even as in the history of England. A society may give the outward appearance of being episcopal (as for example England, with its royal family) while actually it may be quite congregational (democratic). Nevertheless, despite the contradictions between form and function and the conflicts within a society, it is possible to describe many societies in terms of this system. The Tarahumara culture is primarily congregational. There are chiefs, but these do not have much authority. Decisions are made by all the adult males who wish to participate in community meetings. Each one may speak as long as he wishes, but his words increase in value the longer he waits before making his declaration. There are no formal "rules of order" and decisions tend to reflect the consensus of opinion.

Many societies in Africa can be described as presbyterian. Here only the ruling heads of clans or otherwise distinguished persons participate effectively in governing the society. A local chief is usually very dependent upon his elders, and rarely makes an important decision without consulting them. If the people were asked to vote, they would vote strictly along clan lines—even as they do in most church organizations.[39]

One missionary was trying to teach a congregation in the Belgian Congo how to conduct a church meeting along "democratic lines." He had carefully explained in great detail how one should make motions, second the motions, discuss, and then vote, either by ballot or by the show of hands. Everyone present claimed to understand, but when the first matter came up for discussion, there was a huddle of the elders, a few minutes of whispering, nods and telling glances, and then the recognized leader of the congregation got up to announce, "We have decided that . . ." Robert's *Rules of Order* are not a part of the divine revelation nor an obligatory feature of church organization.

Larger states tend to become highly centralized and episcopal, i.e. with a self-perpetuating and largely self-appointing leadership. Perhaps only in a relatively large society is there the isolation which seems necessary to develop ideas of undivided loyalty to a ruler or of divine right of rule. Dictatorships, except for their lack of historical claims, are not essentially different from hereditary monarchies. When a monarchical dynasty is first founded, it is usually nothing more than a dictatorship, an absolute rule without prior sanctions. While kingship is generally associated with such large societies as nations, some small societies, such as in Oceania, have developed kingdoms with almost absolute rule. A very important factor in the absolutism in Oceania was the set of special taboos which surrounded the royal personage and made him sacrosanct.

Societies have, however, always worked out some techniques for handling rulers who proved incapable or unworthy of leadership. In Samoa chiefs could be sprinkled with coconut milk, and in this way all their religious sanctity was removed; after this the people could hack them to pieces with impunity. A slightly more subtle technique was worked out by the Japanese: they succeeded in making the emperor so holy that he was obliged to turn over most of the powers of government to his ambitious noblemen.

Keeping People in Line

When we think of controls for any society, we immediately tend to think of the laws, courts, and policemen. And yet, there is a relatively small part of everyday behavior which is controlled by the edicts of governments. Most behavior is dictated by the socially approved habits which societies develop, and the most effective controls are ridicule and social ostracism. People who have defied governments may sometimes be brought around by the infinitely more effective pressure of public opinion as it expresses itself in scornful sneers or contemptuous glances. The Hopi Indians employ gossip and ridicule as their principal techniques of social control, and the Ngbaka of Congo seem to have mastered the technique of making digging remarks about nonconformists. Some societies, such as the aborigines of Australia, may employ capital punishment for some grievous crime—such as being late for a very important religious ceremony—but generally there is not much capital punishment in primitive society, though in Africa corporal punishment is frequently meted out to repeated offenders.

In some societies there is a definite avoidance of situations which might produce friction. This is no doubt partly the reason for the mother-in-law taboo which exists in a number of tribes, including the Navajos. A Navajo man never addresses his mother-in-law directly. He must speak to her through another person. The Yukaghir of Siberia have an even more extensive system of taboo, in which the daughter-in-law avoids the father-in-law and the husband's elder brother, and the sister-in-law avoids both the father-in-law and the mother-in-law. The avoidance of in-laws is responsible for the fact that in some parts of Africa it is difficult to get parents to attend a Christian wedding. They know they will be expected to greet and be greeted by all the people, but this is sometimes contrary to their tribal custom.

A practice almost opposite to avoidance is the joking relationship, or the sanctioned familiarity. In New Caledonia [40] this joking relationship exists among persons who can potentially be mated. Such persons may not only joke in fun but may also taunt, in this way exercising a degree of social control over the individuals in question. In some instances a person can even denounce a chief, as happened in one case where a young woman publicly accused a chief of treachery resulting in the death of several persons. Such controls as these are strictly informal, that is to say, they are not embodied in law codes. Generally people do not even regard these social pressures as being techniques for control. They just take such matters for granted.

The primitive concept of law [41] and justice boils down pretty much to "an eye for an eye and a tooth for a tooth," with payment of money or valuables as constituting a kind of substitution for some offenses. The Ifugao will accept money in payment for many things but not for the murder of a kinsman. "Who would accept a buffalo as payment for a brother?" one Ifugao exclaimed. In general, primitive law requires that the injured person be recompensed. White man's justice decrees that a thief must be thrown in jail, but this is no justice in the African's eyes. The one whose property has been stolen must be compensated by the thief. It is not enough that the thief pay his debt to society—it is not to society that he owes the debt, but to the man whom he has robbed. Likewise in the case of adultery, which to most Africans is the trespassing of personal property rights, the culprit must recompense the angered husband. A jail sentence for adultery is not regarded as justice in any sense of the term. They generally regard jail sentences as utterly meaningless. The common impression is that jail sentences are imposed primarily to keep men from having relations with women, but they contend that a much more effective deterrent to crime is whipping. We tend to regard corporal punishment as viciously brutal and utterly unjustified, but they insist that jail sentences only make a man maliciously defiant. Our own crime-ridden society might well think twice about its system of law and punishment.

Where there may be no formal systems for settling grievances, some societies provide rather unique ways by which a person may still get satisfaction. Among the Eskimos of Greenland [42] a person who has suffered an injury, such as theft, wanton destruction of his property, or abduction of his wife, may challenge his malefactor to a singing contest in order to denounce him publicly in song. Such singing contests may be continued intermittently for years, but they at least permit the injured party to "get it off his chest." Among the New Caledonians [43] a person may commit suicide in order to get revenge and bring a culprit to justice. This would seem like a sure case of "cutting off one's nose to spite one's face," but New Cale-donians believe that the act of suicide is absolute proof of the victim's innocence and the offender's guilt. Furthermore, as a departed spirit the one who has committed suicide is able to haunt the offender and utterly ruin his or her life.

Primitive justice tends to gravitate toward the ordeal as a means of determining the guilt or innocence of the parties involved. Africa is famous for the poison cup, which is prepared by the medicine man and administered to the defendant. If he dies, it is a sure sign that he was guilty. If he vomits or if the poison proves too weak to kill him (the strength of the poison depends largely on the medicine man), then he is innocent. The strange thing is that many people demand the poison cup in order to prove their innocence. They are firmly convinced that they will not die; but even if they should, they are willing to trust the results of the ordeal, for they reckon that perhaps their spirit did commit such a crime while they were asleep.

Ordeals are essentially of two types: (1) direct and (2) indirect. The first are administered to the persons, and the second are admin-istered to animals, who substitute for the persons; but the person is judged guilty or innocent depending upon whether the animal dies or lives.

The ordeal which involves picking up small stones at the bottom of a basin of boiling water or oil is more difficult to understand, but people insist that they have seen innocent men reach in and pick up such stones without their hands showing the effects, while other persons reaching into the same vessel have been seriously burned.

An Ifugao, who had become a Christian teacher in a Protestant school, was involved in a village quarrel. The only way to settle the matter was to undergo an ordeal in which the plaintiff and the de-fendant were to throw an egg and three darts at each other. How-ever, the people disqualified this young man, for they claimed that he did not have faith in the ordeal and hence it would not be effective for him. They insisted on a substitute for him. The de-fendant's substitute and the accuser were kept awake for two days and nights with various religious incantations and rites. At the end of this time they stood only ten feet apart, but though they both apparently tried, neither one was successful in hitting the other. As a result, the case was dropped.

Even war takes on the coloring of an ordeal with some societies. There may be many warriors involved, but after the death of the first few men the battle is called off. The side which has suffered the most casualties is regarded as having lost the battle while the victors have had their moral rights vindicated and their case supernaturally defended.

All Is Fair in War

Of all human activities it would seem that war, which appears to imply the total absence of law, would be utterly without rules. Strangely enough that is not the case. The Aztecs were very fierce fighters, but their objective in fighting was not utterly to destroy the enemy but to seize victims, especially ones that were still alive, in order to offer them to their gods. The Spanish under Cortez did not fight that way, and they did not waste their energies trying to capture sacrificial victims. Because of their gunpowder and their different rules of fighting, they were ultimately successful, despite their small numbers and the great disadvantage of unfamiliar terrain.

The wars between the Plains Indians could be more properly called raids, for the Indian technique was to come upon an enemy from ambush and to obtain honor, not necessarily by killing him but by demonstrating exceptional bravery. Hence, slapping an armed enemy was counted a greater military honor than carrying off the scalp. The frontiersmen had either to learn the Indian tactics of ambush warfare or to be destroyed by them. These same "rules" were strongly denounced by the British soldiers who fought against the revolting colonists, for such tactics were not in vogue in Europe at that time.

Present-day arguments as to whether it is "moral" to use certain weapons are just continuations of man's attempts to establish a pattern even when all the rest of the social patterns for maintaining peace and security break down.

The "400"

It is doubtful whether one can speak of a truly classless society. Even among the most primitive groups there are distinctions between chiefs and followers, and between respected warriors and recognized cowards. Societies may not overtly recognize such classes, but they exist, simply because people are not all alike.

Americans generally think of themselves as not belonging to any one class, and there is no doubt about the relative fluidity of our social structure. A person born in one class can change his status by education, wealth, and outstanding success. Nevertheless, even some of our small Midwestern towns have three or four fairly distinct classes. The top class consists of the rather well-to-do, the well educated, and the successful business people and civic leaders. These may be subdivided between "the old families," as in some parts of the South, and the newcomers. These groups often form distinct social sets, and if so, they represent different classes. The majority of the people usually belong to the higher middle class and the lower middle class. Below these are the poor, the destitute, the paupers. Members of one class may be quite friendly with those of other classes, but in general the social contacts involving parties, clubs, and private dances reflect rather well-defined cleavages, especially between the high, middle, and low classes. Most dating among young people tends to follow quite closely the pattern of adult society. The exception is always the subject of social gossip and speculation.

The classes in America, particularly in the West, are not as marked as they are in European countries where the population has had many years to solidify into relatively fixed classes, some of which stem from feudal times. The classes of India became completely frozen into castes by religious sanctions. (By caste we mean a class of which the membership is fixed and from which people cannot move to another.) Many cultures of the Orient and Oceania developed very highly complex class systems with many overt indications including differences of dress, ornaments, and even language. So-called honorific language, consisting of special words and grammatical forms used only to and about dignitaries, was highly developed in Thailand and is still employed. In most of the Malayo-Polynesian world honorific language is rapidly losing out since the social structure is no longer so stratified as formerly. Honorific language based on the social stratification arose in Aztec, and in some dialects it is both complicated and exceedingly important, if one is to speak to people without grave social consequences for having used the wrong form.

Other techniques for indicating class distinction and social prestige are (1) display of wealth, such as driving a Cadillac, (2) the number of wives which one has (a matter of some social distinction in certain parts of Africa), (3) the number and quality of one's academic degrees, (4) the use of titles, e.g. reverend, bishop, doctor, monsignor, (5) the possession of sacred objects (as among the Zuni or in many parts of Africa) or the claim of apostolic succession, and (6) war bonnets (for the Plains Indians) and medals and ribbons (for Western Europe). In some cultures the obvious display of such prestige is regarded as unbecoming. A New Caledonian chief refused to wear the medals with which the French had decorated him for being a chief. His comment was, "Who doesn't know that I am chief?" [44]

It is sometimes taken for granted that Western society can be diagrammed as a broad-based pyramid, as the communists teach, with the poorest at the bottom and the few wealthy at the top. This does fit some societies, but not all. In America the lowest class is not as great as the lower middle class, and society is better diagrammed as a diamond lying on its face. Haitian society can be described as a broad-based pyramid with a kind of spire near the top, which contracts first into the second-class elite, who are superseded in turn by the first-class elite. Soviet communist society can be described as a kind of hour-glass structure, with a small bulb at the top and a large one at the bottom. The relatively wide separation of the party membership from the people and the high selectivity of the party membership (with correspondingly greater privileges) make the much discussed pyramid structure somewhat of an anomaly. All totalitarian states tend to develop in this same manner, among them Nazi Germany and Fascist Italy. One essential difference between the teachings of fascism and communism is that the former insists that such class distinctions are in the very nature of humanity and of the ideal social structure (witness such concepts as the superman and the superrace), while the latter declares that it is working toward a classless structure, but that this can only be accomplished through a highly centralized leadership of the proletariat.

Social and Religious Culture

In this chapter we have had occasion to indicate several points at which the social and the religious factors are closely entwined: attitudes toward sex, marriage rites, procreation, law and justice, naming of children, suicide, and class structure. Since we are dealing with social culture in this chapter, we have tried to isolate the social factors in so far as possible, but for many societies this results in quite a wrong picture. For example, Zuni society is essentially a theocracy in which religious factors dominate the entire social pattern. At no point can we touch the social setup without becoming immediately involved in religious matters. The same thing is true of a high percentage of so-called primitive societies. There is no divorcing or departmentalization of social and religious features. The whole socio-religious structure acts as a unit. It is quite impossible to split the culture of a typical Congo African tribe and to say "this is social" and "that is religious." No doubt there are some features of the puberty rites of girls which are predominantly social and others which are predominantly religious, but the entire pattern is interwoven. Therefore, in the study of any one feature of culture, we should attempt to study and grasp it as a whole.

Caste in India is essentially a socio-religio-economic phenomenon, and there is no easy dividing line between the three fundamental features. Socio-religious sanctions forbade outcaste people from drinking water in railroad stations marked "Water for Hindus." By legislation these signs were changed to read "Orthodox water," but the outcaste people still did not drink. As long as the Brahmin class is considered essential for religious blessing upon socio-religious activities and rites, so long will the social and religious structure be interpenetrating. The caste system has suffered a rather general breakdown resulting from legislation which has reflected a progressive social outlook due very largely to Western influence. The caste structure is changing, but such a tightly knit socio-religio-economic structure is not going to be changed overnight.

In a high percentage of cultures in which animistic beliefs are predominant, concepts of immortality are closely tied to the clan. The people believe in a "clan heaven." The immortality of the individual depends upon the faithfulness of such a person's clan. As long as the clan supplies sustenance (offerings of food and drink), the deceased can continue a kind of shadowy existence, but for a person whose clan dies out there is no further provision for the afterlife. In such circumstances one can readily understand why family and procreation take on so much religious importance and why the concepts of clan immortality lead to diversity of religious practice rather than to uniformity. Where the essential religious unit is as restricted in size as the clan, there are almost unlimited possibilities for different developments by relatively small groups.

There is a tendency grossly to misjudge some aboriginal peoples for what appears to be vulgarity and lasciviousness in matters of sex. The typical Akha village in eastern Burma has the figures of a man and a woman at the gate to the village. Often these figures are placed in the position of coitus. This does not mean that the people are crudely obscene in their attitudes. They are not—except by our standards. As in the case of so many primitive peoples sex is regarded as one of the deeply religious mysteries, not to be covered up or disguised but to be recognized openly and to be revered in all its many manifestations. This, of course, is quite contrary to our puritanical tradition and is the source of much misunderstanding.

Christian Missions and Social Culture

No doubt the biggest problem which Christian missionaries have faced in dealing with social problems of different cultures is polygyny. It is all too simple for the missionary to say, "But to become a Christian you must get rid of all but one wife." The immediate question is "Which wife should I keep?" The man has equal responsibilities to all. In some instances women who are turned out by their husbands find they can live only by becoming prostitutes, though in most cases their families will take them in. However, what about the children? What is the father's responsibility to them? It has often been the practice for Christian missions to accept plural wives as full members of the church, including baptism and communion, but not to admit the husbands as long as they have more than one wife. It has not been uncommon for several wives of a man to become Christians and to be admitted into the church, but for the husband, on deciding to become a Christian, to find that he is barred unless he turns out all but one wife. Sometimes he is encouraged to attend church, and he is assured that he is "saved" and hence will go to heaven, but he is barred from baptism, communion, and church membership on the basis of his polygamous status.

Some missions have taken a very strict stand on the matter, and the result has been an outwardly enforced monogamy, with considerable concubinage and prostitution. Missions which have strict rules on legal monogamy may pay little or no attention to extramarital sex offenses, while other missions are quite severe in disciplining sex offenders. Rev. Donald Fraser of the Livingstonia Mission (Church of Scotland) says, "It [disciplinary measures] certainly purifies the body of the Church by removing unworthy members, but it seems to have little reformatory value for the sinner." [45] Still other missions adopt a regular penalty schedule for sins, that is to say, for smoking tobacco one may be put out of the church for two months, for dancing excommunication may be for three months, stealing may draw a penalty of four months, and adultery twelve months. Under this setup it is not uncommon for members to arrange to be caught doing lesser sins, in order that they may not be penalized for major sins which they contemplate committing during their period of excommunication—during which time their behavior is not subject to the same severe discipline.

It must not be implied that because there are so many problems involved in introducing monogamy one is justified in defending polygamy. Polygamy is not desired or defended by responsible African Christian leadership since it not only violates New Testament ethical principles but is found to produce many tragic social problems, e.g. jealousy and antagonism within the household, deep frustrations for less-wanted wives, the tendency for the husband to be unduly domineering in order to preserve order, and the strictly inferior position which women must have.

In order to introduce monogamy some missions have obtained special governmental sanctions for "statutory" or so-called "Christian marriage," in contrast with "native marriage." In many instances this statutory marriage does give prestige, e.g., in the Anglican diocese of the Niger the title of *Mrs.* is used only for those with statutory marriage.[46] In some instances the local African courts treat a statutory marriage with greater respect and will more readily give a woman justice if she complains of an unfaithful husband. However, in other areas the local courts cannot touch cases of this kind and often the woman has insufficient funds to procure the legal aid to present her case to higher courts. Her statutory marriage thus becomes a liability.

A few missionaries have taken the position that polygamy is in some measure like slavery in New Testament times. Hence, on the basis of the Apostle Paul's declaration about the possibility of serving the Lord regardless of one's social status at the time of conversion (1 Corinthians 7:20–22), they are ready to let polygamy die out with the present generation and concentrate their attention on teaching the importance of monogamy to the younger generation. Making the issue of monogamy *vs.* polygamy appear to be the main theme of the Christian message causes many Africans to regard missionaries as home wreckers. What course of action will in the long run prove to be the best is not possible to say at this point. The problems related to polygamy are not easily solved and it is quite unlikely that there is any one formula which should be adopted everywhere. Not only are the particular circumstances varied in different parts of the world, but the reactions of people are not the same. More and more missionaries are coming to feel that in many instances disservice has been done to the cause of the gospel by spending so much effort setting up a new marriage code rather than proclaiming a new way of life. The details of the problem might be worked out better by the people under the guidance of the Holy Spirit than under the discipline of the missionaries.[47]

Another major problem [48] facing Christian missions is one of church organization. It is taken for granted that Presbyterian missions will establish a presbyterian type of church government; similarly Baptists go out to establish congregational types of government, and missions which have episcopal forms of church government generally seek to transplant such social structures in foreign soil. It is not difficult to see why this is done, for matters of church organization and government are generally assumed by the respective missions to be part of the New Testament revelation, rather than reflecting certain historical developments within Western Christianity. The equally important matter to be realized is that in the various countries where missions have established churches these churches may keep the outward form imposed by the missionary group, but for all practical purposes they generally function in terms of the local social structure. As soon as missionary direction ceases, they almost inevitably fall back upon their own cultural processes. The Christian organizations of Japan reflect a number of different ecclesiastical currents: episcopal, presbyterian, and congregational, but they all tend to operate in the typically paternalistic manner of other Japanese institutions.

The United Church of the Philippines has combined episcopal, presbyterian, and congregational elements in its formal organization and its actual functioning. This is not purely the result of a calculated attempt to satisfy all groups involved. It is an inevitable outworking of the various elements of social structure which combine to form Philippine society, which on the local level has a good deal of community participation,[49] but also recognizes strong leadership of elders (a pattern in indigenous Filipino culture), and the pattern for centralization of power (a heritage of Spanish occupation). All of these features of the social structure consciously or unconsciously have affected the development of church life in the Philippines.

In Latin America churches of all denominations, irrespective of their formal organization, have tended to follow the local social structure. Almost inevitably the pattern of Roman Catholicism tends to operate within the Protestant church, with the pastor assuming more and more authority, often for the simple reason that it is thrust upon him. Church conflicts are rarely settled without what is equivalent to a revolution, for the orderly conduct of affairs and the willingness of the minority to go along with the decision of the majority are not patterns of Latin American social structure.[50]

In dealing with the problems of social culture in foreign societies, some Christian missionaries have tended to be occupied primarily with forms and not with content. It has been all too easy to think that by substituting our own social institutions and organizations, one could overcome the sin which poisons all interhuman relationships. Moreover, we have too often been guilty of denouncing primarily the socially spectacular sins, such as adultery and drunkenness, and overlooking the socially cancerous sins, such as pride and backbiting. Furthermore, failure to appreciate fully the fact that God has worked in and through many different social patterns—not only in the history of the church but in the wide varieties of present-day churches—has accounted for some of our ethnocentric blindness. In certain instances, an enamored preoccupation with education and progress prevented some from seeing that the creation, by legislation or philanthropy, of an "ideal social environment" has never and would never lead people to love God nor their fellow men. Only the reconciliation of man with God through Jesus Christ can so change the hearts of men that by the guidance of God's Spirit all human relationships can be sanctified.

The Great Commission and the history of Christendom both point clearly to the necessity of proclaiming the Good News, but neither in Scripture nor in the historical development of the Church does the gospel include the details of social structure or church organization.[51]

DEVILS AND DOUBTS

Some representatives of Western culture flatter themselves by picturing the rest of the world as dominated by beliefs in devils, while they enjoy the sophistication of scientifically founded doubts. It is true that the West has experienced a considerable decline in Christian belief and practice. The schisms within the church, skepticism with regard to the historicity of the Bible, and "the scientific attitude" have all contributed to a decrease in adherence to traditional Christianity. However, these developments seem not to have curbed people's interest in the fantastic or the supernatural. In pulp magazines, and even in the slicks, pseudo science is producing myths by the hundreds to nourish a people who are seeking in science the security which they once felt in God or the church.

Man seems to have always been concerned with the supernatural, but to what extent he seeks to worship God out of pure altruism is quite another question. He is too egocentric to become completely unselfish, even when he thinks that a power greater than his own must be reckoned with. Religious attitudes include not only those of the devotee who lies prostrate in humility before his Maker, but also those of the magician who often in an arrogant manner seeks to control spirit forces by secret rites and incantations. Religion, which is essentially the province of man and his relationship to the supernatural, includes not only the fervent, sincere, and selfless prayer, but also charms, amulets, masks, and even black magic, by which people may seek to destroy their enemies.

Religious experience may be highly intense, as it was traditionally among the Plains Indians, who sought visions at any cost, even to the extent of putting skewers in their flesh and hanging from poles or dragging heavy weights; yet for the most part these Indians developed no world view or cosmology, had comparatively little interest in the life after death, and in general did not believe in future rewards or punishments for deeds done while in this world. But religion is more than philosophy or a world view. It is not only a belief about the supernatural but a response to it, charged with emotion and expressed in such features as rites, ceremonies, prayers, sacrifices, and observances of taboos.

Belief in the supernatural may invade every area of life, even as magic does for the Melanesians; or it may be of relatively little concern to the people, as among the Eskimos. Such people as the Yurok of California have been noted for their almost hypochondriac view of the world, for they constantly surrounded themselves with all kinds of cautions and taboos. On the other hand, the Hawaiians became bored with their religion, and even before the coming of missionaries [1] they abandoned their elaborate religious system of taboos which, for example, made a man guilty of a great offense if his shadow fell on any part of the king's house. All this to the Hawaiians seemed just too burdensome to be worth the effort. The Aztecs of Mexico developed an empire of which one of the dominant themes was the sacrifice of countless human beings provided by tribute-paying subjects, while in South America the Incas greatly reduced the human sacrifices characteristic of pre-Inca culture, devised an elaborate imperial cult, and thus provided a religious symbol for a highly totalitarian empire. The forms which religion may take and the variety of beliefs which it may include are unbelievably numerous.

Complete antisupernaturalism in any and all forms is for the most part only a relatively recent development in modern Western culture, where it has been notably espoused and promoted by some political movements. However, even these have found it necessary to develop such pseudo-scientific myths as state infallibility, racial purity, the "great leader," and the superman, in order to provide symbols for the masses to worship.

Spirits and Gods, Powers and Prophets

There are many ways in which religious beliefs can be and have been classified. No scheme is completely satisfactory, but there are aspects of different types of religions which should be considered, and they are perhaps best treated in terms of a series of dichotomies:

1. Animistic *vs.* theistic [2]
2. Ethical (i.e. moral) *vs.* nonethical (i.e. amoral)
3. Personal supernatural power *vs.* impersonal supernatural power
4. Salvational *vs.* legalistic
5. Mystic *vs.* nonmystic
6. Individual *vs.* collective
7. Revelational *vs.* nonrevelational
8. Exclusivistic *vs.* nonexclusivistic
9. Particularistic *vs.* universalistic

By "animistic" we mean believing in spirits, not only in the spirits of dead persons, but also in spirits which dwell in natural objects, such as trees, streams, mountains, a gnarled root, a perforated stone, or a meteorite.[3] Such objects are sometimes called fetishes.[4] It is often possible when speaking of the religious aspects of many primitive cultures to assign animism a dominant role, but animism is rarely, if ever, the exclusive religious feature. Animistic beliefs are usually traveling companions with many other religious concepts and practices (see pp. 144 ff.).

"Theistic" implies the belief in God or gods.[5] It is not always easy to distinguish between spirits and gods, for they share many characteristics. However, gods are usually regarded as much more powerful than spirits, and they generally have power over some important phase of the cosmos, e.g. Neptune as god of the sea, Pluto as god of the underworld, Mars as god of war. Spirits may dwell in natural objects, but are not "rulers" of such domains.

An ethical religion is one in which there are supernatural sanctions against violations of what is regarded as "correct" or "right" behavior. Christianity, with its system of judgment and concepts of heaven and hell,[6] is an ethical religion. Melanesian religion is essentially nonethical. For the most part there are no special benefits for doing good, nor any great penalties for being bad. The supernatural power of Melanesian religion is simply amoral.

Christianity and Mohammedanism share a belief in a *personal* supernatural power. Allah seems rather chained by fate, but he is still to some extent sovereign. In much of Africa most of the supernatural power is vested in particular spirits. In Melanesia the supernatural power, called *mana,* is essentially impersonal. It exists in all kinds of objects—trees, stones, outstanding persons, magical herbs, and ceremonial knives—and it can be increased or decreased by magical means. It can be used for good or for evil, but it is power and it is supernatural. The *manitou* of the Algonquians, the *wakanda* of the Sioux, and the *orenda* of the Iroquois are all very similar to the *mana* of the Melanesians. This supernatural power has often been likened to electricity, which cannot be described except as it manifests itself in what it does. It is not definable in itself, but it is the all-powerful force behind everything. *Brahman* of Hinduism is not very different from this. It is indeterminate, personless, and all-embracing.[7] *Tao,* the great life force of Taoism, is likewise one of these impersonal supernatural powers.

Christianity, in that it provides a Saviour, is regarded as the prime example of a salvational religion, especially in its emphasis upon grace rather than works or law. Some cults of Buddhism have also claimed to be salvational. For example, the Japanese Buddhist Honen Shonin taught salvation by two means: (1) moral and intellectual achievement, and (2) through Amida Butsu, who by practicing the way of holiness is said to have acquired Buddhahood, suffered for sinful humanity, created the Pure Land of Bliss, and proclaimed a covenant which promises rebirth in paradise to any sincere believer.[8] Most religions offer the believer access to supernatural power or benefits through legalistic means, i.e. by conforming to prescribed ritual, such as incantation, sacrifices, fasting, and secret formulae.

The mystic attitude toward religion, by which we mean the attempt of the worshiper to attain a state of ecstatic communion, overpowering vision, or direct revelation, manifests itself in many distinct ways. The mystic may retire to the secluded quiet of his monastic chamber, or he may beat and torture himself (as the Plains Indians did) in order to obtain his vision, or he may work himself into a frenzy by wild dancing to throbbing voodoo drums. Though such experiences have very different overt psychological manifestations, they represent a very similar characteristic of the worshipers' being "possessed." This highly ecstatic type of worship is quite unknown among the Zuni, for whom religion is also a very important matter and merits equally great concern, since its expression is also the fulfillment of socially imposed responsibilities and requires the calm and poise of beautifully ordered ceremonies.

A religion may lay great stress upon the individual's beliefs, behavior, and response to the supernatural, or it may emphasize the collective patricipation of the society and the benefits for the entire community. The former is true of Christianity, especially in its Free Church forms. Polynesian religion, with its emphasis upon taboo, elaborate ceremonials, and deities which preside over all aspects of human activities: agriculture, hunting, fishing, war, etc., is essentially a collective, or social, kind of religion, which takes for granted the individual's co-operation in procuring the maximum benefits for all. By individual *vs.* collective we do not have reference to whether few or many persons actively participate in leading religious observances, but we are concerned with the degree to which collective participation is essential for the efficacy of the rites and whether the deities deal with persons individually or primarily through the entire community. In Melanesia almost every person is his own priest, for a person's success depends largely upon his personal control of *mana* at all times. In Africa there is more specialization, that is only certain persons—priests, witches, seers, or medicine men—officiate for others. In Roman Catholicism the priest becomes the obligatory intermediary between the people and God.

Judaism, Christianity, and Mohammedanism are the most distinctly revelational in their presentation, but Hinduism and Buddhism also speak of revealed insight. On the other hand, Confucianism makes no such claim, and religions which are primarily animistic generally are not thought of as revelational except as the seer may become possessed of a spirit which makes predictions about the future or as some frenzied devotee declares that the spirit has revealed itself. A religion announced by prophets who claim divine inspiration for their message is to be classified as a revelational religion.[9]

The struggle between Greco-Roman religion and Christianity was on the point of exclusivism. The classical world would have gladly put a statue of Jesus Christ in the pantheon at Rome as another religious leader. But the Christians insisted that he was not "another," but "the only." Judaism, Christianity, and Mohammedanism all believe in the exclusive claims of God or Allah. It was not enough for Jehovah to be the God of the Hebrews—He alone was truly God. This same monotheism is characteristic of Christianity, and fanatically so of Mohammedanism. As far as the rest of the religions of the world are concerned there is no such feeling of exclusivism. When a Navajo states, "Christianity is true and good for white men, but Navajo religion is true and good for Navajos," he is not trying to be evasive. His own religion is not exclusivisitic and hence he finds it hard to understand the exclusivism [10] of Christianity.

The crucial issue which Christian missions face in India today involves precisely this matter of exclusivism. In brief, Hinduism says that all religions are good and lead to the same God. Hence, it is immoral to convert a person from one religion to another. Christianity claims, "There is none other name under heaven given among men, whereby we must be saved" (Acts 4:12). Throughout the history of Christendom, beginning with the opposition of the Roman state, Christians have had to face uncompromisingly the implications of the absolute and exclusive demands of Christ. Anything less than this strikes at the very heart of Christian theology.

Most animistic religions are particularistic in the sense that the deities are strictly those of the particular tribe. It would never occur to a member of such a religious group to try to convert anyone else to his views, for his gods are only concerned with the tribe in question. In this sense Shintoism is a particularistic "tribal" religion, for it is inseparably associated with Japanese national destiny. Though the Japanese demanded respect and "worship" for Shintoism by conquered peoples, such persons could not fully participate in Shintoism, since they were not Japanese. On the other hand, a truly universalistic religion claims that its truths have universal applicability, irrespective of people's racial or cultural backgrounds. The degree of dominance of the universalistic aspect of any religion largely determines the missionary zeal of its adherents. The qualities of particularistic and universalistic outlooks are not absolute, but relative. Buddhism is, for example, more universalistic than Hinduism, and Christianity is more universalistic than Mohammedanism.

It should be noted that in the distinctions which have just been described we have not used "higher" and "lower" religions, as a distinction which is often made. In the first place, the use of such terms implies a judgment which is difficult to justify on any objective basis. For the orthodox Christian it has always been a matter of Christianity vs. non-Christian religions and never a matter of "higher" and "lower." Furthermore, as has been noted in the preceding paragraphs, quite diverse religions may share some traits.

Another feature of our analysis is the avoidance of the weighted word "superstition." It is too easy to miss some important contrast or resemblance by passing off other people's beliefs as "superstitions" and regarding one's own beliefs as "doctrines." In the same way that we avoid "savage" and "native" when talking of social and material culture, we do well to avoid the word "superstition" in talking of religion.[11]

In a sense we are quite unfair to both religious beliefs and to the various religions if we treat them in a purely anatomical manner by analyzing their distinct features and functioning. As in any and all cultural structures we should attempt to grasp something of the totality of the religious belief and expression; and even when we are discussing some of the isolated details, we must keep in mind the larger functioning unit. We may be describing the compounding of magic medicine from the crushed skull of a murdered witch in central Congo, but such a medicine is not an isolated feature of the religious life. It is only one of many medicines, some of which are powerful for preserving health and others for destroying life. The use of these medicines implies certain beliefs in the power of humans to control spirit forces through mechanical, magical means, while the existence of black magic itself means that societies are maladjusted in that men seek to use supernatural means to kill enemies when they do not dare to use physical force. Sometimes the corruption of justice and the failure of any system of judicial equity goads a person on to avenge his wrongs by dabbling in the supernatural. We could go on and on tracing the ramifications of this one concoction of black magic; we would soon be touching almost all the phases of the life of the people. Religion itself is not an isolated compartment in life, and no part of the religious belief or experience can be isolated from the rest of life.

It Just Isn't So

There are a number of popular misconceptions about religion and religions. One of these is that all people believe in God or at least in a "high god." While it is very true that all people believe in supernatural manifestations, and practically all peoples have had ideas about mythological creatures which performed amazing miraculous feats, this does not mean that people believe necessarily in God, certainly not in the same way as we traditionally understand the word. The Polar Eskimos have deities but no supreme being; and the Nama Hottentots believe in the supernatural powers of deified heroes, but there is no high god. In the Orient there are many, many gods, who are often ranged in hierarchies, as in India. These deities are symbolic of various phases of existence. For example, Vishnu is the god of creative production and life and Siva the god of wasting and death. But the ultimate reality in most Oriental religions is not a determinate God, but an indeterminate soul stuff or world soul—the indivisible, formless Brahman of Hinduism, the personless nothingness of Buddhist Nirvana, or the source of life force in Tao, which manifests itself in the supernatural, but the concept of God is not universal.

It is quite a mistake to equate a belief in a high god with the exclusive monotheism of Judaism, Christianity, and Mohammedanism. There are evidences of belief in a high god in many parts of Africa [12] as well as in numerous other areas of the world, but generally he is so remote from the people as to be relatively useless. As one Congolese Mongbandi man explained it, "Why should we make offerings to Him, for we don't know where He is or what He is doing. And anyway He won't do us any harm. It is better for us to placate the evil spirits which harm us, rather than to bother about God."

We erroneously assume that all people believe in a life after death. In one sense they do, but in another, they do not. That is, the beliefs in life after death are so diverse that they offer very few parallels to our traditional ideas. In many parts of Africa it is believed that the soul continues to live on for a time but that it has only a very shadowy existence as a wandering ghost which, when finally neglected or forgotten by the clan, perishes in utter oblivion. Hindus, of course, believe in a life after death—in fact, many lives here on earth in the form of repeated existences, higher in caste and rank if one merits it by proper behavior and religious observance in the former life, but lower if one violates the socio-religious rules. After thousands of such reincarnations, a person may at last be rewarded by being allowed to escape from the limitations of human existence and to be absorbed into Brahman, the world soul. But a person's condition in Brahman is nothing like the Christian's concept of life after death, for in forming a part of Brahman the person loses his individual personality. The soul stuff which comprised the person continues to exist, but not the person. In a sense this is the same as not existing—certainly as far as the individual's consciousness is concerned.

Still a further misconception must be considered if we are to approach the subject of non-Christian religions with a proper perspective. It is assumed that all persons are familiar with the concept of sacrifice for sin—in other words, the presentation of some animal which is killed as a substitute for the guilty person. The Hopis, however, make no sacrifices of any kind, animal or human. They do offer the deities gifts of corn flour, present prayer sticks at their altars, and conduct very elaborate ceremonies; but these are not designed to procure forgiveness for sins, but rather to insure good relations with the supernatural. Sacrifice for sin was prominent among Semitic peoples, occurs still in some tribes in Africa, and was probably a feature of the animal sacrifice of a white dog by the Iroquois. However, most people are much more concerned about placating their angry gods and malicious spirits than they are with worrying about atoning for their sins. The Indian in southern Mexico who sacrifices a chicken on some crude stone altar back in the hills is probably not convicted of his sins; he is trying to placate the spirits who have made some member of his family sick and by this sacrifice he hopes to satisfy their cruel, unpredictable demands.[13]

Idols behind Crosses

Even as idols have been hidden behind crosses, so real religious beliefs have often been masked by outward forms. A missionary traveling in northern Ecuador came upon a village of people engaged in riotous drinking. Many were brawling, others staggering in disorganized dancing, and some had fallen into the muddy gutters along the dirty streets. One of the saloonkeepers, who was more sober than the rest, explained that all this celebration was in honor of John the Baptist. The missionary insisted that of all the saints John the Baptist was certainly not given to drink, for he was under a special vow never to drink. To which the man replied, "Ah, and then we drink to the saints of pleasure," and he reeled off a long list of names, concluding with the boisterous exclamation, "All our saints are drunkards, and so are we." But this type of explanation did not seem to make sense, and so the missionary politely inquired further as to just which saints had encouraged them to dance and drink, to which the man replied in rather sober, earnest tones, "Oh, we really drink to the mountains of this valley," and while reciting their ancient Indian names he pointed in reverence to their lofty peaks. Behind the façade of Christian cathedrals, the symbol of the cross, and the days of the saints, there still remained the ancient worship of the spirits enshrined in the mountains.

The *santería* of Cuba [14] is a strange mixture of outward Christian symbols but with totally non-Christian religious values. The cross is used, and the saints are frequently spoken of—especially Santa Barbara, the patron saint of *santería*. But the real objects of worship are stones, which are said to have the power to reproduce themselves and which are made powerful by being treated each year with the warm blood of animal sacrifice and with herbs mixed with water. It is said that the "saint is fed," but each saint is represented by a stone, and it is the stone which possesses the supernatural power. In addition to the stones there are the symbols of the rooster and the goat, the two animals credited with the greatest sex potentiality. The West African deity Chango (or Shango) is manifest in the male and female counterparts Ifo and Ifi. Here lies the popular appeal in *santería*, for it is fundamentally a fertility rite. Behind the curtain of Roman Catholic respectability exists quite a different set of religious beliefs. The members of the *santería* cult insist that they are Roman Catholics, for they accept the outward forms, but reject the religious content.

In one of the finest Buddhist temples of Djakarta the object which is most worshiped is found in one of the small alcoves just at the edge of the temple proper. It is a stone idol about two feet high, resembling a cat. The workmanship seems crude, but the stone is smoothly finished. The Chinese worshipers tie votive offerings to the statue, pour drink over its body, put food to its mouth, all the while chanting the magic phrases which will insure a proper response from the idol. Time after time the worshiper throws down divination sticks while continuing to fan the incense sticks and to burn paper money. This a far cry from philosophical Buddhism, which was itself a kind of revolt against the idolatry of Hinduism. Behind the outward forms of refined religious concepts one often encounters the realities of animism in some of its crudest forms. It might be said that all men at heart are "animists" in the sense that they are fearful of the supernatural and would like to master the techniques for controlling it.

Man in a Spirit World

Nonliterate peoples have often been described as being animists,[15] but the religions which are generally classified under the title of animism include forms of worship far more different than Christianity and Mohammedanism. In the religion of the Nama Hottentots, the spirits are only those of the dead, including some mythologically enhanced heroes, while the moon is honored by songs and dances and addressed in prayers. On the other hand, the Aztecs had a motley array of spirits and gods, worshiped in a constant succession of elaborate and bloody rites conducted by an influential class of professional priests. These dressed in long black robes, and their unkempt hair matted with dried human blood covered ears made ragged by piercing and cutting seven times each day to meet the insatiable requirements of blood-demanding gods.

But despite the strange contrasts of religious beliefs among non-literate peoples, there are certain beliefs which are present (though often only implicit) in the majority of these religions:

1. Man is essentially a part of nature.
2. Man consists of more than one part.
3. There are supernatural powers.
4. Supernatural powers are, at least in part, controllable.
5. There is no necessary relationship between morality and religion.

The concept of man as an integral part of all nature is reflected in a number of beliefs. The widespread concept of totemic ancestors, e.g. animals, plants, rivers, clouds, and stars, serves as a constant reminder of a people's link with the natural world around them. The Ainu of northern Japan insist that man is no different from animals, plants, and even some totally inanimate objects, since all such objects have souls. When a New Caledonian [16] plants a tree in a hole where the placenta has been buried and then later on tells the child that he will flourish as long as the tree grows, there is more than idle sentiment involved. The child is thus intrinsically linked with the natural world. We must not imply that people regard themselves simply as animals—by no means. Some of the Indians of the Amazon not only believe they are distinct from animals, but take means to show this by removing all body hair. But when one of the same Indians insists that the eating of the heart of a certain animal makes it possible for him to acquire the courage and character of that animal, he has linked himself with the world about him.

So far as is known, all people believe in some part of man which is not completely identical with his body, whether this be called his "soul," "spirit," "breath," or "shadow." The Valiente Indians of Panama believe that every person has an *uyae*, a soul which is regarded as essentially good, and yet when a person dies this *uyae* becomes a *bokoi*, a bad, malignant spirit in the forest. For the Eskimos there are three parts to man: body, soul, and name —all of which have equal importance and combine to make up the total person. The Dahomeans of West Africa believe that every person has three souls, and adult males are endowed with still a fourth.[17] One soul is a kind of guardian spirit, inherited from some dead ancestor. The second soul is a personal one; the third is a small part of the creator god *Mawu*. The fourth is one's "destiny," which must be propitiated with sacrifice at least three times a year.

However the soul or souls may be described, they are generally very real to people even while they are still alive, and may have genuine experiences all of their own, quite apart from the body. Most Melanesian peoples believe that in sleep their souls wander off from the body and actually perform the deeds of which they dream. For this reason, some people have allowed themselves to be condemned for stealing in a distant village even though they could prove that all the time they were asleep at home. If they dreamed that they had stolen, most surely their soul must have done the deed.

In many instances the "animist's" concept of soul or spirit is utterly foreign to our way of thinking. New Caledonians [18] believe that people are either *kamo* or *bao*. One who is living and not ostracized by the society for antisocial acts is *kamo*, but when he becomes very old he may be called *bao*, which also designates a corpse, a spirit of the spirit world, or a deified ancestor. This same word *bao* may designate a fool, who is ceremonially declared dead so that if he does violate taboos, as by treating sweet potatoes with disrespect, he will not implicate all the society. Each *kamo* eventually becomes a *bao*, but it is not just a matter of physical death—it is social death which is more important.

In much of the so-called animist world the souls of people are believed to live on in a kind of shadowy existence, terrifying people by appearing as ghosts, sending plagues if they are not properly conciliated, showering blessings of abundant rains and good crops if they are appeased, and always standing there in the shadows of the spirit world to speak in dreams and to send omens of coming events.

Except among some modern sophisticates, the belief in the existence of supernatural power is universal, but there are wide differences of belief as to the nature of this power. As noted in a previous section, this supernatural power may be an impersonal force such as the *mana* of Melanesia, or it may be quite personal. For the Haida of British Columbia spirits existed everywhere—in the sea, sky, air, stars, fire, mountains, rocks, reefs, lakes, streams, marshes, and plants. But though there were so many spirits and gods very little ritual attention was paid to them. Evidently the people were too busy seeking to increase their wealth and prestige to be much concerned about religious ceremonies for the spirits. In general, the spirit world of the animist is not only populated with nature spirits, but also with those of the dead. The latter may make their appearance in whirlwinds, storms, strange noises, and phantoms in the night. The supernatural powers often include harmless sprites and fairies who take pleasure in clever tricks, as well as ugly ogres who lie in wait to maim and kill.

The belief that supernatural power can be controlled by "mechanical" techniques lies at the root of magic—the foundation stone of animistic ritual.[19] If a Haida was bent on destroying an enemy, he would try to find a few wisps of hair that belonged to his intended victim, or he might get some cuttings from a fingernail, a drop of saliva, a little food left in a bowl, or a piece of the man's clothing—anything which had been a part of, or in close contact with, the person who was marked for destruction. Then by incantations and secret formulae, the man could be struck ill, and in a few days he would die—destroyed by black magic. For Melanesians sorcery is an everyday affair, not just a technique of getting rid of competitors. Regardless of how skilled a person may be, magic is still necessary to insure good luck in business, a safe journey to nearby or distant islands, success in growing huge sweet potatoes—some of which may measure six feet in length. Magic becomes one of the principal ingredients of medicines and healing. The San Blas medicine man concocts a number of excellent medicines of herbs, berries, and roots, but most of his preparations are more magic than medicine. In treating almost any sickness, he files on a crude wooden doll at the place corresponding to where the patient feels the greatest pain. These wood filings are then mixed with water and given to the patient to drink. This medicine, however, is not regarded as effective unless the shaman sings the proper songs, specially composed for each kind of sickness and for each class of person. While the patient lies feverish and restless, surrounded by solicitous friends, the medicine man chants in low, monotonous tones, as he bends over old, dirt-smudged pages on which he has drawn in strange, self-invented hieroglyphics the important themes of the almost endless stanzas.

Magic powers may be employed for purposes other than destroying enemies or healing the sick. The Polar Eskimos insist that the magic power of the shaman permits him to calm storms, to descend into the underworld, and to rise to the sky and walk on the clouds.[20] The voodoo sorcerers of Haiti claim to be able to change themselves into animals, to pass through locked doors, and to raise the dead and make them slaves (these are called *zombies*), who remain utterly forgetful of their past as long as they never obtain a bit of salt. Almost everyone claims to know someone who has seen a genuine *zombi*, in fact whole groups of them, but as is always the case with such beliefs, one never finds the eyewitness and the documented evidence. Nevertheless, one man requested his family to cut his corpse into two pieces to be buried in separate graves, for fear that the local sorcerer, who was his enemy, would bring him to life as a wretched slave. The Haitian government had no valid evidence of the existence of zombies, but it sanctioned the belief by recently passing a law against the supposed practice.

There may be little or no connection between religion and morality. The power of *mana* is entirely neutral in ethical matters. It is only power, and can be used to heal or to destroy. The same person may in one situation use magic to kill and then employ magic to heal. The deities of the Todas of South India are believed to concern themselves with violation of taboo, and by bringing sickness or misfortune they may indicate to the people that sin has been committed. A man may have stolen milk from a dairy barn, entered the barn after having sexual relations during the daytime, or approached a herd immediately after helping at a funeral and without proper purification. All these actions are "sins" and must be confessed and expiated by offerings—made, however, not to the deity but to the other half of the clan.[21] The taboos imposed by Karei, the god of thunder, upon the Semang in Malay, do not include theft or murder, but do forbid the trespasses of undue familiarity with one's mother-in-law, killing a sacred black wasp, mocking a defenseless animal, playing with birds' eggs, and drawing water with a smoke-blackened pot.[22]

Among the Incas the taboos included more of the practices that would be recognized by us as transgressions: adultery, murder, witchcraft. Such sins were regarded as bringing guilt not only to the person but also to the community. The sins had to be confessed and expiation made, usually in the form of ritual bathing, abstinence from salt and pepper and from sexual relations during the time of penance.

There are a number of primitive cultures in which the religion has a definite ethical content. The Kono people of Sierra Leone, West Africa, believe in Yataa as an ethical deity, who punishes wrongdoers. He sees, thinks, and has power to help; and though he may be somewhat removed from the immediate consciousness of the people by virtue of the attention which the ancestral spirits receive as intermediaries between people and Yataa, nevertheless, he remains as both a power and a symbol of the moral order.[23] However, more often than not one finds a situation similar to what exists among the Ovambo people of Southwest Africa. Their deity Kalunga requires good behavior of a sort, but this means conformity to tribal ethics, not to any moral dictates of Kalunga. He objects violently to pregnancy before girls have been properly initi-

ated in the *efundula* rite, but does not object in the least to fornication, incest, and abortion by those who have undergone the rites.
In fact, Kalunga is attributed with being responsible for some
people becoming homosexuals.[24]

There has been considerable speculation as to just how much
feeling of guilt there is among primitive peoples. Even though they
do not reflect our attitudes toward violation of taboos, is there a
sense of guilt? We have to reckon with three different types of
reactions to transgressions of religiously sanctioned codes: fear,
shame, and guilt. It seems that for the most part people are afraid
of being punished or of being caught in the act by some person
or deity. Often there is a sense of shame, expressed as "I'd feel
terrible if anyone saw me doing this." A sense of guilt expresses
itself as an inner feeling of failure for not having lived up to what
the society or the deity expects, irrespective of whether one is caught
or seen. This sentiment of guilt is far less common than might be
supposed. Except for those neurotic persons who magnify their self-
importance by self-incrimination, regarding oneself as guilty is not
in keeping with man's egocentric way of life. Fear and shame are
much more convenient attitudes for self-centered people. Careful
distinctions must be made, however, between objective behavior and
subjective attitudes. Many Americans insist that certain sexual
practices are not sins, but they nevertheless suffer from guilt complexes. The Marshallese, on the other hand, have been taught by
missionaries that such practices are sins, and they affirm their agreement, but many continue to practice them and appear to have no
sense of guilt. Words and actions do not always go together.

Animistic beliefs have been intellectually shattered by scientific
medicine, church and government schools, and the teachings of
missionaries. But they still dominate the emotional life of a vast
majority of people in many parts of the world. The Yoruba in West
Africa have lost their gods, for they no longer have much confidence
in them, but now they are at the mercy of witchcraft, against which
they find no protection. The gods have been dethroned but magic
remains as strong as ever, except in the case of rain-making, where
modern science has taken a hand. To protect themselves the

Yorubas have formed witch-hunting societies that strike with vio-
lence and blindness at suspects, guilty and innocent. The government has denounced these societies, but in doing so it appears to
the people to be on the side of witchcraft, which of course it is
not.

For the most part the religious beliefs of nonliterate societies are
quite unsystematic. As is true in most cultures, the majority of
people have not been critical in the examination of their beliefs,
but have taken them for granted. These beliefs do not, however,
rule out other supernatural powers or forces. From the animist's
viewpoint, it is not contradictory for a voodooist in Haiti to regard
himself as a good Roman Catholic or for a fetichist of West Africa
to claim to be an orthodox Mohammedan. But this is no more
strange than for an agnostic in the United States to pride himself
on being a good church member. However, despite the chaos of
some conflicting beliefs and the motive of fear which dominates
the emotional attitudes, animistic beliefs have become thoroughly
woven into the very warp and woof of the people's daily life. They
justify and strengthen the historical traditions out of which they
have arisen, and they provide an outlook on the mysteries of existence.

Gods and Spirits, High and Low

Not all gods and spirits have the same qualities, functions, or
importance. Corresponding to the Polynesian social structure, the
gods and spirits of the Samoan Islanders likewise have distinctions
of function and rank. The totemic spirits of the families are superseded by the guardian spirits of the districts. Above these are the
gods which preside over various human activities, such as agriculture, hunting, fishing, and war. Next there are the gods of the land,
sea, sky, lightning, and rain, and finally there is the high-god
Tangaloa, creator and benefactor of mankind. The Iroquois believed not only in spirits and the supernatural impersonal power of
orenda, but also in five principal gods: of creation, of destruction,
of rain and thunder, of the sun and warfare, and finally of death.
The Ganda of East Africa have a rather typical array of gods: those

of the clan, the ancient deified kings, and above all the gods of
the nation.

Even where there is a high god, as among the Samoan Islanders,
he may not be worshiped any more than the rest. In some instances
he is very poorly or vaguely defined, as was the sun god among the
Crow. They were much more interested in Old Man Coyote, who
entered into so much of their mythology and seemed to take such
an active place in the life of the people. Among the Dahomeans of
West Africa and the voodooists of Haiti, Legba is a popular god,
even though in the pantheon he serves only as a kind of errand
boy for the more important gods. As a messenger, he is also a kind
of intermediary. His shrine occurs in connection with the temples
of all other gods. He is associated with certain fertility rites and is
represented by a phallic symbol. As a "nearby" god he becomes a
kind of personal mediator and even a personal protector.

From the Sun to a Praying Mantis

From the sun, worshiped by Quechua Indians of the Andes, to
the praying mantis, revered by the Hottentots, there is scarcely any
object in the universe which has not been regarded by some people
or other as being endowed with or indwelt by some supernatural
power. The Quechuas selected as totems such objects as mountain
lions, soaring condors, slithering serpents, and majestic mountains.
An albino animal is thought to be particularly endowed with supernatural power, so likewise is a stone which has fallen and by accident killed a person. For the Ganda the king's umbilical cord is
very sacred.

The sacred objects of the Hopi include *kachina* dolls, ingeniously
made and geometrically patterned representations of the ancestral
spirits of the clans. They also make prayer sticks with feathers
attached, over which they sprinkle corn flour and offer prayer for
blessings. The Plains Indians made medicine bundles out of such
things as dried hides, teeth of much-feared animals, feathers of
awesome birds, and medicinally potent herbs.

New Caledonians treat a sweet potato with worshipful reverence.
They stroke its head, and caress it. They identify some of its parts

as corresponding to the human body, and they claim that its growth resembles the male sexual function. In time of bereavement they may give sweet potatoes to the bereaved as symbols of the promise of life, for even though the extremities die new sprouts continue to live.[25]

Amulets and charms may be kept to ward off evil or to bring good luck. They may be small glass beads which Ngbaka women of northern Congo tie to the front of a baby's head, or Indian-head pennies or rabbits' feet carried by Americans, or leather phylacteries with words of the Koran hung around the neck or tied to the arm of a West African Bambara. In some instances objects acquire sacred power by contagion, as when the cloak of a Maori chief of New Zealand was thought to be too religiously dangerous for a common man to wear since the chief, as the possessor of great *mana,* made the cloak spiritually powerful and hence taboo to anyone else.

In a number of religions there is a distinct difference made between the sanctity of the priest when he is performing his religious functions and when not. That is to say, it is his office and not his person which is sacred.

Objects may be sacred in themselves or become so by virtue of their sacred use or consecration. The bloody human sacrifices of the Aztecs were not required because of uncontrollable brutality. The Aztec worship demanded about 2,500 victims a year,[26] but some of these victims volunteered, and all were highly honored by the people. The latter would dress themselves in the victims' skins, and banquet on the human flesh after the heart had been cut from the body and the corpse flung down the bloody steps of the temple pyramid. By being consecrated as a sacrifice to the gods, the victim was in a measure identified with the god, and those who ate the flesh participated in a kind of spiritual communion with their gods. The Aztec pattern of spiritual participation by eating is not altogether different from the attitude of those Christians who believe in the literal transformation of the communion elements of the bread and wine into the body and blood of Jesus Christ. Following the analogy of sacrifice, in some areas material objects can only be offered to the gods or spirits by the process of "killing." Such objects as vases, precious stones, intricate carvings, or richly embroidered garments must be broken or torn (i.e. ceremonially killed) in order to be offered to the spirit world.

Objects may be rendered sacred by well-known institutionalized ceremonies, or they may come to be sacred by the steady and unconscious growth of tradition. Near the old harbor of Djakarta there is an ancient Portuguese iron cannon in a small grove of trees. For many years it was only a piece of iron—war surplus from olden times—but gradually it has come to be an idol of fertility. The handle of the cannon is a clenched fist of phallic symbolization with the thumb protruding between the first two fingers. This cannon is now enclosed within a small fence, decorated with flowers and small paper umbrellas; a man guards the precinct, and an old woman acts as priestess, warming her hand over a fire of Buddhist paper money brought by the women suppliants, and then transferring this heat to the clenched fist.[27] There are two of these identical cannons in Indonesia, and for many years it was said by Indonesians that if ever these two cannons were brought together Indonesia would become independent. Now that she is independent, the popular belief is that once the cannons are in the same place, there will be world peace.

Blessings, Cursings, Divination, and Communion

Above all else, men seek blessings from the supernatural. They want good health, abundant crops, safety from enemies, forgiveness for transgressions, and progeny to fortify the family or clan. They may not be too particular about whether or not their gain is another's loss, for they may, as in some places in Cuba, pour a little water over a sick person, catch it in a cup, and then throw it out into the street, so that the first person who steps on the dampened earth may contract the disease and thus carry away the malady from the original victim. The Ganda attempt to transfer sickness by making a little clay image, rubbing it on a person, and then burying it in a path so as to infect the first person who passes. This practice contains the two essential features of most magic—imitation and contagion.[28] When the Hottentots dance before a hunt and imitate with incredible skill the movements and habits of the game which they seek to kill, they are employing imitative magic to guarantee their success. When a Haitian makes tea from leaves of the Bible in order to cure rheumatism, it is the magic principle of contagion which is involved. The medical practice in many parts of East Africa depends largely on combined imitative and contagious magic in healing. One part of the ingredients of any medicine must represent the patient: scrapings from a walking stick, if the person is tall, or red bark, for a woman who is known to have bled at childbirth. The second type of ingredient is often of the contagious variety: a piece of cloth from a prostitute to assure success in love, a piece of embryo of a calf to insure that one will not be seen, even as the calf was not seen in the womb, or a small piece of skin from the forehead of a witch, as a protection against black magic.

Spirit power may not only bless but also curse. It all depends upon the techniques and the desire of the one who controls the supernatural force. An Aranda who wished to kill a personal enemy could recite an incantation over a bone, sharpen the point, dab it with rosin, and then point it at the person who was to die a victim of such sinister foul play. The Akha roll a small piece of paper, dip it in water, cast a magic spell upon it, and then hurl it by magic into another person. Unless one can find a witch doctor who is more powerful than the original sorcerer and who can remove the paper by sleight of hand and sucking, the victim is sure to die. He actually does die: he is literally scared to death. In Haiti some of the imprecatory Psalms of the Old Testament are popular as means of bringing curses down upon the heads of one's enemies. Reading such denunciations as David pronounced upon his enemies is supposed to carry the weight of divine condemnation.

If men can only determine what the future is to bring, they seem to think that they can forestall disastrous events. To do this they may watch the flight of birds or examine the livers of sacrifices (as did the Greeks and Romans), or they may heat the shoulder blade of an animal over a campfire to see the way in which the cracks form (as in many parts of Asia), or pierce the thighbones of chickens (as in Southeast Asia). They may also look at the lines in the palm of the hand or tea leaves in the cup (as in Western civilization), or study the position of the stars (as is done in so many parts of the world). In some Buddhist temples the system of divination becomes quite complicated. First a section of bamboo with numbered sticks is shaken. The number of the stick which falls in the right manner is then tested by dropping the two halves of divining sticks. If the appropriate positions are noted, then another series of sticks are shaken, and finally, a piece of paper numbered to correspond to the last determined number is taken as proof of the future. It would seem as though a single act of chance cannot be a guarantee of divine sanction, but that several acts of chance combine to guarantee validity. To our way of thinking, it is as though one were to add up zeros and still come out with a number greater than zero.

Closely akin to divination is the revealing of events which have occurred at great distances. Some of the Mayan Indians in Quintana Roo practice this art with amazing results. One Indian had five clear, glass marbles which he used to divine events by going into a kind of trance. On one occasion he told a friend of the birth of the latter's child at a distance of many miles through the jungle. His incredible ability to tell people about what had happened in distant places from which there was absolutely no possible means of communication is still unexplained.

Communion with supernatural powers through the frenzied hysteria of unpredictable "possession" or the self-induced trance of the seer becomes not only a means for receiving communications about the future from the supernatural realm but also a way of identification and communion with the spirit world. As the dance drums of West Africa beat louder and louder into the long hours of the night and the dancers whirl and leap with ever-increasing momentum and the shrill shrieks of religious ecstasy pierce the mad confusion of song and clapping, sincere devotees believe they find communion with the supernatural. In outward form at least this is not too different from some Christian worshipers who lose consciousness through the hypnotic effect of the singing throng, the contagious rhythm of stamping feet, clapping hands, and swaying bodies.

Communion in religions which are primarily animistic is not entirely a matter of mass hypnosis. A single worshiper may become possessed and show his spiritual power by walking over red-hot stones, eating glass, or piercing his tongue with spikes, without apparently being harmed.[29]

Rites and Ritual

It is not enough to believe in spirits, to own sacred medicine bundles, and to want healing. One has to do something in order to attain the desired results. Religion is belief in action.

The principal ingredients of ritual are sacred objects, sacred words, sacred ceremonies, and sacred persons. Sacred objects have been described on pages 152–54, but we have only touched the matter of sacred words, which are generally regarded by worshipers as an indispensable part of all levels of religion, from magic to intercessory prayer.

Some words are regarded as being so holy that they cannot be uttered, at least not by common people and under ordinary cir- cumstances. By New Testament times, this was the belief of the Jews with respect to the name *Jehovah*, probably pronounced some- thing like *Yahweh*, but we do not know exactly how it was uttered, for the Jews refused to speak the word when they read their Scrip- tures aloud and to avoid its use substituted *Adonai* or *Elohim*.[30] Only once each year on the Day of Atonement the high priest uttered the word inside the Holy of Holies. But even the word for "God" (i.e. Greek *Theos* and Hebrew *Elohim*) had begun to acquire the same magic and mystic value. Accordingly, in order to avoid the use of the word "God" people employed such phrases as "the kingdom of heaven" (used in Matthew, while Luke uses "kingdom of God"), "the right hand of Power" (for "the right hand of God"), and "the right hand of the Majesty" (likewise a substitute for "the right hand of God").

We claim not to believe in the magic power of words, and yet people react very violently to being cursed by someone. If the words were regarded as utterly without value, then the person uttering them should be looked upon as foolish for talking such nonsense.

In order that words may have their full power, some religions, e.g. in Polynesia, have required that the religious formulae be recited with absolute accuracy. If they are uttered properly and everything else is done in accordance with established tradition, then the spirits must act. The Lomas of Liberia insist that upon the completion of proper rites the spirits of their departed ancestors fulfill their obligations, but if these spirits do not comply, they are ceremonially eaten by the people.

There are wide variations in the uses of words addressed to the supernatural. Prayer may be spontaneous or formal, spoken in a natural voice or in chant forms with unnatural enunciation, pleading or coercive. The words of ritual are sometimes purposely archaic or obscure, for they lend a note of magic by the very fact of their being unknown. Much the same religious sentiment prompts the Mohammedan of the southern Philippines to memorize prayers in Classical Arabic (which he does not understand), as induces the San Blas medicine man to sing his chants with strange and unknown words, encourages priests of the Syrian church of South India to use the Syriac Scriptures, and dictates that Roman Catholic priests recite the mass in Latin. The expression *hokus pokus* (or its longer form *hokus pokus dominocus*) is derived from adaptations of the Latin mass. The people could not understand the words uttered by the priest at the most solemn points of the ritual, but they believed that the solemn declarations about the host being "the body of the Lord" were heavily charged with spiritual magic power, and so they coined a Latinlike equivalent.

Just as songs and chants are esthetically embellished words, so religious dances are esthetically elaborated movements. Actions may be free and uninhibited, as in voodoo rites, or very dull and monotonous, as in the Squaw dances among some of the Plains Indians. They may be imitative, as are some of the obscene dances among the Shilluks, or they may amount to little more than processions. Religious dances have an amazingly wide distribution throughout the world, and some of them are highly formalized and elaborate. The Hopi Indians of Arizona have developed a number of ritual

dances, of which the most famous is the Snake dance, performed
by co-operation of the Antelope and Snake societies. On the last
day of the celebration baskets of snakes (containing poisonous as
well as harmless ones) are ceremonially purified by washing in
water and yucca suds and are spread out on sand to dry, while
children play with them and let them crawl over their feet. Then
members of the Snake Society take these snakes either in their
mouths or wrapped around their necks and dance four times around
the town square. It is very rarely that any person is bitten during
this festival.

Perhaps the most emotionally moving ceremony ever developed
in a predominantly animistic religion was the ancient Aztec rite of
Texcatl. A captive youth was chosen for his bravery, physical perfection, and musical gifts as the incarnation of the god Texcatlipoca
for one year. He was decked in costly apparel, adorned with flowers,
served by four warriors and four priests, and honored by both the
people and the emperor. The last month he was married to four
beautiful maidens and was made the guest of honor at numerous
banquets and dances. On the last day of the month he bid good-by
to his wives, and accompanied by his servants, crossed lake Texcoco
in a canoe. Finally, he went to a small temple lying in ruins, laid
off his luxurious apparel, and with only a collar of tiny flutes walked
slowly up the steps of the pyramid, breaking a flute at each step.
Exactly at midnight on the crude stone altar, a black-robed priest
cut out his heart and offered it to Texcatlipoca, as the populace in
the city loudly acclaimed a successor.

Trances, visions, and dreams also reckon as means of religious
expression. Dreams rate particularly high as means by which the
supernatural forces manifest themselves to people. The Bible itself
mentions divine revelation to people through visions and dreams,
and St. Peter's experience recorded in Acts 10 was a trance. Africans, both Christian and non-Christian, place considerable emphasis on dreams, and there are numerous instances where Indians in
Latin America have spoken of dream experiences which profoundly
changed their lives by warning them of dangers, physical or spiritual.

Sorcerers, Seers, Priests, Prophets, and Medicine Men

Religious specialists are of six principal kinds: (1) those who engage in black magic (witches or sorcerers), (2) those who foretell the future (clairvoyants, diviners, seers), (3) those who heal or protect by magic means, detect witches and sorcerers, or reconcile offended spirits or gods (medicine men, witch doctors, shamen), (4) those who represent the people in conducting religious rituals (priests) [31], and (5) those who speak to the people on behalf of the supernatural power (prophets). Of course, one and the same person may practice several of these religious specialties.

In some societies, such as the Witoto of the Upper Amazon, all religious functions are carried out by the same person (usually called in anthropological literature a *shaman*, the most inclusive of all terms denoting religious specialists). Some societies, such as the Crows in the Middle West, have no priests, while others, e.g. the Zunis, have many. Some religious specialists may be professionals in the sense that they earn their living from their religious work, but others are amateurs—though none the less specialists.

In many parts of Africa there is usually a sharp distinction between the medicine man, who is called on to cure the deadly effects of black magic, and the sorcerer, who is guilty of employing it. A medicine man is a highly respected member of society, but a sorcerer is held in deathly fear; and when he dies, his body is often burned in order that no part of it may fall into the hands of those who could use it for compounding more evil medicines.

Among the Todas of India there are sorcerers, medicine men, diviners, and dairy priests. Every dairyman must be a priest, for he is engaged in very sacred business in taking care of the herds. But there are no prophets. In fact, prophets are quite rare in religions, for they are generally against the prevailing religious patterns. They speak to declare truth in the face of vested interests, and as a result they are generally unpopular with the priests, who are usually quite satisfied to retain their religious privileges and the status quo. But prophets do arise, even as they have among the Indians of the United States, who followed such prophets as a Shawnee Tenskwatawa in 1805, a Paiute Wodziwob in the 1870's, and another Paiute Wovoka in the 1890's. Prophet movements have been strong in West Africa and more recently in New Guinea, where they have reflected the breakdown of the old religious patterns and the desperate attempt to find a new solution by re-emphasizing old values.

How a person becomes a shaman in any primitive society depends largely upon the local requirements. The Ainus required that a person be of a nervous, sensitive nature in order to have ready contact with the spirits, but he could not be an epileptic. On the other hand, the Incas preferred epileptics, those born during electrical storms, or those who recovered after being struck by lightning. A San Blas medicine man looks like anyone else, but a Mongbandi witch doctor in Congo wears such emblems of his trade as a leopard skin, a large grimy leather bag, a huge curved knife, and necklaces of bones, claws, and teeth. In general there are long years of apprenticeship before one can become a medicine man, for one must not only master the use of hundreds of medical ingredients and be adroit at sleight of hand, but must also have a profound understanding of human psychology.

It is too often assumed that witch doctors are all fakes and that they know it. No doubt some hoodwink their public, even as some quack doctors operate in our society; but for the most part these men give every evidence of being sincere, even though their activities may be highly "irrational." Barbers in America and Europe, who used to bleed persons as a cure for fevers (from which practice we get the striped barber pole), were utterly sincere in their belief that they were helping the patients rather than slowly killing them. Taking into consideration that in every society a high percentage of persons suffer from psychosomatic diseases, the witch doctor, who specializes in just such maladies, has a large percentage of success. If a man becomes sick and attributes this to black magic cast upon him by an enemy, the ritual performed by the witch doctor to convince the man that he is no longer in danger serves to cure the patient in the majority of cases. The witch doctor does not know that there is no real therapeutic value in pretending to suck out a stick or puncturing the sick man with long bone needles as a method

of letting out evil spirits, but he has learned by experience that this
has led to people's recovery.[32] Results confirm his own belief in the
methods and enhance his prestige among the people. Even though
such medical practices are rapidly giving way to Western drugs
and surgery, it must not be thought that the aboriginal peoples have
basically changed their attitudes toward disease or remedies. It is
only that the white man has more powerful spirits which can provide more spiritually powerful medicines.

Myths and Magic

Polynesians possess many weird myths which describe the miraculous birth of the first human beings, only to be pursued by a
monstrous female ogre who threatens to devour them but who in
the end is utterly frustrated in her evil designs by a culture hero.
Such myths can scarcely be described as constituting a "cosmology"
or a "theology"; and yet, though they are quite unsystematically
formulated, they do reflect basic concepts about the world and the
spirit powers which exist in it. No doubt many of the myths of
nonliterate peoples begin as stories of earthly heroes; and since a
story rarely loses anything in being retold, they gradually acquire
supernatural features and religious significance. On the other hand,
the stories about the gods may become quite secularized, as was the
case with the Greco-Roman divinities, whose escapades of war, love,
jealousy, and intrigue were the object of less and less credence, even
before the time of Christ.

It is difficult for us in Western civilization fully to appreciate
what the myth means to aboriginal peoples. We, of course, have the
remnants of many myths [33] well illustrated by our daily speech,
e.g. "the sun sets," "the moon rises," and "necessity is the mother of
invention." But we are not controlled by such myths. Aboriginal
peoples, however, too often construct [34] a mythical world, only to
find themselves completely dominated by such myths. While the
rationality of the highly educated minority in the civilized world
tends to be more objective and systematic, the thinking of aboriginal
peoples often appears to be more subjective and less critical. We
must not, however, imagine that the thought processes of primitive

men are essentially different from our own. What apparent difference exists is primarily in the content of thought, not the process. The thinking city dweller of the Western world is exposed to so many different modes of behavior and value systems that he inevitably becomes more critical and skeptical in his judgments. His conclusions may not be more true, but the very complexity and diversity leads to conscious comparison, classification, and evaluation. Primitive man, whose range of cultural experience is more restricted, may be equally penetrating in his insights, but his cultural limitations may cause his conclusions to appear naïve. However, his thinking is not childish nor immature. What seems to be so largely subjective is only the reflection of the cultural context.

Our multiform cultural heritage tends to make us skeptical, and our "faith" is frequently with mental reservations. Accordingly, we are somewhat surprised when a new convert to Christianity accepts the stories of the Bible as a living reality, and not as some far-off historical event. The often mentioned "childlike faith" of indigenous peoples does not reflect distinct mental processes, but the freedom from sophisticated skepticism, which is an almost inevitable corollary of "civilized" living. The wholehearted, intellectually unencumbered participation of primitive peoples in religious experience often reaches a high degree of subjectivity. An old Tzeltal Indian in southern Mexico who had formerly been a sorcerer but who had become a Christian was asked to participate in a dramatization of the birth of Jesus. His responsibility was to carry a shiny paper star high on a stick from the back of the church to the platform, but he could scarcely endure the nervous strain of such participation, for he had entered so completely into the subjective reality of this action that for him it was not primarily an historical event, but a vital, living situation.

Not infrequently indigenous myths have prepared people for the acceptance of white men and in some instances even of the gospel. The fact that the Aztecs believed in the messianic return of their god Quetzalcoatl, who according to their legend had departed toward the east, was no doubt a contributing factor in their assuming at first that Cortez was their god who had returned to

rule over them. The Karens of Burma tell stories (with some variations) about the "Lost Book of Life." According to them, Ywa was
about to go on a long journey, so he called his sons to him and
gave them each a book of life. To Karen, his eldest, he gave a Golden
Book of Life, and to the others he gave other books, until finally
to the white man, the youngest brother, he gave a White Book of
Life. The white brother took his book and went away to the west,
never to be seen again. As long as Karen read and followed his book
of life, he was happy and prosperous, but gradually it was neglected,
and one day it fell through the cracks in the bamboo floor and was
eaten by the pigs and chickens below. Without this book, his life
became more and more wretched, haunted by fears, plagued with
sickness, and impoverished by crop failures. But, so the story went,
some day the white brother was to return on the wings of a great
white bird, floating on the water. He would have in his hands the
great white book. The first missionaries, who came in sailing vessels
and brought a book with white pages, were believed to fulfill this
story.

From Birth to Death

There are four major events in the lives of people which are
often associated with important religious beliefs or ceremonies. At
birth, puberty, marriage, and death the mysterious forces of supernatural power may be regarded as present and requiring attention.
Because of the heavy socio-economic aspects of marriage in indigenous societies, it tends to have less religious significance than
either birth or puberty, while death is generally accorded the greatest religious importance, for this is the transition to the spirit world.

More often than not there is no religious aspect attached to normal birth, but difficulties in labor may require magical incantations
or the painful, crude practices of the medicine man. Twins may be
killed, as among the Akhan of Burma, or welcomed with rejoicing
as among the Ganda of Uganda. Women may be left along the road
to give birth and then to catch up again with the band, as is true
of the Syrian Bedouins, or they may be surrounded, as among the
Aztecs, with helping relatives, who rejoice over the birth as much

as over the capture of an enemy by victorious soldiers. The Aztecs considered a woman in labor as equivalent to a soldier in battle and believed that in the event of death of the mother and child, they both went to the most attractive heaven. Similarly, the Germanic tribes thought that a woman who died in childbirth went to Valhalla; but the Batak of Sumatra believed that such a woman was not immortal, even though everyone else was.

The Hopi people regard the new mother as impure for twenty days, during which time she must not taste meat or salt. After this period she is ceremonially cleansed, and the child is carried by the paternal grandfather to the edge of the mesa, where in a simple but moving ceremony prayer is offered, corn flour is sprinkled, and the babe is presented to the rising sun.

Puberty marks a time of great transition, when the mysteries of sex frequently inspire belief in supernatural power. Tribes such as the Semang of Malaya, the Todas of India, and the Eskimos have no formal recognition of puberty and religious rites associated with it; but for most of Africa puberty rites are exceedingly important and the initiation schools figure as an integrating feature of tribal life. Initiation schools take many forms; some are only informal classes conducted in the village, others are camps out in the jungle. For some there are only brief ceremonies; for others there are months of grueling toil, physical hardships, and torturing tests. Initiation schools instruct the young in the traditions of the tribe (the legends, myths, proverbs, and customs), teach the skills of hunting, fishing, and warring, inculcate the beliefs about religion, sex, and responsibility to elders, and test the courage by ordeals, such as whipping with stinging nettles and lacerating with barbed fishbones. A very important part of many of these ceremonies is circumcision of the foreskin for boys and excision of the clitoris for girls. Circumcision is not always regarded as having religious significance, for example among the Samoan Islanders; and sometimes excision is done without the people being able to give any reason for it, as is true of the Shipibos of Peru. Among those tribes in Africa which practice clitorectomy (generally with crude instruments, causing excruciating pain and frequent infection) there are many and sometimes contradictory reasons given for the operation. It is said by some that the clitoris and surrounding flesh must be removed or the woman will be so highly passionate that she will inevitably become a prostitute. Others affirm that this operation is to make a woman more sexually responsive. Among the Ngbaka of northern Congo a woman who has not undergone this rite finds it difficult to obtain a husband; she is scorned and taunted by the women and regarded as sterile. If she should have a baby, tradition dictates that it must be killed before maturity, for in turn it would give birth to a dreadful monster which would bring calamity upon the people.

Marriage is regarded by us as being quite religious in character—in fact, some Christians regard it as a sacrament. But for most peoples marriage is a social contract. Though West Africans may call in a diviner to ascertain whether the intended wife is a good choice, religious sanctions are not very important. Perhaps it is not strange that the Aztecs, who made so much of birth, should also invest marriage with deep religious significance. A black-robed priest tied together the corners of the bride and groom's clothing, and before the marriage could be consummated the young couple fasted for four days, prayed, sacrificed, and drew blood from their ears and tongues as an offering to the deities. As a part of their wedding ritual, a Hopi couple present themselves to the rising sun and offer prayers and the traditional corn flour, symbol of life and blessing.

Sickness and death are attributed to a variety of causes by different peoples. The Aranda of Australia insisted that death was always the result of black magic. For them and for many other peoples there was no such thing as natural death, and hence the search for the guilty person was obligatory. The Semang of Malaya attribute death to both magic and the anger of evil spirits. The Crows had a rather more moralizing view of sickness and subsequent death, for they attributed such events to angry ghosts and to violation of taboos. The Hopis, however, regard death as a perfectly normal transition to rebirth in the lower world.[35]

The Tarahumaras of northern Mexico give the appearance of being quite calloused at death. They have no ceremonial mourning, bury the dead in shallow graves, and may not even announce the death until some later gathering of friends for a community fiesta. The present-day Aztec women in some regions engage in wild mourning, with shrieks of hysterical wailing, while they throw dust into the air and over themselves. The funeral may take place in a local Roman Catholic chapel and if the family has enough money a band may be hired. One such band in Morelos used to play "Yes We Have No Bananas" and "Happy Days Are Here Again," tunes learned from listening to phonograph records. The Igorots of Luzon in the Philippines seat the corpse in the open space beneath the stilt house and watch while it bloats and putrifies. The Thai may place the body in a coffin and keep it in the home for as long as one hundred days. The coffin is specially constructed with a vent to let off the odors and a spigot to drain off the liquids. At last the bones, which have been scraped of their flesh, are burned. Some Africans in northern Congo seize the widow and drag her about the village in a twisting path, shrieking and howling as they go—all for the purpose of confusing the ghost of the husband who may be trying to follow his wife to kill her.

Such practices may seem both crude and foolish, but they are not much more so than ours: huge tracts of hideous stones in the centers of some of our cities (where we ought to have playgrounds for children), fancy coffins (required even when the body is to be cremated), laws, which in some states require that an amputated leg or arm be formally buried, or the practice in some parts of the Western world of adding plaster-of-paris arms and legs to bodies which have previously lost a limb. We may laugh at the San Blas for taking food to the graves of the departed, but this seems no more strange to them than our practice of carrying flowers to cemeteries. We are appalled at the wealth buried with Egyptian monarchs, and at the number of slaves who were killed to accompany their ruler to the next world; but the cost of a beautiful coffin to people in our society, one's best suit of clothes, rings, a favorite tiepin, and flowers, plus perpetual care of a plot are proportionately as expensive and in ways almost as pagan, certainly for those whose much-avowed religious beliefs should contradict such practices.

For the most part primitive peoples believe that the next life will be more or less a replica of this one, but with some minor improvements. The Todas believe they will go on taking care of dairy cattle, but without rats to cause them trouble. The Plains Indians looked forward to a happy hunting ground, with plenty of game; typically enough, the rank-conscious Samoan Islanders believed in two abodes, one for the nobles on a lonely island in the west, and another for the commoners in a world below the sea. The Aztecs insisted on three principal abodes, and none of them had anything to do with one's behavior in this life. Mictlan was a shadowy, sad underworld for those who died from accidents, sickness, or old age. Tlalocan was the earthly paradise of the god of rain, who received those who drowned or were struck with lightning or died of dropsy or leprosy. For those who died in battle or childbirth there was a celestial abode of the sun.

Animists at Heart

At heart the Mohammedan of West Africa is an "animist" when he seeks to be cured of a malady by having the ninety-nine titles of Allah written on a piece of paper, after which he pours water over the pages and drinks the inky liquid. Similarly, the U. S. soldier who thinks that carrying a New Testament over his heart will protect him from enemy bullets is to this extent an animist. The Hindu who chews up his prayers and throws them at an idol, believing that they will be accepted or rejected on the basis of whether or not they stick to the idol, is likewise an "animist"—at least to this extent of his belief. When a Roman Catholic image becomes an idol to the people, they likewise become at least partially animists.[36]

As we shall see in the following section, the religions of traditionally literate peoples often contain many high moral concepts and possess elaborate philosophical systems, which must not be underrated. Nevertheless, for the vast majority of the people these philosophical concepts are relatively unimportant, except indirectly. The average Buddhist in a small town in Thailand is only vaguely aware of the importance of self-mastery by the denial of the ultimate reality of human existence. It is much more important for him to show respect for the spirit house which stands in the yard, to buy a little patch of gold leaf to decorate his favorite Buddha, or to discover his fortune by whirling a numbered wheel after appropriate ritual. Similarly there are Christians who affirm a belief in the sovereign will of God and yet who complain bitterly if they are not treated as deserving special material blessing, particularly if they have consistently given a tenth of their income to the church.

People may at one and the same time hold quite contrary beliefs. In general, it may be said that most Japanese are Buddhists. They may not be active members of some strict Buddhist sect, but they usually plan on being buried as Buddhists and for all practical purposes are in agreement with most of the Buddhist tenets. A high percentage of these same people would regard themselves also as Shintoists (at least adherents to national Shintoism), and they are likely to be married with Shinto ceremonies. Philosophically, Buddhism and Shintoism are not reconcilable—at least not in terms of our Western system of logical analysis—and the priests of Buddhism and Shintoism are quite competitive. Not only are the masses of people in a sense both Buddhists and Shintoists, but many of them also engage in purely animist practices, such as placing offerings in groves or along water courses in honor of the dead spirits which return in midsummer. These offerings, which include such objects as cucumbers (made into the form of horses with little sticks for legs), eggplant, rice, tomatoes, beansprouts, and onions, have their origins in practices which antedate both philosophical Buddhism or organized Shintoism.[37] It can be said of many Japanese that they are Buddhists, Shintoists, and animists, and most of the people do not see any essential contradictions.[38]

Inside the Roman Catholic church, the Indians of Chichicastenango in Guatemala may pay their respects to images of the saints; but on the steps of the church, where they wave pots of burning incense, they worship the rising sun. The Chol Indians of southern Mexico bury their dead within the sacred precincts of the church cemetery, but they insist on helping the soul go to heaven by shooting off rockets. Animism is far from dead, even among those who profess a higher religion. To some extent people in so-called advanced cultures are still exhibiting animistic attitudes when to avoid bad luck they refuse to walk under ladders or to sit down at a table of 13, and when they shudder at black cats, worry about breaking a mirror, and buy horoscopes by the millions.

The So-called World Religions

When did Japanese tribal animism become what we would recognize as the religion of Shintoism, with its nature myths, its cultivation of ancestors, and its belief in national destiny? How are we to decide that Taoism is to be classed with Buddhism and Hinduism as one of the great religions of the East, rather than simply as an elaborate form of animism, with paper gods, dragons, firecrackers and magic concoctions to make one live to a ripe old age? There are no fixed lines of demarcation, no definitive criteria, no qualitative distinctions. We do, however, generally class Shintoism, Taoism, Confucianism, Buddhism, Hinduism, Mohammedanism, Judaism, and Christianity [39] as world religions. Though it is difficult for us to define neatly the distinctions between these religions and those of so-called primitive peoples, nevertheless, we find it both convenient and important to recognize certain essential differences. The following features of the religions of traditionally literate peoples are significant, though in greater or less degrees, depending upon the religion in question:

1. A more or less systematic organization of beliefs.
2. The existence of some unifying principle (or hierarchy of principles) or deity (or hierarchy of deities).
3. A written formulation of beliefs and supernaturally sanctioned traditions.
4. The belief that existence has some meaning, even if, as in Hinduism and Buddhism, the goal is escape from personal existence.[40]

For the most part anthropologists have left the study of the so-called world religions to specialists in comparative religion. However, it is impossible wholly to neglect these elaborate religious systems, even though within the scope of this chapter we can only touch upon some of the more salient features and certain of the broader patterns. Since the essential features of Judaism and Christianity are familiar enough to the average reader in Western culture, we shall not treat them here.

Mohammedanism, in company with Judaism and Christianity (from which it borrowed so largely) and in contrast with other religions of the East, believes in a determinate immanent God (Allah to them), one who has a definite personality and who was operative in creation. For one who believes in Allah, it is quite impossible to conceive of the separation of church and state. As one Mohammedan in the Anglo-Egyptian Sudan explained it to me, "The fact that British officials try to be neutral when it comes to religion is nonsense. If a man is really a Christian how can he be neutral? If he tries to be neutral, it is either heresy or hypocrisy." In the doctrine of the infallibility of the Koran, it can be said that "the word became a book" in contrast with Christianity which declares that "the Word became flesh." [41] It is now heresy for a Mohammedan to say that Mohammed wrote the Koran; rather, one must believe that the Koran is a word-for-word copy of the pre-existent, eternal Koran which is in heaven. An infallible Koran and an immutable social structure have frozen the socio-religious culture and given it incalculable strength and defense against penetration.

Without a doubt Mohammedanism is more successful than Christianity in gaining converts in Africa. This is due to three principal reasons: (1) the prestige of a world religion which is relatively devoid of racial discrimination, (2) an easy cultural transition (in many areas a recent convert may continue to live exactly as he has, but must promise to educate his children as Mohammedans), and (3) the greater missionary zeal on the part of the average Moslem, who often demonstrates a genuine pity for the animist's fears and tries to convert him.

In Hinduism, Taoism, and Buddhism there is no personal, supreme, all-powerful deity, but rather, a formless, timeless reality: the Brahman of Hinduism, the Tao of Taoism, and to some extent the Nirvana of Buddhism. Hinduism and Buddhism teach a pantheistic identity of the human soul with the world soul or primeval oneness. The Tao of Taoism is likewise an impersonal force, and ultimate happiness and prosperity come from perfect adaptation of oneself to this cosmic power. In a sense Confucianism is somewhat more of a philosophy than a religion, because it does not insist upon the supernatural as a sanction for human behavior or life; but in its teaching of the ultimate validity of its canons of social ethics (in contrast with the personal ethics of Taoism) and loyalty to family (which on a practical level becomes ancestor cultivation), it is a kind of religion, even though a very earthy one.

A significant feature of Oriental religions is their cyclical interpretation of life. The constant succession of morning, noonday, evening, and night—the endless repetition of spring, summer, fall, and winter—the ever-present transition from birth through puberty and adulthood to old age and death—all this has given rise to the concept of the cycle of existence and the wheel of destiny, where all objects and states of being are transitory and where there is no such thing as actual progress, for soon the cycle will move on around and all will be the same again. If life is thus so fleeting and if material changes are unreal, escape lies only in exalting the spirit over the body, finding tranquillity in the midst of uproar and beauty in the midst of squalor. Hence the priest meditates at the edge of the noisy market place, and the temple has the appearance of a neglected stable.

Hinduism recognizes the four aims and phases of life: (1) *artha*, man as an acquisitive being, with all his material needs, (2) *kama*, man with his sensual natural needs, (3) *dharma*, man in the social pattern and duty of caste, and (4) *moksha*, the training of the life and soul, directed at deliverance and salvation.[42] This last aim of man is what Yoga tries to attain, but even with all the help of enforced conformance to religiously sanctioned social taboos, people recognize far more evil in their lives than good. Hence, rather than being optimistic about their chances of graduating into Brahman, they cannot conceive of deliverance in less than thousands of reincarnations. How discouraging is life for an outcaste when his drinking from a high-caste well would pollute it and incur horrible penalties for him, both here and hereafter, while if a dirty goat falls into the same well and drowns, that is of little import.

Buddhism was a kind of intellectual revolt against Hinduism. It promised emancipation from the plague of ignorance and outlined a way of moral self-conquest as the answer to the blight of human desire. The good news which Buddhism brought was escape for the ego-soul into the nothingness of Nirvana. But though Hinduism had assimilated all kinds of alien ideas and adapted them, it expelled Buddhism, not because of its philosophy, but because of its threat to the social structure. It is not the heresy of ideas, but of actions, which entrenched religious leaders fear.

Among intellectuals in the Orient all religions are coming under increasing attack for being basically irrational, traditional, instruments of exploitation (whether this is the Hindu sanction for the economic disabilities of caste or the Christian approval of some aspects of colonial imperialism), other-worldly, and negativistic—the very criticisms which many intellectuals of the West have leveled against Christianity. But despite such objections, which are propaganda fodder for Communism, one witnesses a tremendous rebirth of local cultures, with religious concepts playing an important role. Politicians in Thailand are vying with each other to make truly spectacular the closing years of the 2,500-year era of Buddhism in that ancient land. Communists claim that their philosophy will be the creed of the future era, while saffron-robed Buddhist priests rally young people in festivals, Sunday Schools, and discussion groups. With hymns such as "Onward Buddhist Soldiers" and "Silent Night, Holy Night" (depicting the birth of Buddha), they diligently instruct the people in social responsibility and new ways of earning merit.

Mixed Wine in Patched Wineskins

All religions resemble patched wineskins filled with mixed wine. Even the exclusiveness of Christianity has not kept it from such accretions as various forms of church government, rules about behavior of its members, regulations for its priesthood and ministry, and diverse forms of the sacraments. Most religions, however, have no special objection to additions. Many of the Dinkas in the Anglo-Egyptian Sudan would readily agree to add certain "Jesus-taboos" in order to procure the supernatural aid of such a respected person. The American Indians of the Middle West who took up the ceremonial eating of peyote, a button from the top of a small cactus growing in the Rio Grande Valley and northern Mexico, declared that the spectacular visions, like kaleidoscopic patterns of brilliant light, were from the Holy Spirit. On one occasion some Comanches protested when a missionary preached against peyote, and they solemnly warned him to cease his "blasphemy." Their convictions were supported by the fact that within a few minutes a whirlwind completely destroyed the tent in which the missionary was speaking. Peyote worship has employed symbols of the Thunder Bird as well as the Cross. The peyote narcotic is regarded as God's gift to man by which he may obtain the Holy Spirit. Such combining of cultural elements, in this case religious traits, is generally called syncretism and is to be found throughout the world.

The average devout Buddhist who climbs to the lofty gleaming pagoda overlooking the city of Chiengmai in northern Thailand, worships in a manner quite foreign to the teaching of Buddha.[43] In one of the most sacred shrines sits a glittering statute of Buddha, looking out upon the courtyard with a blank, meditative stare. Those who wish healing from dysentery or malaria come especially to this Buddha. In order to know whether their prayers will be heard and they will recover, it is necessary before worshiping to measure the distance from fingertip to fingertip on a stick handily placed near the shrine and to put a small piece of wax on the stick so as to mark the distance. The worshiper then pours over the head of the Buddha the water which he has carried up the several hundred dragon-lined steps. The water flows over the statue, then down through a pipe, represented as the hair of a female deity seated below the Buddha. Finally, the water drains out beside a Taoist Chinese lion, which is smeared with gold leaf, especially on its bulging eyes. After prayers, supplications, and the offering of flowers, a rickety prayer wheel is spun, a coin is dropped into the nearby case, and one's fortune is taken from a numbered box. If it is number seven, it reads as follows:

This card number seven will bring you luck. It has to do with happiness. Your entire household and all your friends should receive this with joy. But you are suffering from the results of your accumulated deeds, which is unfortunate. Therefore, make merit for yourself by giving alms to help your soul. This will be satisfying to your mind and heart. Do not embrace the world too much. If you do, you will suffer. Listen to what the people of old have taught.

The tract ends with admonitions to plant fruit trees near the house and to seek a lovable spouse.

After the ritual is completed, the worshiper again stretches out his arms along the same stick, and if the wax appears to have moved down the stick, that is to say, if he cannot reach it, the prayer will be answered—all of which adds up to a neat psychological trick.[44]

When Christian teachings have filtered through utterly different sets of beliefs, they may seem quite strange and unrecognizable. This is true of the stories about St. Thomas, who is the cultural hero of the Tzeltal Indians living near Oxchuc in southern Mexico. He is credited with bringing the people corn and having gone through the land, touching the ground with his staff so that springs would burst forth. He is believed to be the one who prevents a hateful god from destroying people and putting their counterparts here on the earth, and who is supposed to keep the antichrist chained to one of the four pillars which support the flat world. Jesus only enters the story as one who sent a flood because the Jews had tied him up.

The persistence of old beliefs takes on an almost comical aspect at times. In the state of Coahuila, Mexico, in June, 1949, the local authorities hired a U. S. firm to produce rain by using dry ice or silver iodide to precipitate moisture. One such experiment was so successful that it rained for ten hours. One woman, who thought it would never cease, carried a crucifix around the town in order to stop the downpour, but she was forthwith imprisoned for sabotage.[45]

Syncretism is not absent from Protestant missionary work. Consistently higher collections on communion Sunday, even though the crowds may be just the same, may indicate that people are "paying" for spiritual benefits, thinking that without payment the sacrament loses some of its value. One of the most subtle difficulties involves the tendency to lay great emphasis upon baptism, church membership, and communion by making them the result of a period of trial and proof of worthiness. Too often the new convert interprets his attaining church membership as being more or less equivalent to initiation into some secret society. Church membership then becomes the goal and reward for good behavior, not the beginning of a new fellowship with other believers. Being put out of the church for some major sin just confirms the man's belief that membership is what counts. Too often the missionary, who sets out to be a prophet of God's Good News, ends up by being a judge of deportment.[46]

Social Structure Influences Religion

The direct and indirect effects of religion upon society are constantly indicated, but what about the effect of society upon religion? It is quite understandable that the Plains Indians, who emphasized so much the attainments of individuals, should also lay great stress on individual religious experience. A Crow, who would risk his life to gain a military honor, would not hesitate to chop off a finger in order to obtain a vision. Religion and social structures have reinforced each other in the caste system of India, the family life of China, the struggle for national destiny in Japan, and the position of women in Islam.

Some religions are distinctly puritanical, i.e. they not only advocate certain customs but force their acceptance upon those who may not be entirely in accord. Protestantism has treated certain aspects of sex in this way, while Islam has taken such an attitude toward the eating of pork and the representation of living creatures in art. There may be a wide gap between real and ideal behavior, for though a Mohammedan is not allowed to drink wine or gamble, both practices are widespread in the Islamic world.

It is sometimes assumed that women are always more religious than men. This depends largely upon the culture. Among the San Blas the men are in many respects the conservative element, despite the fact that they have much more contact with the outside world.

They dominate the social and religious life, and the men's lodge constitutes the bulwark of tradition. However, the San Blas situation is the exception, for men generally have many more contacts with the outside world than do women, and it is only to be expected that in traditional matters—of which religion surely is one of the most important and most deeply entrenched—women would reflect their more limited associations, and hence be more adverse to change.

A severe social maladjustment and a real threat to an indigenous society may provoke a "nativistic revival" or "messianic movement." In the United States during the period of 1870–90 a number of Ghost Dance movements broke out. Similar movements with promises of utter destruction of the whites, supernatural help from the dead, and mysterious protection from the white man's bullets have incited uprisings and revolt in West Africa and more recently in New Guinea. These extreme religious manifestations are grim evidences of a dying culture—the last agonies of a disintegrating society, which makes one final attempt to rally the past to solve the problems of the future.

Christian Missions and Non-Christian Religious Beliefs

Throughout this chapter we have touched upon significant problems for Christian missions, and still others will be considered in the last chapter. However, we should perhaps note at this point some situations in which the religious culture of a people is strikingly important for the approach of Christian missions.

What is one to do when more than 10,000 people claim to accept Christianity within the space of just a few months and with scarcely any instruction, as was the case in one tribe in southeast Asia? A former medicine man heard enough of the gospel to tell the people that they should not smoke opium or drink beer, and that they should be good. He proceeded to baptize whole villages of people, and the missionaries co-operated by sending Gospels of Matthew, Mark, and Luke to the people. These were highly prized and put in bamboo containers and the people celebrated their new faith with huge feasts. Not long after this, the same medicine man married a second wife and left the movement, taking a large percentage of the people with him. All that remains of the movement is a fear of having one's name erased from "the book," in which case the person will go to hell, but if apologies are made three times (in some places seven times) before the assembled villagers, the name is written again and he will not go to hell.

Such mass movements leave many missionaries skeptical as to whether there can be a really genuine mass movement. When a man in West Africa told the missionary he would return the next week with his family, he did and brought forty-seven persons with him (five wives and forty-two children), all of whom insisted that they believed. In some of the mass movements in India entire villages have seemed to respond as a single person. We who lay so much stress upon individual action and decisions find it hard to conceive of people acting as a unit; yet in societies with a highly integrated social structure, people do act together in a remarkable manner. The missionary must not underestimate the importance of such socially conditioned decisions nor fail to appreciate the individual's part. There are both dangers and advantages to mass movements. However, they should not be judged in terms of our responses, but on the basis of the culture involved.

Insistence upon the separation of church and state is fully defensible, for no church should employ the state as a means of enforcing conformity. However, the separation of church and state does not mean that religion should be excluded from community life, nor that the religious convictions and resultant behavior will not and should not have their influence upon the total structure of society. Some of the major contrasts between the Catholic and non-Catholic countries of Europe and America stem from the differences of religious belief. Patterns of behavior which become recognized mores sanctioned by religious conviction and reflected in formal legislation are quite different from regimented conformity based upon "absolutes," as claimed by any one church or religious group.

Some missionaries insist on a total repudiation of any and all "pagan" practices. So complete is this dissociation that some doctors have refused to treat infections arising from rites such as excision. To save a life under such circumstances is considered by them as condoning the practice. But other missionaries have seen that the death of a few more persons is not going to stamp out a practice which has taken its toll of life for many generations. Such practices cease only when people find something which they regard as better to put in their place.

Legislating or ranting against socially harmful practices is not likely to have much effect. Preaching itself is relatively useless unless it offers something distinctly better. For as long as anyone can remember, the Aymara Indians on the shores of Lake Titicaca have had annual festivals at which groups of young men from different villages challenged each other to fight with sticks, stones, and fists for control of a selected hill. This was "King of the Mountain" with a vengeance, for usually one or more young men were killed or maimed for life. The young men of Guatajata who had become Christians as a result of the work of the Canadian Baptist Mission in that region decided that this fighting to show brute superiority was not right, but changing such an old custom was not easy and certainly was not to be accomplished by denouncing the other villages for engaging in such fights. Accordingly, the young Christian men from Guatajata proposed that a soccer tournament be held as a substitute for fighting on the hilltop. So enthusiastic was the response that the soccer tournament is now one of the biggest events of the year, played at the festival of the Bolivian national holiday. A functional substitute is the real answer to problems of promoting desired cultural change.

Should the missionary have anything to do with the local medicine man? What if he has some very good remedies? Missionaries among the San Blas Indians have made friends of the local medicine men, and as a result these men have co-operated with visiting physicians by bringing in samples of the urine of pregnant women who are their patients. Some of these medicine men are employing increasingly better techniques of treatment. The fact that the medicine man's bedside manner is a little weird and spooky is no sign that he is incapable of learning to do a better job. A friendly and understanding approach often succeeds where denunciations only drive practices underground.[47]

The first reaction of any missionary faced with a belief in black magic or ghosts is to deny their existence. I was discussing such spirit phenomena with some brilliant young students from West Africa who were studying at the University of London. I expressed my doubts about such matters as they were describing, to which one of the men replied, "How can you tell me spirits don't exist when I have seen them with my own eyes!" What is a missionary going to do when his most valuable helper announces to him that he has dreamed that he will die and when all past experience confirms the people's belief that anyone who dreams in this manner is certain to pass away within fourteen days? When Ephraim Alphonse was working among the Valiente Indians of Panama, his assistant made just such a dire announcement. Mr. Alphonse realized immediately that to deny that the man would die was quite futile, for in past years he had known of several vigorous men who had claimed to have such a dream. In the panic of their morbid belief, they had refused all nourishment and died, literally scared to death, within two weeks. Sensing the psychological situation, Mr. Alphonse said to his young helper, "But you must not die in two weeks, for you owe me some money. You will have to work off that debt, and it will take you at least three weeks." Having convinced the man that he would have to work to pay off the debt, Mr. Alphonse told two of his own sons to go out and work with this young man and not to leave him for a moment. He insisted that the man must eat well so that he would be able to work off the debt before he died. When the two weeks had passed, during which time not a word of skepticism was expressed about the meaning or ultimate consequences of the dream, Mr. Alphonse and all his family joined in laughing at the belief that this young man was doomed to die. The young man himself, realizing that the dream had not come true within the fated fourteen days, was convinced of its fallacy. Then Mr. Alphonse explained carefully to the young man exactly what he had done and why the dream brought death to others but not to him. This was the key to freeing many others from their morbid fear of fateful dreams.

The answer to religious problems is not always the same, but real solutions result from presenting the truth within an understandable framework of the other man's experience.

DRUMS AND DRAMA

No one can fully appreciate the Congo until he has wakened in the dead of night to hear a melancholy melody skillfully played by the night watchman on a crude little instrument made of steel umbrella ribs and a squarish wooden resonator. The lofty Andes remain just huge monuments of stone until a lone shepherd's flute makes the whole countryside come to life. The piping notes soften and float away as they echo faintly from cliff to cliff, only to be answered by another shepherd high up on the snowy ridge. The peal of West African drums dexterously beaten in weird rhythmic fugues of contrasting and blending beat cannot be duplicated in the Western world.

Thailand is not Thailand without the riotous colors and exquisite beauty of its dazzling pagodas. The fierce snarling of its stone lions and griffins and the expressionless placidity of its Buddhas are almost forgotten in the blaze of golden pillars and polychrome friezes. Contrast this with the exquisite loveliness of three small flowers and two wisps of fern arranged with typical Japanese artistic taste. The low ceramic dish which holds the flowers is scarcely noticed, for its restrained elegance and delicate coloring are in perfect harmony with the silky sheen of the wall painting, in which the wispy mountains seem not to touch the earth below. The Balinese express their esthetic sense in the inimitable gracefulness of dancing girls and the exquisite idealism of their wood carving, unsurpassed anywhere in the world.

Modern man is not the only one who has sought to beautify the objects around him or to give expression to his esthetic sense. The polychrome painting and carvings in stone and bone of prehistoric animals in Western Europe give abundant evidence to the skill and the artistic sense of people who lived when bison, mammoths, and rhinoceri roamed in France and Spain. The many-colored, intricately designed pottery of the pre-Inca and Inca cultures of Peru reveals unbelievable skill in modeling the human face and in the elaboration of ceramic forms. The tapestries of these same cultures are comparable, if not superior, to the best that Europe has produced.[1]

All Men Are Artists

The expression of an esthetic sense is one of the universals of human behavior, but whether it takes the form of rock paintings, as it does among the Bushmen, or realistic imitative dances, as among the nearby Hottentots, is not predictable. Some people, such as the Marshallese, may be very fond of flowers; others, such as the Ifugao, have little appreciation for them.[2] But in one way or another, all people express an esthetic sense, which may, however, be so foreign to our modes of behavior and way of thinking about beauty that we fail to appreciate it. Western women decorate themselves with elaborately designed cloth, conspicuous pieces of jewelry, and eye-catching, frilly hats, if they happen to be in style at the time. The Dinkas of the Anglo-Egyptian Sudan insist on daubing their heads with clumps of red and white clay, circled with bright-colored beads, which blend with rich ornately beaded collars, and ivory bracelets, spaced with coils of brass and copper, while the face and chest are painted in fantastic geometric figures with white chalk and red ochre.

We are so familiar with the supposed distinction between fine arts and applied arts that we sometimes forget that our Western culture has introduced a distinction which is quite unknown in most of the rest of the world, certainly so in the nonliterate world. Even in our own society the artificial distinction is losing its hold upon people's thinking and we recognize more than formerly that beauty of design can be found in the lines of an automobile just as well as on a canvas. We have thought of artists only in the sense of those who make a living at it, or who daub canvases and load down their friends' walls with amateurish efforts. Our culture has produced artistic specialists, just as it has produced specialists in all kinds of occupations; but the esthetic sense is not solely the possession of professional artists, though they may have a higher natural aptitude (this should be true, though sometimes it is debatable) and have increased their skills through careful study and practice. Nevertheless, the harmonious arrangement of furniture, the wearing of blending colors, the making of a beautiful chair, the decorating of a birthday cake, and the planning of an attractive flower garden are all responses to our esthetic desires. The particular manner in which one expresses these esthetic tastes is determined largely by the culture, which has already established the major patterns for esthetic expression. However, individuals may make some changes and adaptations, depending upon their originality and skill.

Culture Dictates the Style

Woodcarvers from Ponape, Bali, and Congo may be equally skillful and equally artistic, but they do not carve the human head in the same way. The Ponapean carver is used to straight lines, angular faces, and long noses, with highly stylized ornamentation. His results are massive and strong, if not a little haunting. The Balinese artist carves with unusual attention to exquisite detail, but he overlooks defects as he carves the Balinese "ideal." There is something ethereal about his work by virtue of its idealism. The Congolese carves with sweeping lines, elongated features, and seemingly strange distortions; and yet he captures a mood and tells more than may appear to the casual observer. We must not think that these Ponapean, Balinese, and Congolese artists employ their respective styles simply because they have inherited certain biological capacities which make them incapable of doing anything else. They carve as they do because that is the style of carving in their respective cultures. Each artist expresses something of his own personality in what he does, but the major form of artistic expression is dictated by the culture.

Do not styles change? Of course they do, but within certain culturally prescribed limitations. Styles of women's dresses change with amazingly rhythmic succession.[3] The length of skirts increases and diminishes; dresses switch from full skirts to narrow; and the carrot-shape, the hour-glass, and the elongated pyramid designs come and go, but still American women do not dress in Indian saris, Japanese kimonos, or Shilluk half-sheets and aprons.

Within the style dictated by the culture each artist is free to make important personal contributions, which may eventually add up to radical changes; but such changes do not come overnight, any more than the cracker-box Ford sedan of the early 1920's became the streamlined fishtail car of the early 1950's by one huge leap in design. Navajo rug weavers have considerable freedom of design, so much so that seldom will any woman ever weave exactly the same design twice, and many women can recognize the blankets of neighbors and friends by the style of weaving and the type of design. However, rugs adhere strictly to geometric patterns, while Navajo jewelry made by the men exhibits not only many geometric patterns but several realistic motifs, especially the squash flower. Are Navajo women incapable of weaving squash-flower designs? Of course not. It is just that blankets are thought to require one style of design and silver jewelry may follow another.

Primitivism Is Not Childish Art

Ignorance, compounded with bigoted ethnocentrism, has led many people to regard the art of "primitive" peoples as being nothing more nor less than childish scribbling or daubing. Several reasons have contributed to this impression, but certainly one basis for error is our enslavement to Greek concepts of art which glorified the human form and sought to portray it with minute idealistic exactness. This is a very laudable esthetic goal, but it is not all of art. The Mayans could also carve the human form, as they demonstrated so well with some of their highly expressive human faces done in huge blocks of hard stone. However, they did not decorate their temples with motifs of ivy, dancing nymphs, or parading gods. For the most part they choose to reproduce textile designs in sculptured and fitted stone, which cast varying lengths of shadows throughout the day, producing an ever-changing but always harmonious blend of design.

Sometimes our judgments of "primitive" art are based on incorrect viewing of an object. The stone faces carved by the Yipounou people of the Gabon appear at first to be grotesquely out of shape. A huge topknot of hair dominates a bulging forehead. The nose is disproportionately long, the lips and mouth are strangely small. However, in order to view this stone carving "correctly" it must be laid flat on a table and viewed on a level with the surface of the table.[4] From this perspective the various features display a startling realism. It is just as wrong to view this Yipounou stone carving from the incorrect angle as it is to complain about the daubiness of some modern oil landscapes when seen at a distance of twelve inches rather than twelve feet.

African art in particular has had a very profound effect upon contemporary Western art. Not only are examples of African sculpture and painting reproduced with little or no change for European and American markets, but the basic motifs and art forms have influenced many European and American artists. Perhaps the most outstanding example of this is to be found in the work of Picasso and his followers.

Aboriginal people have been described as being only artistic children because when given pencil and paper, they have produced drawings which are little better than what children do in our society. A San Blas woman cannot draw with a pencil, but she can sew unusually elaborate and intricate geometric designs depicting monkeys, men, lizards, and fish—all with a riot of color and unusual taste for harmonious arrangements. No Western artist could in any way match this skilled needlework. Artistry is not simply a capacity for design but a skill in using certain materials. Eskimos are failures with pen-and-ink drawings, but they can cut designs in ivory with a simplicity and realism which has made their work world famous.

One popular misconception about geometric or conventional designs is that they are much easier to make than realistic drawings. As a result they are thought by some to represent a lower form of art. Nothing could be further from the truth. Esthetically satisfying designs employing only curves and straight lines are just as difficult to make as are equally acceptable realistic drawings. Conventional designs often develop out of realistic ones, and vice versa.[5]

There is a tendency toward esthetic elaboration to the point of losing any utilitarian value. Women's hats illustrate this point in our culture. For the most part they no longer shade the eyes or protect the head. They seem to be as exotic as human imagination can conceive them, and still make them fit the human head; but no one should regard them as filling any useful function other than attracting attention and supporting the millinery industry. Toward the end of the days of chivalry sword handles became more and more ornamented, to the point where one could no longer grasp such a sword to use it in fighting. The Shipibos are a very down-to-earth people with plenty of needs for practical, useful pottery. But they spend a lot of time and energy making exceedingly thin, perfectly round glazed bowls, decorated with black and red designs, so simple that they seem easy to reproduce until one attempts to do so. These delicate pieces of pottery are not strictly necessary objects in the Shipibo household, but they reflect a desire to express an esthetic sense, which overrides the dictates of mere usefulness.

Artists with Words

Artists may work with pencil and paper, paint and canvas, thread and looms, chisels and stone, or clay and a potter's wheel, but there are others who work with words. They may be poets who sing the epics of their people or chiefs who chant the wisdom of the tribe. Their minds may be the storehouse of ancient proverbs and riddles, or they may contain the intricate religious ritual, memorized from the lips of old men who long before learned it from a previous generation. Their purpose may be to teach the young to entertain guests around the evening campfire, or to win the applause of people by virtue of the sheer beauty of their poem or song, but whatever the source or whatever the purpose of this skill, the artist of words is to be found in every society.

Legends, myths, and fables are the most common forms of word artistry. Many stories go in cycles, such as the Uncle Remus and

Br'er Rabbit yarns of West Africa, the exploits of Reynard the Fox in Western Europe, or the tales of Old Man Coyote among the Plains Indians. Some stories have literally circled the world. One of the most famous of these is the "Magic Flight," a story which has many forms but whose essential structure calls for a maiden (whether alone or with an escort) fleeing from an enraged father or a cruel uncle (or some other dire enemy). The pursuing fiend comes closer and closer; and when all seems lost, the girl throws down a mirror (or a brooch), and this becomes a lake. Soon, however, the enemy in hot pursuit catches up, and the end is near—when the girl hurls her comb behind her, and instantly a forest (or a cactus patch) separates her from her pursuer. She may have to throw down a number of such articles (usually, however, only three) which become obstacles to her enemy, but at last she arrives in safety. This story has been found in Europe, Asia, Africa, and North and South America. The corresponding details are entirely too numerous to think of its being invented independently in many different places, especially when the variations themselves show marked and characteristic gradations from one place to another.

When it comes to stories, it seems that there is nothing new under the sun. The warning "If you have heard this before, stop me" has been applicable for a long, long time. When visiting among the Tarahumara Indians of northern Mexico I heard what seemed to be an original story. A Tarahumara, who habitually wears only a scant shirt and a kind of loincloth resembling baggy shorts, was reported as having been asked by a Mexican, "Why aren't you cold? Why, there is snow on the ground and here you are without clothing to protect your body!" The Tarahumara is supposed to have said, "But you have nothing to cover your face. Is your face not cold?" To which the Mexican replied, "But that is my face." Finally the Tarahumara declared, "But I am face all over." When I told my father that story, he smiled and said, "Well, son, I heard that about Indians in Oklahoma when I was a small boy." This was quite a letdown, but imagine my surprise to find this very same story told by the Roman Claudius Aelianus, who in the second century A.D. wrote this anecdote about the Scythians who lived north of the Danube.

In the same way that artistic designs are modified by new groups who borrow and adapt them (compare the Japanese adaptations of Chinese motifs), so stories become adapted to the local culture. Among the Valiente Indians the story of the "Fountain of Youth" develops some interesting local touches and moralizing features:

An old medicine man, enfeebled by long illness, wrinkled by time and famine, and suffering the loss of memory in his dotage, dreamed one night of finding the Fountain of Youth and Wisdom. He set out the next morning, walking through the deadly silence of the jungle, and at last he heard a voice saying, "Why do you seek the Fountain of Youth and Wisdom?" To which he replied, "If you know what I am seeking, you also know the way." Whereupon the voice like a wisp of a cloud led him to a clear pool, from which he filled his gourd and drank. Almost instantly his feeble limbs became strong, his wrinkles disappeared, and his memory returned—he was young again. The voice instructed him to take a gourd of water with him and to share it with all he met. Elated with his new powers, he noted well the location of the pool and raced back to his village, heedless of all others and only intent on demonstrating his new physical and mental prowess. His reputation spread far and wide, and men made long journeys to be healed by him and to hear his wisdom. Soon he noticed old age creeping upon him again, but a few sips of the carefully concealed water revived his youthful powers.

At last the water was gone and his threatening weakness drove him out into the jungle again to seek the fountain. Finally he found it, and he eagerly reached down to dip up its sparkling water. But suddenly his gourd was filled with mud and slime, and the voice said to him, "Because you did not share this water with others, you cannot have it for yourself."

The stories people tell and the proverbs they recite reveal cultural attitudes. We talk about "locking the door after the horse has been stolen," but a West African equivalent, "They built the bridge after the prince fell in the water," reveals a subtle touch of class distinction. We use such contradictory proverbs as "A rolling stone gathers no moss" and "A setting hen never gets fat." Similarly, some West Africans declare, "No one should tie a new horse to an old picketing peg," but they also affirm, "He who ties to a new picketing peg is a fool." [6] A dominant theme of West African philosophy is revealed by "A dry leaf does not laugh when his neighbor falls." Not infrequently a proverb is quite unintelligible apart from a knowledge of its local context. When an African says, "One who hunts elephants never sleeps cold," he means that one who undertakes large enterprises will always find additional and supplementary rewards, just as a man who hunts elephants has no difficulty finding sticks and logs broken by the elephants into convenient sizes for firewood.

Nonliterate peoples have not been without their poets and bards, some of whom, like Homer, developed immortal epics. The following translation of a pre-Columbian Peruvian Quechua poem indicates something of the profound religious and esthetic sentiment characteristic of these Andean people: [7]

Viracocha, Creator of Man

The world awakes
And is filled with light
To worship thee,
O Creator of man.

The lofty sky
Sweeps away her clouds
In homage to thee,
The Maker of the world.

The king of the stars,
Our father, the sun,
Submits to thee
His power and might.

The wind lifts up
The tops of the trees
And waves each branch
In tribute to thee.

From the shadowy woods
The birds sing out
To render praise
To the Ruler of all.

The flowers show forth
In brilliant array
Their vivid colors
And pungent perfumes.

In the depths of the lake,
In the watery world,
The fish proclaim
Their joy of thee.

The dashing stream
In bursting song
Exalts in thee,
O Creator of man.

The cliffs are dressed
In glowing green,
And the canyon walls
With flowers gleam.

The serpents come
From their forest abode
To thee they pay
Obedience due.

The wary vicuña
And mountain hare
Come down from the heights
And are tame before thee.

At the dawn of the day
My heart sings praise
To thee, my Father
And Creator of man.

When the Polynesians describe in great detail the elaborate hierarchy of their mythological heroes, they are also describing their own highly class-conscious society. When the pioneers of the western United States told tall tales about Paul Bunyan, they were express-

ing the same unlimited optimism and abundant energy which
characterized the men who pushed out into these rich unexploited
regions. Stories may reflect either an actual practice in a society or a
psychological revolt against traditional mores. For example, one must
not think that the sexual vulgarities of Old Man Coyote reflect exactly that way the Plains Indians lived. Psychologists have found
that very frequently people express their inner resentment against
binding moral codes by constructing heroes who defy all such
restrictions with impunity.

Rhythm and Melody

Some missionaries have said to their home constituencies, "But
when the natives are converted, they change from minor to major
music," citing this as evidence of some profound psychological transformation in the people. The truth of the matter is that most
peoples in the world simply do not have our musical scale, and
accordingly their music often sounds like a lugubrious chant in a
minor key. Before we can fully appreciate the music of other societies we must bear in mind several significant facts about the music
of so-called primitive peoples:

1. The notes of the music do not necessarily have fixed pitches.
   Very frequently, of course, the intervals between notes are
   relatively fixed, but in some musical systems the interval between notes may spread or contract depending upon the emotional attitude of the singer or instrumentalist. It is the relative contrast, and not the fixed positions, which counts.

2. In contrast with the rhythm, melody may be a much less
   significant feature of the music. The melody, sung or played
   on a relatively weak instrument, seems to bobble along on the
   waves of the rhythm.

3. Harmony of rhythm may correspond to our harmony of tones.
   One missionary thought she would be very popular in Africa
   with her accordion, which she played with a good deal of
   skill. However, the people much preferred her poorer violin
   playing, because they could appreciate single melodies but
   not the "jumble" of different notes. The missionary was

equally at a loss to appreciate the polyrhythmic drum music, which seemed to her like staggering clashes of chaotic banging.

People who specialize in rhythm will find no difficulty in reproducing the rhythm of Western music, but they may hopelessly "murder" the tune. The workmen in the mission station at Karawa, Congo, sing each morning in chapel before going to their respective tasks. The exact reproduction of the rhythm of such hymns as "Onward Christian Soldiers" and "Lead On, O King Eternal" makes it possible to identify what the men are singing, but the tunes bear only a rather accidental resemblance to those with which we are familiar. The tunes and harmony have been completely recast in the people's own scale, which has its own powerful beauty and is equally valid as ours. It is just different.

Some missionaries have felt constrained to make Western music compulsory in the church. This is a pity, for the people often find it hard to sing such hymns, which remain forever a more or less artificial feature of the church service. More often than not, the missionary sings out the first line of a hymn and the people try hard to follow, but by the second line the swelling volume of the congregation tends to drown out the missionary's voice, and by the third line even the missionary has begun to accommodate himself to the people's musical scale. On the other hand, the rich resources of the musical heritage of the Western church should not be kept from other peoples. Polynesians have shown remarkable capacity for appreciation and mastery of Western vocal music. Some of the choirs of Fiji are deservedly world famous. Though the voice quality of Marshallese church singing leaves much to be desired—especially the squeaky voices of the women—nevertheless, the congregation sings complicated four-part music far beyond the skill of the average small-town church choir in America. One must not underestimate the musical potential of primitive peoples or fail to appreciate their distinctive contributions. One Easter morning in Tanganyika, as bright streamers of crimson streaked across the sky and splashed with brilliant color a natural rock amphitheatre nestled in a hill overlooking the town of Singida, I listened and wept as the African Lutheran congregation sang with incredible sublimity some of the heart-moving German chorales.

Dance and Drama

Dancing involves the rhythmic movement of the body—in the subtle gestures of the hands and arms (an essential part of Balinese dancing) or in the frenzied hysteria of West African fertility cults. Dances may be highly formalized, as they are among the Zuni of New Mexico. The twisting and turning may seem like dull repetitious shuffling, as among the Tarahumaras of northern Mexico, or the dance may take on an individual character, as in the sword dance of French Guinea, where the individual is free to develop all manner of special features, such as appearing to thrust the sword into his eyeball and to gouge out the eye amidst hideous shrieks and facial contortions. Ecstatic dancing was a part of ancient Jewish worship, as evidenced in David's dancing before the Lord (2 Samuel 6:16–22).

In many societies the dance is an integral part of drama, the most emotionally stirring of all esthetic forms, since it often combines design of masks and costumes, legends and songs, music and motion, and provides for the participation of the people, either directly in the representations or as eager spectators. The Snake dance of the Hopis is more than just a dance. It is drama since it consists in acting out a supernatural relationship. The Easter festivals in many villages of Mexico are dramas. There are the "Jews," the "Centurions," the conquering Spanish, the Indians in ancient plumes and masks, Death (often dressed in long white underwear with bones painted in black), and Judas. The dances and processions, the mock battles and buffoonery—all are part of the drama. The mass of the Roman Catholic church is likewise a type of drama—in fact, a very powerful one because of the beauty of the pageantry, the mystery of the Latin language, the claimed miracle of the host, and the participation of the communicant.[8]

One of the most moving and appealing features of the Pentecostal movement in Chile is the unconscious use of drama.[9] In the large Evangelical Pentecostal Church of Santiago as many as 1,500 people

gather each Sunday night to hear a simple message and to participate in a moving drama, which may not seem to be a drama unless
one studies carefully what is happening. The pastor begins his
message by talking about a Biblical hero. He describes a person such
as Zacchaeus, who earnestly desired to see Jesus but felt that he
could not because of his physical disability. Nevertheless, he made
every effort to see the Master. Then the pastors turns to the en-
raptured audience and says, "Who of you want to see Jesus this
night! You who have been prevented because of the trials and
tribulation of life, you who wish to see the Master, come forward
and pray." Immediately hundreds of people flock to the altar and
others kneel in the pews, but all raise their voices crying to God for
a chance to see the Saviour. After a few minutes the pastor rises
to his feet, the people go back to their seats, and the next episode
of the drama is unveiled. At this point Zacchaeus is pictured as
eagerly awaiting the Master from his vantage point in the sycamore
tree. At the crucial moment, Jesus looks at Zacchaeus. He has not
only seen the Lord, but the Lord has recognized Zacchaeus and has
filled his heart with unspeakable joy. Again the pastor asks the
people, "Have you found the joy of seeing the Saviour and being
seen by him?" A burst of joyful shouting goes up from the congregation, and people fall to their knees again, this time with shouts of
joy and a note of victory. Again the pastor continues with the story
of Jesus in Zacchaeus' house, the confession of discipleship and the
promise to make retribution for sin. This time the pastor pleads
with the congregation and says, "Are you willing to be disciples
of the Master and make retribution? Will you pay the price of
victory that Zacchaeus had to pay?" Again hundreds move to the
front and all kneel. Some are overcome with grief, others are trans-
fixed with joy, hundreds plead with earnestness and unquestionable
sincerity.

These people, who come from the poorer classes of the sprawling
city, whose lives are so often crushed by monotonous grueling
labor, and whose material circumstances scarcely provide the necessities of life, much less a chance for social recognition, have all participated in the same experience of victory that Zacchaeus had. They

have identified themselves with one who did find release from oppression, and by this dramatic identification, they themselves experience the soul-warming and life-sustaining emotion of triumph. The only staging of this drama is the moving description of the pastor, but the congregation acts out the emotional content, which after all is the heart of drama.[10]

Christian Missions and Esthetic Culture

Perhaps in the matter of esthetic culture more than in any other area of life, Christian missions have, usually unintentionally, stifled indigenous practices. For the most part missionaries have assumed that those habits of worship which are approved in their own home churches have universal validity. Even the order of service becomes for many a matter of doctrine. All this is quite unfortunate, for too often the indigenous esthetic resources have been denounced. The ethnocentric principle of transplanting churches has overruled the Biblical principle of sowing the seed.

There is a certain measure of truth in the affirmation made by some missionaries that without some controls "the natives would run wild." However, our own church services are a far cry from the services of the early Christian church. It is interesting to note that all revival movements—Methodist, Quaker, and Pentecostal— have been accused of "running to excess." There seems also the possibility of being so "respectable" as to be lifeless.

In many parts of Africa it is a common practice for one person to tell a story in song, leading out with a line which is repeated by the chorus. This is an excellent way to review a Sunday School lesson, but some missions have hesitated to use such a method because it has seemed "too pagan." The fact is that the Africans do this very thing constantly with both religious and secular themes, not infrequently using this method for good-natured grumbling about their tasks and poking fun at the missionary's queer ways.

A missionary executive arrived in West Africa and was told by the local church authorities that they had prepared a three-hour dance in his honor. What should he do? Should he disapprove by denouncing the long prepared dance drama and by refusing to attend, or should he go? He went. And there before his eyes the people enacted with consummate skill the coming of the white man, his difficulties with the language, his trials and tribulations with travel—especially in old motor cars—and lastly the message of the gospel and the transformation of the lives of the people. All this was enacted before an audience of thousands of people, who, in a more effective way than any preacher could use, learned exactly what it meant to be a Christian.

John V. Taylor [11] points out that African drama is better when enacted outdoors in natural surroundings with the people supplying the "script" spontaneously. The greatest appeal of African drama is its religious and spiritual theme, which holds the audience spellbound. Even the patches of burlesque and humorous satire are not regarded as out of place; they only seem to heighten the effect of the expressive movements of whole groups of people who express their deep emotions in dance forms.

In the Southern Sudan some of the converted Dinka minstrels have gone about the country singing the stories of the gospel in traditional Dinka style. These songs have become so popular that they form part of the Dinka hymnal. Dramatic plays have been exceedingly effective in Bishop Tucker College in Uganda. Dramatic representations have sometimes failed, but generally this seems to have been due to too much coaching and too much rigidity imposed by missionary instructors. The words which the actors use may not always be strictly Biblical, but a certain amount of freedom will permit the drama "to come to life." Dr. Taylor describes [12] the "terrifying and unforgettable experience" of seeing the Fall of Man danced by three players at Buloba College, Uganda:

Adam and Eve, dressed like peasants in bark-cloth, were seen cultivating in the shade of a great tree. Adam became weary, and throwing himself down slept while Eve continued digging with slow, tired movements. Then, far away one small drum began to throb, menacing and horribly insistent; and to the rhythm of it a girl, swathed in a scarlet cloth, with a long, green train dragging behind her over the dry grass, danced out the Temptation. It was an extraordinary dance of undulation and slithering movement, with her two hands keeping up a ceaseless flickering at the level of her eyes. And opposite her Eve also danced her reluctant, frightened, slow surrender to fascination and desire. Louder and louder grew the throbbing of the drum, more intense the serpent's hatred, until Eve, who was already fondling the fruit that hung from the tree, suddenly tugged it from the branch and sank her teeth into it. At that instant the drum was silenced, and the snake slid quickly away into the surrounding darkness.

The degree to which the esthetic accomplishments of people can be employed in any Christian society depends very largely upon the attitudes of the indigenous Christians. Nothing artificial and foreign should be forced upon them, nor should they be robbed of anything which has value. In other words, under the guidance of the Holy Spirit (and not by the dictates of the mission) the people should be given some chance to choose for themselves those types of esthetic expression which are most truly consonant with their new faith.

QUEER SOUNDS, STRANGE GRAMMARS, AND
UNEXPECTED MEANINGS

"The language which you are to study has only about three hundred words and no grammar," wrote a self-styled missionary linguist to a young missionary under appointment. If such a statement were true, learning the language would be a cinch, but there is no tribe of people anywhere in the world which does not have thousands of words in its vocabulary and an intricate, systematic way of putting words together into phrases and sentences, i.e. a grammar.

Of course, people do not have words for things with which they are not acquainted. The Shipibos had no words for a motor launch or an airplane before they saw such objects, but when steam-driven, wood-burning river boats first came up the Ucayali River, the Shipibos called them "fire-canoes"; and when airplanes first landed on their broad, swollen streams, they called them "flying-fire-canoes." Some amateur linguists have miscalculated the number of words in a language because they have tried to compare languages by using a dictionary of some European language. They select pages at random out of some well-known dictionary, ask the people for equivalent expressions, and then calculate the average correspondences per page, mutiply this by the number of pages in the dictionary, and conclude that they have determined the extent of the indigenous vocabulary. Nothing could be better designed to distort the truth. The Marshallese have over sixty terms just to describe different parts of a coconut tree and its fruit. The stages of growth and maturity of the coconut are described by twelve different words. Equivalent terms are not to be found in an English dictionary, while conversely the Marshallese have no words for the numerous parts of horse-drawn carriages, though on some of the islands they have borrowed or made up words for parts of automobiles, trucks, and airplanes.

Those who have made thorough studies of the vocabularies of aboriginal languages have found that these languages have rich resources of available words. The Maya language of Yucatan has at least 20,000 words, the Aztec of central Mexico about 27,000,[1] and the Zulu language of South Africa possesses more than 30,000. Some other languages may not have as many, but the vocabulary of any language, irrespective of how primitive the people may seem, must be reckoned in thousands, not in hundreds of words.

The accusation that some languages have no grammar may result from ignorance of the language or ignorance of what is grammar. The Aymara language has no adjectival endings to show agreement with nouns, nor does it distinguish between masculine, feminine, and neuter forms; but the language could scarcely be accused of lacking a grammar. Aymara verbs invariably begin with a root, to which may be added various combinations of twenty-three sets of suffixes, indicating such features as cause, direction, mode, condition, number, location, negation, size, aspect, tense, subject, object, and emphasis. Perhaps the most interesting suffixes are those which indicate direction of the action, e.g. -cata "up to," -ka "away from," -naka "back and forth," -nta "inward," -su "outward," -tata "expanding," -thapi "contracting," -quipa "change of location," -ranta "covering of a surface," and -ra "distributive." If one is talking about a fire going out, then -ra is the proper suffix, for there are scattered flames darting up from the dying embers. However, this suffix is not appropriate for describing the extinguishing of a candle, which goes out in a single action. For this latter action one must employ the suffix -t'a which denotes "punctiliar (i.e. instant or pointlike) action. The Aymaras speak of hail falling "inward" toward the earth (using -nta), but a house is built "outward" (using -su). It is not unusual for a verb form to consist of as many as ten or more elements; e.g. awist'ayaniwayarapipjjämawa, meaning "I will have him notified for you on my way here," consists of the following parts: *awis-* "to notify," *-t'a-* punctiliar action (meaning that this event is viewed as a single action), *-ya-* causative (i.e. the subject causes someone else to perform the action), *-ni-* motion toward the scene of speech (i.e. "here"), *-waya-* "on the way," *-rapi-* benefactive (i.e. the action is performed for the benefit of someone else), *-pjja-* plural participants, *-ä-* future tense for the first person singular, *-ma-* "I" subject and "you" object (two referents combined in a single suffix), and *-wa* emphatic particle. Almost any verb root in Aymara can occur in at least 100,000 different combinations.

There is a popular impression—perhaps resulting from memorizing Greek and Latin paradigms—that masculine, feminine, and neuter genders have something sacrosanct about them, that they embody some universal grammatical truth which all languages should hold inviolate. The truth is that most languages do not distinguish gender though it does occur in such widely scattered languages as Hottentot of South Africa and Chinook, Coast Salish, and Pomo languages of the Pacific Coast of North America.[2] Even in the expression of gender there is certainly nothing logical or rational about what happens in Greek. Why should a word such as *hodos* "road" look like a masculine word (it ends in *-os*) but actually be feminine? Why should it not be neuter? Of course, there is no strictly "logical" answer, any more than there is a biological validity for treating German *Frau* "woman" as feminine and *Fräulein* "young lady" as neuter.

Those who regard the gender system and grammatical agreement of Greek as being the perfect expression of human thought may need to think again when they discover that some Bantu languages have as many as twenty classes, with remarkable sets of agreement, including not only all the adjectives which modify a noun, but even the pronominal particles which are prefixed to the verb. The following sentences in Ilamba of Tanganyika illustrate this point: [3]

1. *ke:nto   kiakoe keko:lu kemoe kiameke:la   eno:mba.*
   "Thing   his   big   one   is greater than (a) house."

2. *lokani   loakoe loko:lu lomoe loaoke:la   oo:ta.*
   "Word   his   big   one   is greater than (a) bow."

These two sentences mean (1) "His one big thing is greater than a house" and (2) "His one big [i.e. important] word is greater than [i.e. has greater strength than] a bow." These sentences cannot be thrown together in any old way; each word must come in a specific order and begin with a prefix which indicates the system of modification (or attribution).

We are sometimes confused by languages which fail to distinguish the categories that we regard as necessary. Tarahumaras in northern Mexico use the word *towiki* to mean both "boy" and "boys." They regard distinctions between singular and plural as both unnecessary and queer. Why should one form designate a single object and another include any number of objects, from two to infinity? We must admit that it is all quite arbitrary—even as languages essentially are. We are accustomed to thinking that only verbs indicate tenses, e.g. past, present, and future time, and accordingly, it may be hard to adjust ourselves to the fact that a language such as Mongbandi, spoken in the northern part of the Belgian Congo, indicates the time of the action by changing the tone on the pronouns. For example, *mbi* "I" or *'e* "we" spoken on a low tone means past time, a middle tone denotes present, and a high tone is future.[4]

Some of the categories which other languages express could well be adopted by us, though this would be as unlikely as having Americans give up eating steaks and go in for whale blubber. The Wintu Indians of California have special forms which indicate whether a statement is (1) hearsay, (2) a result of direct observation, or (3) inferred, with three degrees of plausibility. If politicians, newscasters, and columnists were only required to use such tiny particles to salt down their extravagant remarks, all of society would be immensely benefited.

"Just a Jumble of Sound"

To the inexperienced ear any unknown language seems like a jumble of sound spoken with incredible speed. But languages are not jumbles of sounds and the average speed of utterance is about the same for all languages.[5] Of course, languages may have unusual and queer sounds, which seem to pop, explode, hiss, rumble or whistle. Germans trill the uvula (the tiny bell-shaped piece of tissue which hangs down at the back of the mouth), and the Spanish trill the tip of the tongue, while the Yipounous in the Gabon trill their lips. A number of the languages of South Africa have clicks, a variety of popping sounds made by forming little vacuums between the tongue and the hard or soft palate. The so-called glottalized consonants (named for the fact that the glottis, the opening between the vocal cords, is shut off tightly during part of their production) also seem to pop and explode, but they have a "deeper resonance" than the clicks. Queer consonants are bad enough, but vowels are equally difficult, and the tones almost make us give up hope of learning to speak some languages. We may hear a Navajo word which sounds like *anii*, but one time we are told it means "face," another time the people insist that it means "nostril," and still another time it may mean "waist." The people are not trying to deceive us, for though we may have properly identified the vowels and the consonants, we have probably missed the tones. The vowel and consonant sounds, when spoken on a low tone, do mean "face," but when spoken on a high tone the meaning is "nostril." If the first syllable is spoken on a low tone and the second on a high tone, then the meaning is "waist." The Navajo word *atsos* (spoken with low tones) means "feather," but if the second vowel is drawn out (i.e. lengthened), the word means "veins." If, however, some of the sound of the long second vowel comes out through the nose (a nasalized vowel), the word means "sucking." We are simply not used to such distinctions in sounds, and so we conclude that other languages are disorganized jumbles of incoherent sounds.

The science of phonemics [6] has shown quite clearly that behind the apparent hodgepodge of sounds there is a very intricate system of units which distinguish meanings. All languages have a limited number of distinctive sounds, somewhere between a dozen and sixty. Though these sounds may at first seem to glide almost imperceptibly one into the other, there are definable differences between them.

A common remark is, "If you just knew Latin, you would understand English grammar." Perhaps one would understand some of the terminology used for describing English grammar: gerunds, gerundives, infinitives, gender, and case, for these terms make some sense in Latin, whereas for the most part they do not fit English. However, Latin is not the original language, nor is Greek. Even Sanskrit is just one of the Indo-European languages, which include the Germanic languages (Icelandic, Danish, Norwegian, Swedish, German, Dutch, Flemish, English, and Ancient Gothic), Romance languages (Latin, and its present-day successors: Spanish, Portuguese, French, Italian, Ladin, and Rumanian), Celtic languages (the languages of Caesar's Gaul, and present-day Breton, Welsh, Irish, and Scotch Gaelic), the Balto-Slavic languages (Lithuanian, Lettish, Polish, Russian, Bulgarian, Serbo-Croatian, and Slovene), Greek, Albanian, Armenian, and Indo-Iranian (the Indic languages include Ancient Sanskrit and modern Gujerati, Marathi, Panjabi, Western and Eastern Hindi, Oriya, Bengali, and the language of the Gypsies; the Iranian languages include Persian, Kurdish, Pushto, Baluchi, and Ossete).[7] Ancient Hittite is related to these Indo-European languages, and some persons believe (though the concrete linguistic evidence is very tenuous) that the Hamitic-Semitic languages (including many of the languages of North Africa, Arabic, Hebrew, Coptic, and Amharic) are distantly related to the Indo-European ones.

There are nine great families of languages [8] which include close to 90 per cent of the world's population: Indo-European, Sino-Tibetan (including Chinese, Tibetan, Burmese), Semitic-Hamitic, Dravidian (the languages of South India, e.g. Telegu, Tamil, Malayalam), Ural-Altaic (including languages as geographically distant as Turkish, Tartar, and Yakut), Japanese, Malayo-Polynesia [9] (including languages from Madagascar through Indonesia, Micronesia, and Polynesia to the Hawaiian and Easter Islands—not far from North and South America respectively), Bantu (almost all the languages in Central and South Africa), and Austroasiatic (Mon-Khmer, Palaung-Wa, Semang-Sakai, Nicobarese, and Vietnamese). These great families are by no means all, for there are such isolated relics as the Basque language of the Pyrenees, which cannot be related to any other language of Europe,[10] and the remarkable variety of tiny languages in the Caucasus. We cannot overlook the Nilotic languages of the Sudan, the Hottentot-Bushman languages of South Africa, and the multiplicity of languages and dialects in the Sudan, New Guinea, western North America, southern Mexico, and the Amazon valley. We must reckon with no less than twenty families of languages in the Eastern Hemisphere and on the basis of our present knowledge we undoubtedly need thirty to forty families to classify the languages of the Western Hemisphere. Obviously, not all languages go back to Latin, nor even to Sanskrit.

"Broad Lips and Broad Vowels"

"You can't tell me those broad Southern vowels don't come from those broad Negro lips," declared a Yankee visitor in Georgia, despite the fact that some very thin-lipped Southern aristocrats use vowels just as "broad." There is simply no relationship between the biological heritage of facial features and the type of speech sounds which people make. Some Negroes speak sonorous Parisian French with perfect skill; others are equally adept in reproducing the staccatolike rippling of Spanish phrases, while still others cannot be distinguished from Lisbon-born Portuguese. One's speech habits depend not on one's racial physiognomy, but on the speech community where one has been reared. Of course, a person with poorly fitting false teeth will have no end of trouble in trying to sputter the clicks of Zulu, Xhosa, or Hottentot, but all normal human beings can learn to speak any language without a "foreign accent" provided they begin early enough.

The belief that primitive peoples speak distinctly "primitive" languages is utterly untrue if one means by "primitive" anything that is unusually simple, limited, deficient, or "primeval." The remarkably extensive vocabularies (reaching into tens of thousands of words) and the intricate structures of words and phrases which are possessed by all types of languages mean that there is absolutely no correlation between linguistic structure and cultural complexity.

During the last century there was a popular evolutionary belief that
languages had evolved from monosyllabic structure (such as Chinese) through the agglutinative structure of such languages as
Bantu and Aztec to the "highest form of speech," the inflected
languages of Europe. Such blatant egoism has been found utterly
without any basis in fact. Even Chinese, which was cited as such
a primitive language, was discovered to have possessed some inflec-
tion in its earlier history. As for "primitive languages," they have
been shown to exhibit all the types of structure found in any language spoken by "civilized peoples."

As an antidote to the numerous false impressions about language,
we need to consider some of the pertinent facts, which not only
permit us to appreciate languages more and to learn them more
readily, but which enable us to understand better their relationship
to culture.

Languages Are Arbitrary Systems

There is nothing in the nature of sounds themselves which makes
it obligatory for them to carry particular meanings. The Spanish
word *ni* means "nor," but the closest equivalent combination of
sounds in English is *knee*. In Congo Swahili *ni* is a prefix to affirmative verbs and means "I," while in Navajo it is a suffix to verbs and
indicates complete action. Even exclamations show no basic similarities. We yell "Ouch!" but a Spanish-speaking person cries *"Ay!
Ay!"* Our dogs bark *bow-wow* but the Kipsigis of Kenya insist that
dogs say *u'u'*.[11] It is entirely arbitrary as to which sounds are to be
employed to represent particular ideas or emotional responses. Nowhere in all the phases of culture is the principle of selectivity so
obvious, for each language has an almost unlimited number of
potential combinations of consonants and vowels, and yet only
certain ones of these are used to convey meanings. Why should we
have the words *bill, pill, kill, till, mill, sill, dill, fill, gill, hill, jill,
nil, rill,* and *will,* but not use the combinations *vill, zill, xill,* and
yill? There is no reason for such limitations, other than the essentially arbitrary selectivity of language.

However, languages, like all parts of culture, are essentially arbitrary systems. This "arbitrariness" includes not only sounds and corresponding meanings, but also grammatical structure. If we wish to emphasize something we may repeat it, e.g. *very very good*. But in Hiligaynon, spoken in the central Philippines, a repetition of an expression makes it less strong than if it were said once. Hence, the "verily, verily" of the Bible has to be reduced to one "verily" if the people are to understand it as a strong affirmative. In Indonesian the repetition of a word indicates plurality; *tuhantuhan* (sometimes written simply as *tuhan2*) means "lords." However, in Hiligaynon, a member of the same language family as Indonesian, the repetition of the Spanish borrowing *Dios* "God" in the form *diosdios* means an "idol" (i.e. something less than God). Repetition in San Blas conveys a meaning of diminutive as well as of repeated action. *Mua* means to rise and *muamua* means to rise and fall repeatedly on large waves, while *muamuamua* implies bobbing about on little ripples.

We take it for granted that people describe experiences as we do, and hence we assume that they should employ our idioms. It is all very well for us to talk about the "eye of a needle," but the Eastern Otomi in Mexico insist that it should be the "ear of a needle." The Kekchi Indians of Guatemala call it the "face of the needle." Still other people call it the "nostril of the needle," "hole of the needle," or even the "foot of the needle" (in contrast with the "head," which is the point).

In some of the Quechua dialects of Peru and Bolivia one speaks of the future as "behind oneself" and the past as "ahead." Such interpretations of time have given rise to remarks by foreigners that the Quechuas have "a perverted philosophical instinct." However, the Quechuas argue, "If you try to see the past and future with your mind's eye, which can you see?" The obvious answer is that we can "see" the past and not the future, to which the Quechua replies, "Then, if you can see the past, it must be ahead of you; and the future, which you cannot see, is behind you." [12] Such an explanation does not mean that the Quechuas worked out a philosophical interpretation of the past and future before talking about it, but it does suggest that there may be equally valid, but opposite ways of describing the same thing.

To our way of viewing psychological phenomena "a big heart" means generosity, but the Huaves in southern Mexico insist that it means "bravery," while the Tzeltals, also living in southern Mexico, interpret it as "forgiving." However, the Shilluks of the Anglo-Egyptian Sudan say that a person with "a big heart" is stingy, while someone with "a small heart" is generous. They explain the idiom in cultural terms by saying that a stingy, selfish man has accumulated all that he can and has put all this in his heart; therefore it is big. On the other hand, the generous man has given away almost all of his possessions, and hence his heart is small. The Akha of Burma have these same figures of speech, but they use the phrase "a big heart" to describe a conceited man, while one who has "a small heart" is cowardly.

Despite all the arbitrariness in the use of sounds, the type of grammatical structure, and the meanings of idioms, there is nevertheless some system within languages. Were this not the case, no one would be able to say anything which he had not already heard from someone else, something we can all do. The speaker of any language knows (but cannot necessarily explain) the way the sounds go together to make up the words, and the patterns of constructions in which the words go together to make up phrases and sentences.[13] In English we say *his white house,* but Spanish has the order *su casa blanca,* literally, "his house white." Ilamba in Tanganyika has the order "house his white." One order is as logical as the other; the important thing is that each language has a pattern for such expressions, though, of course, there may be several alternative orders, each with its own special value. There are, however, certain preferred ways, which are regarded by the people as the "natural ways" of speaking. If we know the patterns of a language, it is possible for us to predict with reasonable accuracy how other similar phrases will be formed. We must, however, expect all kinds of irregularities in languages (and English is no exception). The most irregular verb in our language, *be, is, are, am, was, were, been,* is also the most common verb of all. Such irregularities illustrate the arbitrary character of language, but they do not invalidate the fact that despite all such utterly obnoxious discrepancies (obnoxious from the viewpoint of the learner) there is nevertheless a structure to language, even as there is a structure to culture.

Languages Are Constantly Changing

√ All living languages are constantly changing. *God be with you,* the greeting of an earlier century, becomes the *good-by* of today, while today's *let's go eat* is rapidly becoming tomorrow's *skweet.* One only needs to read the first lines of Chaucer's *Canterbury Tales* to realize how much English has changed since the fourteenth century:

> Whan that Aprille with his shoures soote
> The droghte of Marche hath perced to the roote
> And bathed every veyne in swich licour,
> Of which vertu engendred is the flour

We can recognize many of the words, because of the archaic character of contemporary English spelling; but if we heard these lines recited by a Middle English poet, we would probably not recognize a single word or phrase.

Not only sounds, but also grammar changes. We used to have nominative, genitive, dative, and accusative cases in English, but now there are only six remaining words which show objective case forms: *me, us, him, her, them,* and *whom* (and the last word is rapidly losing its -*m*). Verbs used to agree with the subject in person and number, but now only a singular present-tense -*s* remains, e.g. *runs, hits,* and *walks.* However, English is not alone in changing—all languages change. Some seem to be getting more simple, while others appear to be getting more complex. In fact, simplicity and complexity seem to run in cycles and in different stages, for while one part of the language may appear to be getting more simple, another part is becoming much more complicated. The same is true of all aspects of culture. While the complex social organization of African tribes crumbles, due to urbanization, the economic organization becomes much more intricate. Modern French has much simpler nouns than Latin, but the verb phrases are considerably more complex.

It is easy enough to understand that languages must undergo changes in their vocabularies because of cultural modifications and word borrowing from the outside world. But rarely do we realize how extensive these vocabulary changes can be. Though English is basically a Germanic language, nevertheless, it has a vocabulary which is more than half derived from non-Germanic sources. We have borrowed thousands of words from all over the world, e.g. *chant* and *village* from French, *spaghetti* and *bologna* from Italian, *calaboose* and *vamoose* from Spanish, *consul* and *senator* from Latin, *theology* and *hippodrome* from Greek, *chocolate* and *tomato* from Aztec, *coca* and *jerky* (*charqui*) from Quechua, *tattoo* from Tahitian, *thug* from Hindustani, *squaw* from Algonquian, *succotash* from Narraganset, *kimono* from Japanese, and *checkmate* from Arabic (*shah mat*, meaning "the king is dead").[14]

Literate peoples are not the only ones who borrow words from other languages. The Aymara of Bolivia and Peru speak a language which has many striking structural similarities to Quechua, but it is generally regarded as belonging to quite a different language family. Nevertheless, there are hundreds of words in common between Quechua and Aymara. Similarly many of the languages of Mexico have hundreds of Aztec words, borrowed freely from the Aztec-speaking colonists who were scattered throughout the country to form centers of Aztec influence and power. The Tagalog language of the Philippines includes some three hundred religious and philosophical terms borrowed from Sanskrit hundreds of years ago, at a time when the islands were in relatively close cultural contact with the religions and philosophies of India.

Languages may keep the same words, but change their meanings. *Vulgar* used to mean "common" or "popular" and *awful* meant "inspiring with awe," but now *awfully vulgar* means "very uncouth." The King James Bible speaks of the "Holy Ghost" and "seeing a spirit." The words *ghost* and *spirit* have switched meanings. *Spirit* used to mean a "phantom," but now *ghost* has this meaning, while *spirit* has taken on the meaning formerly expressed by *ghost*.

It is popularly supposed that unwritten languages change with greater speed because they are not "fixed" in form by writing. But as far as we can observe, writing has relatively little effect in slowing down changes. In fact, languages seem to change in proportion to the density of communication and the intensity of outside cultural pressures. Writing may popularize some particular dialect which is chosen as the literary medium and it may seem to give permanence to a language (since spelling so often lags behind changes in pronunciation, as it has in English); but reducing a language to writing will not stop it from changing.

Meanings of Words Reflect the Culture

The Quechua word for "year" is literally "tying up the sun." Such a phrase makes no sense apart from the cultural context in which this expression arose and in which it fits perfectly. As we noted on page 82, the Quechuas used *quipus*, multicolored cords to record all sorts of facts, including astronomical ones. When the year ended, the *quipu* designating the sun was evidently tied in order to indicate the passing of the time. Accordingly, the phrase "tying up the sun" acquired the meaning of "year."

If one wishes to translate the phrase "wagging their heads" (Mark 15:29), it is necessary to know just how people in the culture in question express derision and mocking. The Subanun of Mindanao in the southern Philippines use a word which means to move the head up and down, for this is the way the Subanun people indicate contempt. However, the Ifugao in the northern part of Luzon have a term which means to wag the head from side to side, for this is their equivalent cultural expression. The two manners of moving the head are different, but the meanings of the corresponding words are equivalent.

The dependence of meaning upon cultural context is perfectly obvious when children are in the process of learning a language. The little girl who defined *amen* as meaning "Now you can open your eyes" understood unconsciously the relationship between language and cultural context. The Quechua Indians in Bolivia who decided that the patron saint of a new missionary was "Oh Boy!" were being very logical, for they heard this phrase in precisely the same contexts in which most people called upon their favorite saint.

The connotations of words abound in cultural influences. When a person is denied a visa to enter a country as a "missionary" but is granted entrance later when he applies as a "pastor" or a "preacher of the gospel," [15] it is perfectly obvious that the real trouble lies in the cultural associations of the word "missionary," implying, as it does, to most people, an irksome superiority-inferiority relationship. There is nothing intrinsically wrong with the word, but it cannot be isolated from the cultural environment, of which it is an inseparable part.

Language: a Part, a Mechanism, and a Model of Culture

When an Arab affirms that "Allah gave the Frenchman a head, the Chinese hands, and the Arab a mouth," he is indicating what many other peoples express in different ways, namely, the deep significance of language for the people in question. Language is not only a part of human activity, it is the most characteristic feature of human behavior, and the possession of distinct languages is certainly one of the most obvious features which distinguish human cultures. Societies may include more than one language, as does Belgium, which is almost equally divided between Flemish (a dialect of Dutch) and French. The U.S.S.R. has officially recognized within its boundaries forty-six nationalities speaking distinct languages, and certainly the Roman Empire included many more. On the other hand, people speaking the same language may belong to different societies, e.g. English speakers in the United States, Great Britain, Canada, Australia, and New Zealand, or Spanish speakers in numerous countries of Latin America.

The significance of language as a cultural dynamic and symbol is fully evident in the attempt by the Irish to re-establish their own Gaelic tongue, and the more apparently successful endeavor of the Jews to reintroduce Hebrew. Efforts to promote nationalism through the use of one's own language may even result in a complete tour de force, as happened in Turkey, during the time when the new, self-conscious nation was trying to vindicate its distinctively Turkish past and to forget its Arabic and Persian heritage. A law was passed that no newspaper or magazine could use any word that was not 100 per cent Turkish. Publishers, editors, and writers were completely at their wits' ends, for one could scarcely write a sentence in intelligible Turkish which did not contain some of these forbidden foreign words. Dictionaries were rapidly made up, listing Turkish paraphrases or archaic terms for everyday common words, and scores of employees translated news releases into the artificial language which the readers could not understand, unless they in turn used the same dictionaries to retranslate the totally unfamiliar Turkish into the everyday language. Day after day the situation went from bad to worse until at last one clever person dreamed up a marvelous scientific hoax. He insisted that primitive man first worshiped the sun, which he called *ag*, a word which was declared to be Ancient Turkish (the Modern Turkish word is utterly different), and from which all other words in all languages were descended. Accordingly, if present-day Turks borrowed from Persian, Arabic, or any other language, they were just taking back what was originally Turkish anyway. With the official endorsement of a couple of properly coached outside "scientists" and with strictly controlled internal news coverage, the Turkish government was able to extricate itself from an awkward situation and at the same time reaffirm the strong cultural link between language and culture.

As a mechanism for the transmission of culture, language has A-1 priority. Artifacts can be seen and studied, but their manufacture often requires verbal explanation. As regards a very high percentage of the social and religious culture language is an indispensable instrument for transmitting not only the outward forms but the inner content and the subjective evaluation. Perhaps the best evidence of the essential function of language as a transmitting mechanism is seen in the almost total failure of meaningful cultural contact when effective communication is lacking. In one area of South America missionary work has been going on for more than thirty years, with a total of slightly more than twenty different missionaries working in the area at different times. In all these years none of the missionaries has learned to speak the Indian language with any degree of intelligibility. In fact, only one missionary has made any marked effort to do so. The result has been that there are not more than sixteen Indians who are said to be "converted" and more than half of these are regarded as having "backslidden." If a culture cannot and does not transmit its own concepts except by language, how can missionaries expect to inculcate wholly foreign concepts without using the only language which the people really understand? [16]

If languages are a part and a mechanism of culture, they are also, in a sense, a model of culture. The use of honorific language (see page 127) by and about the respective classes of a culture so closely reflects the social structure that we can describe the linguistic usage as a kind of model of what happens in the society. If, as in England, one's accent betrays his social class and certain positions in business or society are restricted to those who possess the culturally acceptable accent, language becomes, in a sense, a model of this social classification.

In the language of New Caledonia [17] there are two different ways of expressing possession. One system is used with words such as "foot," "belly," "head," "life" (in the sense of one's descendants), "totem," "liver," and "mother," while another system is employed with such words as "heart," "intestines," "thought," "personal life," and "father." This distinction reflects a basic distinction in the New Caledonian interpretation of culture. The first set of words identifies intimate and culturally essential features of one's life, while the second list includes the less intimate and less essential. In this matrilineal society the mother is the indispensable cultural fact, while the father is not so culturally important. The liver is regarded as more significant than the heart, for in sacrifices it is a substitute for the animal. One's own personal life is not as culturally essential as are one's descendants who perpetuate the clan. It would, however, be quite wrong to assume that we could take any and all grammatical facts about languages and derive some cultural interpretation from them. There have been too many injudicious attempts to do this sort of thing with the various Indo-European languages, as well as others. At certain historical periods in the development of languages such grammatical distinctions have usually had some degree of cultural validity, but whether they are models of present-day cultures depends primarily upon the cultural, not the linguistic facts. Even in the case of the New Caledonian data cited above, the socio-religious bases for the grammatical dichotomy are rapidly disappearing but the grammatical structure will continue as a relic without functional correspondence in contemporary life.

Present-day expressions may give us clues and confirmations of earlier cultural situations. When we find that the Mayans in Yucatan call a sheep a "cotton-deer," we have corroborative linguistic evidence that the Mayans, who did not have sheep before the coming of the Spanish, were describing the sheep in terms of features which they did have in their culture. A number of the Indians of northern Canada use the same word for "horse" which they do for "dog." When horses were introduced into their regions, they were used to transport loads tied to a framework, of which two poles dragged along behind. Dogs had been used to transport smaller loads in the same manner. Accordingly, it is not strange that the new animal which was used in quite a similar manner should be identified by the older, familiar word. We have used the word "ship" in speaking of an object which navigates through the water or through the air, even though the *Queen Elizabeth* and a jet fighter have little resemblance. Our days of the week, Sunday, Monday, Tuesday, Wednesday, Thursday, Friday, and Saturday, are relic witnesses to the ancient worship of the sun, the moon, the god of war, Woden, Thor, Frija, and Saturn, respectively.

Languages in Competition

The American woman who has to decide whether her next dress will be one designed in Paris or Hollywood has to make the same kind of decision as the Filipino on Panay who has to decide whether his child is to have some good indigenous name or be given a Spanish one, including not only common Spanish names, but less usual ones, such as *Concepción, Resurrección,* or even *Circoncisión.*[18] What has more prestige, Hollywood or Paris, Hiligaynon or Spanish? The ancient Romans who wanted to have some cultural standing went away to study under famous Greek professors in such places as Athens, Rhodes, and Alexandria. Americans think they are "cultured" if they listen to operas in some language they do not understand, and a Liberian woman called her twins Syphilla and Gonora, terms taken from an impressive-looking pamphlet on venereal diseases distributed in Liberia during the last war.

In the clash of two languages, as when the conquerors and the conquered live together, the conquerors may impose their language upon the conquered, as in Hungary, or they may learn the language of the conquered, as in Bulgaria. The Romans imposed their language on most of France, but the Norman conquerors of England finally gave in to English—after loading it down with thousands of words and some hideous spellings.

Matters of efficiency seem to be relatively unimportant in determining which language or system of writing wins out in the long run. During the fifteenth century Korea had an honest-to-goodness alphabet which was very efficient, infinitely more so than the clumsy adaptation of Chinese writing which was also in use in those days.[19] However, only the shopkeepers and the common people used the alphabet, while the Chinese characters were the possession of the elite. In the end the alphabet died out, and the Chinese characters remained. Not what people can use with greatest ease but what they want to use for the sake of social standing largely determines the course of cultural events. A very efficient "scientific" alphabet was worked out for the Quechua Indians of Bolivia. Theoretically it was perfect, but it was not acceptable because the people insisted on having something which was more like Spanish, the language of prestige and culture.

Prestige (backed by economic considerations and sometimes force) seems to be the determining factor in the conflicts between languages. However, we must not underestimate the tenacity of minority languages. Breton, a Celtic language, has lived on in France for about 2,000 years since the Romans first began to introduce Latin into Gaul. Theoretically speaking, the Basque language should have disappeared hundreds of years ago, but it still thrives. When a century ago there were fewer than 10,000 Navajos, anyone could have felt justified in predicting the extinction of the Navajo language within a generation, but there are now more than 40,000 monolingual Navajos.[20]

Talking and Making Sense

Being able to speak so that people identify the words may be quite different from being able to speak so that people understand the meaning of what one is trying to say. A missionary in the Philippines was preaching on the theme, "Get thee behind me, Satan!" but he used a word for "getting behind" which implied "follow me and be my helper." A missionary in Latin America thought he had found the right word for "sin" in an Indian language, for it included such acts as "stealing," "murder," and "adultery." However, after a few years it was discovered that this word also meant "marriage." Certainly he did not want to imply that marriage was a sin. What did the word mean anyway? At last the truth was discovered. This word meant primarily to "spoil something," and it could be employed just as well for "gathering ears from an unharvested cornfield" as for "stealing another man's wife." Marriage of course implied spoiling the virginity of the bride.

Not only single words but whole phrases may be misleading. In English it is all very well to translate Romans 4:7 as "Blessed are those . . . whose sins are covered," because we know enough of the Semitic idea of "covering sins" to realize that this implies forgiveness. However, in Hiligaynon this expression means that the sins are hidden from God's view. The phrase "generation of vipers" (Luke 3:7) is an obvious reproof to the hypocrites of Jesus' day, but the Balinese would interpret such a phrase as a great compliment since they regard the viper as the sacred animal of their paradise. For them the equivalent expression is "offspring of creeping vermin." We are somewhat mystified by the psychological phenomenon implied in the words "power had gone out of him" (Mark 5:30), but we are scarcely prepared to realize that in Tojolabal, spoken in southern Mexico, this phrase would refer to having sexual intercourse.

Proper translating from one language to another never consists in matching phrases or sentences word for word. The results are not only absurd and misleading, but usually quite unintelligible. One Polynesian who was asked about the very literal translation of the Scriptures in his language produced a masterpiece of understatement, "It is a little bit clear." True translating reproduces the closest natural equivalent, first in meaning, and secondly in style. Even in this there are two possible approaches: one follows the standard traditional equivalents, but still in completely natural idiom, as does the *Revised Standard Version* of the Bible (1946–52); the other reproduces the contemporary psychological equivalents, such as has been done by J. B. Phillips in *Letters to Young Churches* (1947) and in *The Gospels* (1953). The type of translation which one employs depends very largely upon the audience and the purpose of the translation.[21]

The following problems involving culturally significant features of equivalence must be understood if one is to communicate accurately and effectively.

1. *Two and Two May Not Equal Four*

One cannot always add up words and come out with the meaning of a phrase. The meaning of "heaping coals of fire on one's head" is not to be understood by adding up the meanings of the individual words. That is what some aboriginal peoples have done with their translations of the Bible, and they have concluded that the Scriptures advocated a very diabolical method of torturing people to death. The meaning of this phrase is more than the sum total of the meanings of the individual words, that is to say, it is an idiomatic expression. Of course, most phrases in any language are understood by the simple process of adding together the meanings of the component parts. Because of this fact, people may badly misunderstand idioms, for they try to understand them as straightforward statements of fact. In 1 John 3:17 "close up his bowels" just means in Chol, a language of southern Mexico, to become constipated. In order to suggest a psychological interpretation of the expression, the translator suggested "close up his heart," only to discover that this was a Chol idiom meaning "to have epileptic fits." The final result was to drop the Greek idiom and say quite simply "he does not give him anything."

2. Deceptive Similarities

In the apparent cultural correspondence which one finds there may lurk numerous deceptive similarities. Some Zanaki people of Tanganyika knock on doors; but if they do, one can be sure they are thieves. These approach a house in the dead of night, knock on the door posts, and then if they hear any movement inside they dash off into the darkness. An honest man will come to a house and call the names of the people inside. By doing this he causes his own voice to be identified. If one literally translates the words of Jesus "Behold, I stand at the door and knock" (Revelation 3:20) this could only mean to Zanakis that Jesus was a thief. Accordingly, one must say in the Zanaki language, "Behold, I stand at the door and call."

When some Ifugao speakers were asked if they had a word for an "oath," they instantly suggested what they regarded as an equivalent. In the sense that their word meant "a solemn promise" it was similar to corresponding Greek and Hebrew terms, but actually the Ifugao word has a very restricted usage. It is not used to confirm declarations, but is a bargaining technique whereby the supernatural powers were promised benefits on condition that they first perform their part of the contract. The Ifugao people have no idea of letting the deities get the better of any bargain.

We understand the word "under" in the phrase "under the law" (Romans 6:15, 1 Corinthians 9:20, Galatians 3:23, and elsewhere) as referring to the jurisdiction of the law. The Marshallese also use a word meaning "under" and they have a term for "the law," but for them the phrase "under the law" means "illegal." The Marshallese equivalent of the Biblical pharse is "those who must do what the law says."

3. A Part Is Not Enough

A missionary was so intent upon describing "salvation" as being "rescued from drowning" or "saved from a burning building" or "snatched to safety from an angry mob" that the people suggested as a translation of the word "salvation" an indigenous term meaning "a place to hide." Before realizing it, the missionary had embarked on a thoroughgoing escapist theology, not having considered that the corresponding term in Greek implies not only "to rescue" but also "to heal" or "to restore to health." Finally, it was realized that the best equivalent in the language in question was "to receive new life," a close reproduction of the Greek area of meaning.

4. Meaningless or Ludicrous?

The missionary who translated "Holy Spirit" as "Clean Breath" was saying something quite meaningless. He had found in a dictionary that the Greek word *pneuma* could mean "breath," but for the people in that part of Africa a "breath" is not a spirit. The translator had just taken for granted that holy objects could be understood as "clean" (assuming as universal the dictum "cleanliness is next to godliness"), but "clean breath" was so much nonsense.

One can translate literally in Chol "If the light . . . is darkness" (Matthew 6:23); but "How can light ever be darkness?" a Chol Indian will inevitably ask. In English such an expression is possible, but in the Chol language it is nonsense, and hence the rendering must be "If the light . . . be shaded over," which is perfectly understandable and very close to the Greek original.

Sometimes what is not meaningless may nevertheless be ludicrous. The translator who, without realizing it, rendered "gird up the loins of your mind" as "put a belt around the hips of your thoughts" was providing some local humor—not translating Scripture. Similarly a translation in one of the Micronesian languages reads, "Opened his mouth wide and taught . . ." (Matthew 5:2). The people always chuckle to think of anyone trying to talk with his mouth stretched open. Their way of saying this is "He began to teach . . ." which is substantially the meaning of the original.

5. Let the Borrower Beware!

Where indigenous terms have been lacking or have seemed wholly inadequate, it has been a common practice to borrow foreign words—especially for technical religious expressions having few equivalents in other languages. In English we have borrowed *priest, church, presbytery, bishop, theology,* and *synod* from Greek, and *virgin, pulpit, preach, lectern, Scriptures, sanctify, justify, predestine,* and *congregation* from Latin. However, borrowing is a dangerous business. For one thing, the people may already have borrowed the term in question. The Zapotecs of the Isthmus of Tehuantepec use the Spanish word *domingo* "Sunday" in the form *dumingu,* but for them it means a "dance." The Aztecs of Tetelcingo, Morelos, Mexico, have adopted the Spanish word *gloria* "glory," but it signifies a drunken fiesta and brawl, and Ecuadorean Quechuas call a child's doll a *santo,* which also means "saint." Borrowed words are under no obligation to retain their original meanings—in fact, the evidence is quite to the contrary. Spanish priests introduced the word *Dios* "God" into many languages of Latin America; but since it was a strange term and hence apparently equivalent to a proper name, the Indians assumed that it was only a foreign title for their own local deity. Accordingly, for the Aztecs of Mexico the word *Dios* is merely a name for the sun, and the word *virgen* "virgin" has in many instances become a religious designation for the moon. Borrowed terms soon acquire the distinctive imprint of the borrowing culture, even as Chinese art styles have been adapted by the Japanese, and Roman Catholicism has taken on distinctive forms in Cuban *santería.*

6. Cultural Barriers

Cultural differences are ever-present barriers to communication. The Bambaras of West Africa cannot understand the apparent disrespect which Moses showed when he announced to his father-in-law Jethro his intention to return to Egypt (Exodus 4:18). No Bambara would treat his parent-in-law with such unceremonious abruptness. Likewise the Kpelle people of Liberia are shocked at the record of people putting branches of palm trees in the path of Jesus when he rode triumphantly into Jerusalem (Matthew 21:8). In order to prepare for the entrance of any Liberian dignitary, the pathway must be painstakingly cleaned of all branches and leaves. An even more serious problem is presented by the cultural evaluation of "hope" among Hindus, who regard it as essentially an evil which the mystic sage must renounce if he is to experience the complete cessation of desire. Cultural differences between people will always pose some barriers to communication, but these should be reduced as much as possible by an effective use of cultural equivalents, sometimes in the form of descriptive phrases. The Huastecos in Mexico have no technical term for idols, but they may describe them as "gods of wood and plaster." Barrow Eskimos do not keep sheep, but they may speak of them in terms of culturally known objects, either as "hornless goats" or "woolly goats." Similarly they may call a pig "a queer deer." The Valiente Indians of Panama have no word for "corruption" (Romans 8:21 and elsewhere), but they can say "become food for worms"—a vivid equivalent of dying.

In the expression of psychological phenomena and related spiritual concepts, many languages have surprisingly rich resources. The Mazahua Indians of Mexico find it quite natural to speak of repentance as "turning back the heart," of salvation as "healing the heart," of conversion as "a change of the heart," and of peace as "resting in the heart." In the Valiente language the difficult term "sanctification" is translated as "to wash and keep clean," a phrase drawn from the experience of the Indian women who wash their clothes in the jungle streams and then put them in special baskets reserved for clean clothes.

Where the rapid growth of the people's religious experience outdistances the existing terms, new expressions inevitably arise, many of which reflect penetrating insights. When a Chol Indian of southern Mexico speaks of the response of a new believer to the message of the gospel, he says, "He answers the Word"; those who reject, "Pass by the Word." The catechumen is one who "learns the Lord," and those who continue true to their new faith "have entered in."

7. Keys to the Heart

Translation is not merely conveying information, but expressing in an equivalent style something of the emotionally charged character of the original. The parallelism of Hebrew poetry has an almost exact counterpart in the songs of Indonesia, and the bold figures of Old Testament proverbs strike fire in West Africa. In the Valiente language it would be possible to speak of a teacher as "one who instructs children," but the more meaningful indigenous term is "a mind-engraver." In the Shilluk language of the Sudan one could explain "He must increase, but I must decrease" (John 3:30) as "He must be more important and I must be less important," but the most effective natural equivalent is the poetic idiom, "He must come in out of the morning and I must go out into the night." The "way of peace" (Romans 3:17) becomes in the Chol language "the road of the quiet heart."

Linguistic parallels are even more striking because they reveal some of the subtle underlying differences. In English we may be told "to mind our own business," but an Uduk in the Sudan tells his bothersome neighbor, "Go sit in your own shade!" We can describe an obnoxious person as "a pain in the neck," while the Marshallese will talk about the same kind of pest as "a fishbone in one's throat." Our phrase about "butterflies in the stomach" is not very different from the way the Chontals of Oaxaca, Mexico, describe nervous worry as "butterflies in the heart."

Learning a Foreign Language

The numerous problems and techniques for learning a foreign language are quite beyond the scope of this discussion,[22] but we should note briefly the fact that failure to learn foreign languages results primarily from false attitudes toward culture. A superiority complex fortified by a paternalistic air is about the worst liability for effective language learning. Our ethnocentrism makes it difficult for us to "let ourselves go," for we dread making mistakes, not realizing that languages cannot be mastered until we have thoroughly murdered them. Perhaps our most serious fault is a failure to listen to the language. Since we have always conceived of language learning as a schoolroom and textbook technique, we fail to appreciate the fact that language is a speaking-hearing phenomenon. In order to learn to speak, we must listen. This requires exposing ourselves to situations in which we can and must listen;

as long as we maintain a cultural isolation, we cannot expect to learn a foreign language. Learning to speak an African language well means endless hours of sitting around the village campfire, listening to blood-curdling tales of former wars and hunting expeditions, long arguments salted down with innumerable proverbs, and rollicking stories of wise and stupid animals and men.

Linguistic training is of great help, but it is no substitute for cultural submersion. One Indian who had been trying very hard to teach a missionary the indigenous language explained with great distress, "I do not know what to do. I have been teaching this missionary for a long time, but she just sits and studies, and seems to learn nothing. Why, a Spanish-speaking girl married one of the Indians in our village, and now in one year's time she talks very well. Why is the missionary so ignorant?" The problem is not one of ignorance but of cultural isolation, of learning a great deal about the language but not learning the language, of studying but not speaking.

The beginner will inevitably make many mistakes. A missionary may point to a tree with his finger and say, "What is that?" to which the reply is more often than not, "Your finger." One missionary asked an Indian, "How do you say, 'I will pay you'?" But the Indian, who had had some dealings with whites before, replied, "You are fooling." The beginning notes of any language investigation—and in some instances the published comments of short-time investigators—will be replete with similar misleading expressions, which only the intimate speaking knowledge of the language can correct.

Languages can and must be learned if the Word of God is to be communicated in the words of men, but this cannot be done outside of the total framework of the culture, of which the language in question is an integral part.

OLD CUSTOMS AND NEW WAYS

"We know that the younger people will abandon our ways," remarked an old San Blas chieftain, as he lamented the rapid changes which were being introduced into the islands by schoolteachers, traders, missionaries, and politicians. No group of people, whether primitive or civilized, has a completely static culture, for everything is subject to and in the process of change. This is true of our own culture even though we may not recognize it because we are flowing imperceptibly with the tide. Our own lives are constantly changed by streamlined automobiles, indispensable dishwashers, time-consuming television sets, ever more efficient vacuum cleaners, push-button elevators, and automatic garage doors. But more important than these mechanical features of life are the factors of millions of people flocking to our impersonal cities, the rising juvenile delinquency, the breakdown of home life, and the general replacement of religion by popularly understood science as an explanation of the origin and purpose of life. The tempo of change may vary, but whether slow or fast, life never remains the same for succeeding generations.

Primitive and Civilized

The most definitive characteristics of primitive peoples may be summarized as follows: (1) small, isolated groups of people living in a more or less face-to-face society, (2) fundamentally homogeneous culture, (3) practically no full-time specialists, (4) a strong sense of group solidarity based on the sentiment of kinship, (5) relationships between people based upon the status of family and personal acquaintance rather than wealth or symbolic reputation, (6) a high degree of co-operativeness in procuring such basic necessities as food and shelter, and (7) an implicit adherence to the moral order.

One of the most marked characteristics is the primitives' unquestioning acceptance of the moral order [1] of his culture. The primitive peoples of any one culture have essentially the same goals and standards of value, and the basis of their society is not formal political organization but the moral order, consisting of the shared sentiments as to what is right and wrong.

In contrast with primitive cultures, civilizations may be characterized as consisting primarily of (1) large groups of people, some of whom live in cities, (2) great diversity in occupations and outlook, (3) political relationships (in place of family connections), (4) a strong emphasis upon improvements and changes in the technical order, and (5) the tendency to criticize and to be skeptical of the moral order. Certain secondary features of civilization include (1) tribute and taxes, with accumulations of wealth by the state, (2) public works, including cities, (3) the art of writing (or some means of calculation and the keeping of records), (4) science, e.g. astronomy, geometry, mathematics, (5) organized trade and commerce, and (6) a ruling class.[2]

The differences between primitive and civilized cultures are so great and "antagonistic" that cultural conflict is inevitable whenever primitive and civilized societies come in contact with each other, whether by military conquest or by peaceful growth and expansion. The impact of civilization upon primitive society consists not only of a frontal attack on the primitive technologies but also a flanking ambush of the moral order. The heterogeneous elements of civilization provide the basis for phenomenal developments and progress in technical lines, but they also introduce the factors for the demoralizing decline in the moral order. The writer, philosopher, scientist, and artist can no longer take things for granted. Their questioning results in greater systematization of knowledge, the tendency to compare opinions and ideas, and an inevitable skepticism as to the bases of the primitive moral order.

The "halfway stations" between the isolated primitive cultures and the civilized ones are the folk cultures such as the Indians of Mexico, the peasants of India, and the fellahin of Egypt. These peoples do not live in primitive isolation, but they are not full participants in civilization. They are the peasant hangers-on to the city civilizations. These folk cultures take account of the city: economically, they are related to it in buying, selling, borrowing, and taxation; and politically, they are dominated by it. They may be entertained by professional bands or troops of dancers who come from the city, and a few people in each village may acquire some of the education of the city (that is, they may learn to read and write). But fundamentally, the peasant remains suspicious of the city—proud of his rural piety and indignant of the city wickedness. He concedes that the city dweller may be more successful in business, possess greater social prestige, and have more authority in politics; but in industry, thrift, honesty, and sex morality, he rightly feels himself superior to the city dweller. The life of the folk culture is more implicit, with less skepticism and more religious sentiment.

We must not imagine, however, that the city is all bad, and the folk culture unqualifiedly superior. What we define as the "moral order" for any one culture is by no means an ideal moral order, for it may include human sacrifice, trial by ordeal, condemnation of innocent members of a family along with guilty persons, unsocial use of black magic, harmful religious practices such as scarification and clitorectomy, cruelty to the physically and mentally unfit, and complete intolerance of strangers and new ideas. Out of the conflict of technologies and concepts which are the inevitable results of civilization have come some of the "driving" ideas of the modern world: (1) the rights of man to justice and the full development of personality, (2) the responsibilities of man to all men, not merely to the in-group, (3) humane treatment of others, (4) national destiny, (5) economic and social reforms (primitive societies undergo changes, but rarely are they consciously directed reforms), (6) the necessity of subordinating the technical order to the moral order, and (7) the desire and planning for world peace.[3] The impact of civilizations upon each other and upon primitive and folk cultures and the dynamic interplay of all these factors are of utmost importance if we are to understand the processes of cultural change.

With or Against the Stream

What about the individual in the stream of culture? What chance does he have in conflict with what seem to be the inexorable laws and requirements of society? In this age of the mass-man is there any place left for the individual? It is true that culture is supra-individual, in the sense that people live and die, while institutions continue. The reigning monarchs of Great Britain die, but the "kingdom" remains. However, individuals not only live within a culture, but culture itself is lived by individuals. A megalomaniac paperhanger with an ethnocentric view of history can make a horrifying difference in the lives of millions of people, even as Hitler proved. Yet Hitler was not the whole of Nazism; he was primarily the focus and the clever manipulator of cultural forces nurtured by such symbolic figures as Bismarck and Nietzsche.

Man's ideal role in the world may be viewed quite differently by various cultures. In the classical Greco-Roman culture man was viewed by the philosophers as being in harmony with nature, while modern Western man often imagines himself in conflict with the status quo, forever combating obstacles to progress and pleasure. Despite the fierce fanaticism which may characterize a Mohammedan's outbursts, he is essentially resigned to a fatalistic view of life. The mystically inclined Oriental tries to find tranquillity of spirit in the midst of the endless cyclical successions of events. For many Africans the friendly, jovial appearance covers (or compensates for) a fearful apprehensiveness of inimical spirit forces. Generalizations of this kind hold true for many persons in their respective cultures, but just as there are contradictory persons in our society so there are in all societies—especially in the sprawling metropolitan regions, where people are physically close together but often culturally far apart.

Some societies such as the Northwest Pacific Coast Indians put a premium on the individual's capacity for conflict and competition, while others, such as the Pueblo Indians of the Southwest, discourage the "outstanding-personality" complex. For us "good personality" usually means personal magnetism, charm, the typical supersalesman breed, but for the Marshallese, the "good personality" is one who makes others happy by friendly helpfulness and charming wit. What, however, is characteristic of people on one level of behavior may not be typical of another. The ruthless businessman may be a very kind, doting father, while Mr. Milquetoast may make up for his humble office role by being a bear at home. We make much of rugged individualism in economic affairs, but we do not prize this quality in the church or country club.

The biologically endowed potentialities of the individual are quite definitely channeled or diverted by the culture. The visionary psychoneurotic with a religious bent was a venerated person in medieval society, while in our contemporary culture he is merely a pitiable fanatic. Such a person would have fared reasonably well as a Plains Indian, but would have found life much less pleasant as a Pueblo Indian. In one country of Central America a young girl of a Protestant family has had innumerable fantastic visions, but she has met with very little approval. On the other hand, had she been in a Roman Catholic household, she would have been highly acclaimed, even as others in that country have been, who have had much less spectacular "gifts."

Insanity would seem to be one area of experience which would be completely personal and individual, but even here the reciprocal relationship of the individual and the culture results in patterns of experience. Malayans are said to "run amok," while certain Indians of Canada engage in cannibalistic aggression. A common form of insanity in Southeast Asia is "weretigers," and in Siberia arctic hysteria is predominant. A proportionately high percentage of mental aberration among Sumatrans is described as "pig madness," while the lower classes in the United States suffer more from schizophrenia and the upper classes from manic depression.[4]

In small primitive societies each individual participates in a high percentage of the cultural activities. In our own complex civilized societies the role of the individual becomes increasingly more specialized. This permits a higher degree of creativeness on the part of gifted persons since they are not required by a low subsistence level to hunt, fish, farm, make their own clothes, or build their own houses. However, for the masses of the people anything beyond the narrow confines of factory and home is likely to be a symbolic experience, either religious or socio-political. Modern national states have proved to be very adept in creating a dreamworld participation by efficient mass-propaganda techniques.

The roles of individuals within a society may be well organized, and the goals of the culture may be well defined; but it is always easier to judge such matters in retrospect than in the contemporary scene. For this reason we tend to exaggerate the present lack of integration in our own society, for we see so many conflicting tendencies and opposing pressures. What we have not fully realized is that there are quite different patterns of behavior and standards of value for the privileged "400," the labor organizer, the race-track devotee, the professional politician, the bookish intellectual, the member of the National Association of Manufacturers, and the Midwest farmhand. Within each subculture there are quite well-defined roles and goals, and as long as these can be constructively developed within the ethos of the total culture, well and good. If not, society either distintegrates or goes through a convulsive revolution.

Cultures Exhibit Personality

In much the same manner as individuals and small societies show distinctive qualities, so larger societies—including whole nations—may be said to have definable characteristics. Kroeber [5] has described Burmese men as vain, lazy, pampered, gossipy, and when active, very often violently destructive. In contrast with this, the Siamese men are characterized as cheerful, gay, jolly, and easygoing. On the other hand, Burmese and Siamese women are much more industrious, dependable, and stable than the men of their respective countries. In contrast with the easygoing Thai, the Vietnamese are aggressive and bustling. Benedict [6] has described the Plains Indian temperament as Dionysian, that of the Pueblo Indians as Apollonian, the Dobuans as paranoid, and the Kwakiutl as megalomaniac. While such conclusions are certainly true of many dominant features of the respective cultures, one must not assume that there are no exceptions among the people of these societies. Furthermore, most societies are entirely too complex to be described by single dramatic terms. However, in all cultures there are certain aspects which seem to characterize the peoples' thinking and reactions. In the United States the focus of culture is technology and business; in ancient Greece it was philosophy and the arts; but the neighboring and conquering Romans were far more interested in government and armies. The Chinese not only prized education highly and honored the scholar, but they made a classical education the principal prerequisite for civil service and social prestige. Ancient Hebrew life was dominated by theocratic considerations, while medieval Europe was primarily ecclesiastical in outlook.[7]

The focus of a culture is not necessarily the most important characteristic, but it is the most talked about and the most conscious aspect of the people's corporate life. For the Todas of India the focus is certainly their religiously tended cattle, while for the Ponapeans the cultivation of huge sweet potatoes constitutes the central dynamic. In West Africa the cultural focus has been religious experience, and hence it is not difficult to understand how such a dominant interest in religion and a belief in the superiority of the conquerors' deities set the stage for large-scale conversion of these Negroes to the religious beliefs (at least in outward form) of the various countries to which they came in this hemisphere. The focus of the culture is not equivalent to the over-all ethos (the system of values), but it does contribute much to the tone.

On the basis of themes, foci, and ethos Kluckhohn has ingeniously described the culture of the United States as paying high tribute to physical comfort, bodily cleanliness, finance capitalism, and material generosity. It loves humor by exaggeration (in contrast with British understatement), has chivalrous and "pampering" regard for women, possesses strong faith in the rational, and insists on moralistic rationalization. There is a general optimism, a romantic individualism, a cult of the common man, a quest for pleasure, and a high valuation of change.[8]

Once we have had such matters pointed out to us, it is not too difficult to see the reasons for the characterizations, but arriving at valid analyses of a culture is not easy. To do a thorough piece of work we must undertake a painstaking survey of all aspects of the culture, but we can sometimes make valid observations by noting the premiums which cultures offer. The Chipewyans of northern Canada reserve their greatest praise and prestige for the successful hunter, while the Palauans of the South Pacific consider a rich man as having attained the pinnacle of social prominence. A measure of success in the United States can be judged by the number and make of cars which one owns, but in some countries distinction is proportionate to the number, fame, and beauty of one's mistresses. Among the Kekchi Indians of Guatemala distinction is not symbolized by having a better home, finer clothing, or more food, but by the ownership of more land, from which the resultant wealth makes it possible for a person to head up more fiestas (the leader of a fiesta pays a considerable part of the cost) and hence to obtain more public offices.

Cultures Change

Cultural processes include inertia (the stabilization and preservation of existing patterns) and momentum (growth and change), which expresses itself in additions, losses, and displacements. The changes which take place are often so slow as to be almost imperceptible. The development of the so-called "scientific attitude" in modern life was not accomplished in a day. Even at best our historical memories are short. Many people in our day are quite surprised to learn that there was a time when books were written by hand, and some have thought that the "artillery" mentioned in the Bible (1 Samuel 20:40) was nothing less than a heavy machine gun. A small child in a Sunday School class was asked to illustrate the story of the fall of Adam and Eve and their subsequent punishment. The child drew a picture of a car and three persons in it, with the explanation that this was "God driving Adam and Eve out of the Garden of Eden."

Changes may be so cumulative that we do not know at what

point they become complete modifications of the original pattern. On other occasions changes may be formalized by laws and regulations. In the late 1920's in Long Beach, California, there were strict laws against any male wearing a topless bathing suit. A few people tried to break the law, but they were heavily fined. However, one winter the city council passed a ruling permitting men to wear bathing trunks without tops. The next season a high percentage of the men wore trunks, and within two or three years' time the male who was seen with an "old-fashioned bathing suit" was regarded as queer. Sentiment for such a change had been building up for a long time; only the outward change seemed to be rapid.

Frequently we are quite unaware of culturally profound changes which consist not so much of new objects but of new ways of regarding old happenings. For many years only women were supposed to admit suffering from nervous breakdowns. Within the last ten years a nervous breakdown has become for some a symbol of the "dynamic executive." Sex is certainly not new in American life, but during the 1920's some profound changes took place in people's attitude toward sex. Repression gave place to expression, and a hush-hush subject became an everyday topic and a commercialized theme for the advertising world.

Changes tend to be most numerous at the focal point of the culture. In our own culture technological changes occur constantly, but political and religious changes are looked upon with great suspicion. Those features which change least in a culture are the implicit ones, phases of life which people take for granted. In American life they are such matters as a belief in God, abounding confidence in the common man, optimism about the future and the nature of man, and the prevention of cruelty to animals and children.

In a culture which is undergoing rapid change, not all aspects reflect the same acceleration or speed. For instance, television has become nationwide in relatively few years, while the use of contraceptives has met with resistance from a number of religious and ethnic groups.

The rate of change in any society can be accurately measured only by careful historical studies, but some valid general impressions can be gained by analyzing the tensions between the older and the younger generations. Do the elderly people constantly accuse young folks of a lack of discipline, breakdown in morals, and a wholesale abandonment of the old way of life? Do the younger people deeply resent parental domination, deride the "old-fogy ways" of their parents, and exhibit a rebellious antagonistic spirit? A certain amount of misunderstanding is to be expected between successive generations, for the older generation usually tries to hang on to privileges and prestige as long as it can, and a typical defense lies in denouncing the cultural heterodoxy of the newcomers. However, this more or less expected opposition can be discounted, and the more serious tensions can then be analyzed. Another approach to the problem of rapidity of transition is to study the discrepancies between real and ideal behavior. Where behavior theory and practice are so far separated as to produce numerous and serious frustrations, one can be sure that the culture is undergoing a period of rapid transition.

When a society cannot resolve the tensions of conflicting interests produced by too wide a gap in the participation (real or imagined) of all persons in a culture, a revolution is inevitable. However, the momentum which is necessary to carry through a full-scale socio-political revolution [9] is so great that almost inevitably it goes too far. For example, in the early days of the Communist state Russia instituted easy divorce and legal abortion, but these features have now been eliminated.

So great is the cultural "drag" that though a society may change the essential content of an action, the old form may be retained. The Afuge of the Lake Nyassa region [10] used to expose twins in a basket left at a road crossing. Now they carry the twins in a basket to the road and leave the basket but keep the twins. In Latin America it is sometimes almost a matter of life or death if one refuses to drink with a drunken braggart staggering down the road or swaggering in a saloon doorway. However, anyone who does not care to drink or who has religious scruples against doing so, can put his thumb over the end of the bottle and tip it to his lips. In this way he goes through the gesture and thus satisfies his insistent (and sometimes threatening) host. Daylight saving time is also a technique for changing the content (getting up earlier), while keeping the old form (the customary hours). On the other hand, one may preserve the old content while adopting new forms. The Buddhists in Japan have a Y.M.B.A. (Young Men's Buddhist Association), Sunday Schools, a Salvation Army, a Federation of Buddhist Sects, street and radio preaching, and even a Kingdom of God movement.[11] In Thailand the Buddhists have published the "Sayings of Buddha" in Thai (to compete with the New Testament), have organized flood relief (formerly unheard of), have attempted to introduce hymn singing, and in some instances have tried elaborate initiation ceremonies (to compete with Christian confirmation and baptism).

All Cultures Are in Debt

Even the simplest cultures are in debt to others for important contributions to their life. Composite cultures, such as our own, are monumental agglomerations, resulting largely from the process of borrowing. Our language is Germanic, but more than half of our vocabulary has been borrowed from non-Germanic sources. The Christian religion had an origin in Jewish culture, and the Bible was written in Hebrew, Aramaic, and Greek. Our philosophy came originally from Greece, our coffee from Ethiopia, our alphabet from Semitic languages, our tea from Asia, our "Irish" potatoes from South America, our tomatoes from Mexico, and the signs of the zodiac from ancient Mesopotamia, which also contributed many of our weights and measures. But we are not the only composite culture. Japan borrowed Buddhism, a religion developed in India, acquired a system of writing devised in China, and more recently added the industrialism of the Western World.

Borrowing does not imply that the "debtor" culture will use the new cultural feature in the same way as the "creditor" culture did. The Western World was not content to restrict gunpowder entirely to use in firecrackers when it could serve as a useful weapon for political expansion. Likewise, Europeans felt no compunction about dropping the religious connotations which tobacco had among many American Indians. Chickens were apparently domesticated in Southeast Asia with primary interest in their use in divination, but except for breaking "wishbones" (a practice not found in Southeast Asia) the chicken is kept by us only for its economic value.

Borrowing from one culture by another is essentially the action of individuals. In general, men are more likely to introduce innovations than are women, for men tend to have more outside contacts. Similarly, people who travel about are more likely to acquire new traits than the "stay-at-homes." In the ancient world the seafaring Athenians were conspicuously more alert to cultural borrowing than the isolated Spartans, who made a virtue of the status quo. It is not always necessary for the borrowers to travel; they may simply be alert to contacts which they have with travelers. Accordingly, one finds that throughout South America the people living along the seacoasts are generally more progressive in material culture and more liberal in thought (compare Guayaquil with Quito, Lima with Cuzco, and Barranquilla with Bogotá). Cultures which have already actively borrowed a great deal are also more likely to be interested in further borrowing. Such a practice develops a momentum which helps people adjust more and more readily to new features. However, borrowing is not blind, but selective. The Japanese exhibited a phenomenal capacity to acquire material aspects of our culture, but they almost totally rejected our ideas. On the other hand, the Filipinos have in many ways manifested greater readiness to assimilate some of our ideas about progress, democracy, and education, than to acquire our industrialization.[12]

The atmosphere in which borrowing takes place does not seem to influence the situation appreciably. Friendly traders or enemy raiders are all imitated. In fact, competition and strife seem only to add to the pressures for taking full advantage of technical improvements. German gas warfare was soon copied during World War I, and blitzkrieg tactics were rapidly imitated during World War II. Professional spies are incontrovertible evidence of planned "borrowing" from actual or potential enemies.

In describing changes which take place by the process of borrowing we need to distinguish between borrowing specific objects, processes, or ideas by relatively isolated groups of people, and the broad cultural exchange which takes place when two peoples live in continuous and relatively intimate contact. This last process is generally spoken of as acculturation.[13] In Yucatan, Mexico, a long period of acculturation has resulted in the assimilation by the Indian population of innumerable objects and attitudes of Hispanic culture. Because of the patterns of social prestige, economic advantages, and political dominance, the borrowing has been primarily by the Mayan Indians, but not without many changes. In large cities such as Merida people of Indian background go to Spanish schools, are usually well-instructed in the Roman Catholic religion, and may become mechanics, shopkeepers, day laborers, or servants. Some have distinguished themselves to such an extent as to be completely assimilated into the Spanish-speaking society, but many of the women continue to wear their distinctive dresses and to speak Mayan more than Spanish. In smaller towns such as Dzitas the Hispanic influence is much less in evidence, but there are some Indians who attempt to imitate the Spanish-speaking people in dress, language, religion, and business. In the still more remote villages Hispanic influence is very greatly reduced, and except for manufactured or processed articles such as cloth, lamps, kerosene, salt, and sugar, and the influence of the local school, the irregularly visiting priest, and the more recent political interests of some of the inhabitants, the life is predominantly Mayan. They may revere the cross, but not primarily as a symbol of Christianity, since for them it is a kind of magic object endowed with inherent spirit power, quite unrelated to the atonement of Christ. They may welcome the appearance of a Roman priest who makes sporadic visits through the country to baptize and perform marriages, but the local shaman is in most instances the actual religious leader.

In Cuba the Negro population has been steadily assimilated into the Hispanic culture in almost every aspect except religion. For the most part the Negro population is nominally Roman Catholic, but at heart it is largely devoted to the cult of the West African god Chango, worshiped as a "saint" (under the symbolism of Santa

Barbara) by all strata of Cuban society. Except for the activities of a very rapidly growing Protestant movement and a struggling reform movement among some of the Roman Catholic clergy, there would be a very good chance for *santería* [14] (the cult worship of Chango and related spirits) to become the nationally recognized religion of Cuba. Already many persons have affirmed that *santería* has more believing adherents in Cuba than does Roman Catholicism. Borrowing is thus not a one-way affair, for though the Negro population approximates the Hispanic culture in dress, language, formal education, politics, and occupations, the religion of these West Africans has made deep inroads into the non-Negro population.

Diffusion of Traits

In some instances cultural traits are borrowed over wide areas with the rapidity of an epidemic; at other times the process is slow and spotty. After discovery of the New World by Columbus the use of tobacco spread like wildfire, first to Europe, then to Africa, Asia, and the East Indies. In remote regions of Africa and New Guinea primitive tribes of people who had never seen a white man were found to have tobacco and to be convinced that their ancestors had smoked it from time immemorial—a striking proof of people's short memories and ethnocentric attitudes. Tobacco reached Alaskan Eskimos not from Indians to the south, but by way of Russian traders who brought it from Siberia. The Spanish had taken it to the Philippines and thence to China, from which point it had traveled north to Siberia. However, tobacco did not make much headway in the Andean areas of South America, for coca chewing was a well-entrenched competitor.

The chain-reaction borrowing of Indian corn (maize) had a somewhat similar history, though by no means as spectacular. It was grown by Indians in the Western Hemisphere all the way from Chile to North Dakota, but in Europe it was accepted primarily as feed for animals. In Africa it was widely adopted by many tribes and in some instances incorporated into religious rites. In some regions of Asia the cultivation of rice proved too competitive, but the raising of corn became firmly established in the East Indies.

The diffusion of cultural traits is not a steam-roller process. Each group selects or rejects depending largely upon whether they regard the new feature as valuable. The peyote cult [15] spread rapidly among the Plains Indians who had traditionally placed great emphasis upon personal religious experience, and whose tribal life by that time had rapidly disintegrated under the pressure of the expansion of white settlers. Both peyote and alcohol constituted a kind of escapism for which the cultural situation was ripe. However, the Pueblo Indians were not culturally conditioned for such interest in personal excesses and neither alcohol nor peyote made much headway. The cultural situation in pre-Columbian Mexico no doubt explains in some measure the popularity of "Virgin worship" among the Indians, whose own female fertility deities were certainly more attractive and more the focus of worship by the common people than were the male deities of war and conquest. Diffusion may, however, meet serious cultural obstacles. For example, Mohammedans have not been good prospects for life insurance salesmen, for insurance has seemed too much like gambling with Allah, and gambling is forbidden by the Koran.

Diffusion commonly flows along lines of relative prestige. In eastern Peru Spanish cultural traits are taken over by Shipibos, who in turn pass them on to the Cashibos. In the ancient world many of the cultural accomplishments of prestige-laden Egypt became a part of the culture of classical Greece, which after the time of Alexander the Great "re-exported" to all the eastern Mediterranean world many of its own prized possessions: language, philosophy, literature, and science. However, we must not conclude that just because ancient Egyptians and pre-Columbian Mayans built pyramids that the Indians of Mexico and Guatemala learned from the Egyptians. Superficially their constructions may seem similar, but fundamentally they are very different. The Egyptian pyramids were constructed as gigantic tombs, while the pyramids in Mexico and Guatemala were elevated altars. In Chichen Itza there are three successively built pyramids,[16] each one built over and including the previous. The high altar of the second pyramid, which may have served as a secret sanctuary of the third pyramid, contained a fierce-looking, life-sized, stone jaguar with awe-inspiring onyx spots and gleaming eyes.

In order to determine whether two similar objects are really the result of borrowing or of independent invention or development, one must consider (1) the number of similarities, (2) the relationship of the similarities, (3) the percentage of nonutilitarian features (which are least likely to appear independently, and hence, if they are present, point more clearly to a common origin), and (4) the possibility of communication. The pyramids in Egypt and Mexico do not meet these requirements, but the piston bellows for iron smelting which are found in Madagascar and Sumatra do give every evidence of having a common source. The similarities of construction, the identity of use, and the fact that Madagascar is populated by people whose language is related to that spoken by Sumatrans, all provide abundant evidence of diffusion, despite the thousands of miles of water which separate these two large islands. However, it is quite unnecessary for us to conclude that the use of coal as fuel by Indians in the Southwest United States was a trait borrowed from Europe (or elsewhere). The process is entirely too simple and the chances of independent discovery too great. New Caledonians have periods of five days which constitute a kind of ceremonial week, beginning with sacrifice and ending with dancing.[17] The ancient Mayans had a commercial week of five days, and some Guatemalan and southern Mexican tribes preserve a five-day rotation of markets. However, the unit of five (obviously derived from counting by fingers) is so common in various numerical systems that we would be entirely unjustified in concluding that the New Caledonian and Mayan "weeks" had a single origin. Similarly, accidental resemblances between languages are inevitable. One must not conclude that the Totonac language of Mexico is related to Zulu in South Africa simply because one finds the following kinds of "correspondences": (1) Zulu *luku* "of violent moving and tossing, as of anger" and Totonac *lukuj* "violent, easily angered," (2) Zulu *maka* "slap in the face with the open hand" and Totonac *makan* "hand," and (3) Zulu *tanu* "of separating the legs indecently" and Totonac *tanu'* "separate." On the other hand, the word *kitabu* "book" in Swahili (compare the Hebrew root *ktb* meaning "to write") is borrowed from Arabic. This fact, however, does not cause us to classify the Bantu language Swahili as a Semitic language, simply because of the many Arabic words which it possesses. We surely do not regard English, which is a Germanic language, as Semitic by virtue of its having borrowed directly or indirectly from Arabic such words as *algebra, alchemy, alcove, alcohol, alkali,* and *alfalfa.*

New Meanings for Old Traits

Reinterpretation of culture resulting from new forms or new content is an everyday practice. On Ponape present-day missionaries may be deluged with presents in the month of October, since earlier missionaries made gifts to the Ponapeans at Christmas time. Such gifts were interpreted purely in terms of the local system of gift exchange, which was not a matter of simultaneous giving but of advance giving, with the hope that the return gift would be even more valuable than the one previously presented. The Tongans [18] reinterpreted Christian teaching about Sunday observance in such a way as to include prohibitions against plucking flowers or breaking branches on that day. They also concluded that the church was so "taboo" that social gatherings should not be held in it and that rain water from the roof should not be collected or stored. Haitians have interpreted the Dahomean deity Legba as being San Antonio; Damballa, the West African rainbow serpent, has become San Patricio; and Erzulie, a water goddess, has become Mater Dolorosa, one aspect of the Virgin.[19]

The tendency to interpret anything new in terms of the old system of reference has resulted in a number of Roman Catholic traits coming over into some of the Protestant churches in Latin America: special gifts to the pastor in order that he may pray for the suppliant, flowers presented at the altar as a symbol of repentance (equivalent to candles), and fasting, not as a means of grace, but as an expression of penance. In Tetelcingo, Morelos, Mexico, the people have adapted pre-Catholic fertility rites to church saints. They bring together a male saint and a female virgin saint for a period of two months, after which they wait for nine months and then perform birth rites for this "virgin saint." A recent syncretistic development in the Micronesian Islands of Palau is the Modekgnei movement, with a reported membership of about 900 persons in 1952. Adherents are drawn from both Protestant and Catholic constituencies, and its avowed purpose is to unite the Palauan people under a code which is claimed to include the best of the old and the new, reinterpreted in a Palauan context. The primary emphases are preservation of old customs, maintenance of family and clan privileges, increasing the value of native money (much prized old beads and cylinders of glass and porcelain), application of a strict, puritanical moral code, and an interpretation of God, the Virgin, and Christ in terms of "father," "mother," and "uncle." The religious symbols are the fishing spear and the sacred wine cup, and the holy men are supposed to forecast the future, appease the lesser gods, and provide cures for sorcery, illness, and sterility.

Such instances of syncretism reflect the universal tendency to reinterpretation, in which we give new meaning to old traits or attach old meanings to new events.

Something New under the Sun

Life is not merely borrowing traits from neighbors or giving new meanings to age-encrusted objects or actions. We must also reckon with inventions and discoveries, but the stories of many of these developments have been lost in history, e.g. the discovery of fire making, the wheel for use in transportation, the balance, domestication of the dog, development of corn, pottery making, iron smelting, and tattooing. Because of the numerous techniques for making fire, such as bow and drill, flint and steel, and fire piston, we probably must reckon with several distinct inventions at different places and times. The same is probably true of the balance and pottery. Even such a complex accomplishment as the invention of zero has occurred no less than three times. The Greeks and Romans were seriously hampered without a symbol to represent zero, "the significant absence of something." The Hindus, however, did invent zero some twelve or fifteen hundred years ago. The Mayans of

Yucatan also employed zero and positions to represent numerical values, but the Mayan accomplishment antedates the Hindu discovery by several hundred years. Recent archeological discoveries point to the fact that the Semitic Neo-Babylonians also developed zero several centuries before the Mayans ever thought of it. All of these inventions of numerical placement and zero were quite independent, despite their complexity.[20]

A high percentage of so-called inventions consist of elaborations and new interpretations. The steamboat was not solely the brainchild of Robert Fulton. A number of other people had preceded him with various and ingenious designs, including one with a kind of mechanical webfoot for power. Fulton, however, profited from others' failures and partial successes and made a boat which would not only run but which would be economically feasible, and hence acceptable to the culture. Accordingly, he gets the credit. Many inventors and discoverers have paid a rather high price for having been ahead of their culture. Copernicus and Galileo were both fiercely denounced, and the monk Mendel died in complete obscurity. His fundamental laws of genetics, published in 1866, went entirely unnoticed until the end of the century, by which time the evolutionary rage had settled down to more serious analysis and evaluation.

Some inventions are only adaptations of ideas to new circumstances. Sequoya, a Cherokee Indian, also known as John Guest, learned about reading and writing, but he never learned English. However, he made up a number of symbols and adapted others, borrowing from various alphabets, of which some letters were written correctly and others as though they were seen backwards in some store window. All these symbols were organized into a syllabary for his own Cherokee language. Its use spread rapidly, and not only were the Christian Scriptures and hymnbooks published, but also periodicals and several volumes on law and customs. Even today there are several hundred Cherokees who read and write Sequoya's alphabet.

From the vantage point of a backward look, invention often seems to be born of necessity; but necessity is not the mother, only the doting aunt of invention. The true arch (in contrast with the corbeled arch) was known in Ur of the Chaldees as early as 3000 B.C., but its potentialities were not realized. Only when the Romans took over the arch from the Etruscans and began to exploit its uses in large buildings did people become aware of its structural value. In twentieth-century America we regard the automobile as a necessity, but its invention was rather a novelty and its first use was largely for sport. The airplane was not invented as a direct response to a necessity to fly, but rather because of a desire to do so. By now the car is a cultural "necessity" and horses are largely retained for sport. Similarly the bow and arrow gave way to the more destructive gun, but they have stayed on as instruments of recreation.

For the most part changes in culture represent additions, but there may also be losses, especially of some ancient skills whose secret is buried with those who possessed them. The startling megalithic fortresses of the Andes exhibit a skill of stone construction with which present-day Quechuas are unfamiliar. The huge stone idols on the shores of Easter Island are mute reminders of a culture which is quite forgotten by modern inhabitants. The elaborate rituals and beliefs of pre-Columbian Mayans are hinted at in some of the ancient codices and can be reconstructed in part from contemporary customs, but much of this culture was lost in the deliberate attempt by early Spanish ecclesiastics to stamp out every vestige of the conquered culture.

Well-entrenched Resistance

Riots in Greece over the translation of the New Testament into modern Greek and the recent burning of the *Revised Standard Version* by well-intentioned zealots (a heartening improvement on the former practice of burning the translators) are convincing evidence that cultural inertia is firmly entrenched in religion. But what is true of religion is also true of other aspects of culture. Being able to amass a big bank account, freedom from abuse because of one's skin color, and the distinction of having a low number on one's auto license plate can be ends equally prized and violently defended. The inertia of long-established habits, a sense of belonging in familiar surroundings, and the almost pathetic degree to which we imitate others (keeping up with the Joneses) all conspire to make most of us culturally right-wingers. We know perfectly well that English spelling is a chaotic, inefficient mess, resulting in endless time wasted in learning to read and in consulting dictionaries in order to spell in the conventional way. Nevertheless, each adult generation seems quite willing to condemn succeeding generations to the same unjustifiable waste of human energy, simply because they are in a comfortable rut of cultural laziness. We know perfectly well that dozens, gross, inches, feet, yards, miles, bushels, acres, pints, quarts, and gallons are all clumsy ways of measuring distance and volume, and yet most people shy away from the metric system as though it were some foreign disease.

Knowing our own traditionalism (except in such matters as late-model cars, radios, football rules, and 3-D), we should not be so much inclined to denounce primitive peoples for lack of progressiveness. Moreover, other peoples may have very valid reasons for their resistance to change. Among the Conob Indians of Guatemala there has been a long and persistent opposition to reading. This is not, however, simply a part of the total pattern of resistance to Hispanic culture, but arises from bitter experience during the days of General Barrios. Anyone who learned to read in those days was likely to be appointed as mayor of the local community. This meant that he was made responsible for carrying out all government edicts. Any mayor's failure to comply with government demands not infrequently resulted in his being shot to death in front of the people. It is no wonder that a deep-seated prejudice arose against "book-learning."

Our cultural attitudes become so deeply rooted that we often excuse or explain behavior as being "in the blood." It most certainly is not in the blood, but in the very fabric of our thought. Lutherans, who protested so magnificently for the freedom of conscience against the tyranny of ecclesiasticism, were still "the children of their age" when they persecuted the Anabaptists by fire and sword. The Church of England denounced the papacy, but took a papal attitude toward the "Methodist heresy," which in turn was not sympathetic to the evangelistic outbursts of the Nazarene church movement. Long-practiced habits of thought and action combine with vested interests to make us emotionally rebellious toward change. Social pressures may succeed in imposing a measure of accommodation, for though the average Mohammedan Indonesian first directs his prayers to Allah, in the event of a prolonged crisis he implores the *dewata*, the older gods of Hinduism. Finally, in extreme necessity, the indigenous pre-Hindu deities are appeased through well-known but officially ignored medicine men. It is almost pathetic to hear a tradition-bound old Ifugao in northern Luzon complain of the endless, impoverishing sacrifices required by his father's way of life. "We are old," he says, "and we were born in this. The young may and should change, but even though our beliefs are burdensome, all we ask is to be left alone."

Growth and Death

Cultures resemble organisms in that they are either growing or dying—they do not remain static. Growth occurs by the infusion of outside influences or by the steady accumulation of traits arising from individual differences of behavior. Since no two people act precisely alike (either as a result of environment or heredity), it is only logical that other things being equal (which they seldom are), the greater the size of the group the greater the variation in behavior. Where there are specialists, such as priests, prophets, blacksmiths, musicians, sculptors, or philosophers, the very diversity tends to prod the society into cultural momentum. However, societies may suffer the creeping paralysis of cultural morbidity, brought on by such factors as conflicts of rival classes, loss of vitality from pestilence, disease, wars, and malnutrition, and subjugation by enemy powers, who may destroy the dynamic spark through brutal enslavement. Within a few years many proud Plains Indians became drunkards and parasites of frontier communities, living in pathetic indifference and purposelessness. The former focus of life—namely, prestige through valor in fighting—had been destroyed. The average semi-nomadic hunting and warring Indian could not adjust himself to an agricultural economy based on money values. Only now, after about two generations, are young Indians adjusting themselves to American patterns of life and taking places of leadership in keeping with their inherent capacities. The Inca empire was methodically enslaved by Spanish overlords who dealt a death blow to the highly centralized government and killed by forced labor and white men's diseases fully two-thirds of the indigenous population. Under such conditions of cruel serfdom the Indians retreated culturally and found escape as well as defense in drunkenness, debauchery, irresponsibility, and sullenness. Extreme alcoholism, which is generally in direct proportion to the level of anxiety and frustration, can be a rather accurate index of cultural morbidity, if not of the whole society, at least of the class in question. In contrast with the Quechuas of Peru, Bolivia, and Ecuador, the San Blas Indians of Panama exhibit considerable dynamic, for they have their own chiefs, police system, co-operative work, organized village life, and religious ceremonies. They are alert to new things: literacy in their own language, the use of radios, Panamian politics, and medicines such as sulfa drugs and penicillin. It is true that the San Blas men drink at fiestas, but their wives stay sober in order to see to it that they do not fight. Their drinking has the quality of social hilarity and not of morose escapism.

The people of Micronesia have suffered more or less from cultural morbidity for two or three generations. New diseases (especially smallpox and venereal diseases), inadequate nutrition, and loss of morale (due to the vagaries of Spanish, German, and then Japanese administrators) all resulted in lower birth rates and higher death rates. The last few years have witnessed a marked change: populations are increasing, new leadership is coming to the front, and the momentum of life is quickened, directly and indirectly as the result of World War II.

Profound dislocations may occur in societies without one being fully aware of what is happening. The Belgian government has trained a number of Congolese young men to be agricultural supervisors. They not only advise the people concerning what and how to plant, but see to it that each man tends his allotted acreage (or that he has his wives hoe it for him). Such officially backed power makes the young agriculturalist even more important in some ways than the chiefs. In many crucial issues the Belgian government finds it necessary to back the young agriculturalist, even at the risk of incurring the deep hatred of some jealous chief. Little by little power over the economic life makes inroads on the social structure, and the government-educated Africans become a new elite, a new center of influence, and a new focus of prestige. The older chieftainship, based on clan ties or heroic leadership, succumbs to the more impersonal power of foreign-sponsored petty officialdom.

If cultures are to be changed effectively without boomeranging dislocations, functional substitutes are essential.[21] Anthropologists in Papua succeeded in introducing a pig instead of a human body in a fertility rite and a football to replace a spear in working off hostilities between embittered factions in a tribe.[22] A missionary in Congo was faced with the problem of rival clans who consistently and persistently split on all matters of church government. The solution to this age-old problem was not to be found in simply denouncing the practice. The missionary arranged for the students in the school to be organized into dormitories, in which members of each clan were represented. Each dormitory functioned and was recognized as a unit in athletic contests, academic honors, and general deportment. New associations brought new loyalties, and with these came a realization that differences of opinion about church matters should not be resolved by blind adherence to clan membership.

Is There Progress?

A generation ago the question "Is there Progress?" would have been regarded by many as unabashed heresy and stupidity. However, the shock-treatment experience of two world wars, the insidious spread of totalitarianism, the revival of slavery in the form of forced labor, and the horrifying power of the propaganda lie, now leave serious doubts. The god of Progress has been worshiped alike by crass materialists, visionary intellectuals, and the incurably optimistic devotees of "bigger and better" whatever-it-is. However, Progress is still a very young "deity," born in an age of great material achievement and swaddled in the hypotheses of social evolution.

Most societies look back to a Golden Age, which may reflect the nostalgia of older people for a time when they enjoyed somewhat greater prestige or may be the dream fulfullment of an ethnocentric pride.[23] In view of the serious maladjustments in modern life, dire threats to personal liberty, and the hideous fear of atomic destruction, are we justified in seeing any substantial progress in human culture?

A careful appraisal of developments within the last five thousand years (the period for which we have relatively reliable archeological and historical evidence for several areas of the world) cannot fail to reveal certain significant developments.

In the matter of health there is less superstition and magic and more use of medicines and hygiene. The witch doctor and the shaman are giving way to the physician and the psychiatrist. Though there are still millions who read horoscopes and accordingly make foolish judgments, plagues are no longer left to destroy the people while diviners seek supernatural intervention by watching the flight of birds or inspecting livers.

Psychologically abnormal people addicted to visions and trances are more and more regarded as socially useless or harmful, and not as fit persons to lead others in religious worship or to guide them in important decisions. However, these same psychologically or physically handicapped people are not so likely to be exposed to die on bleak hillsides or in vermin-infested jails. They are increasingly the object of more scientific care, despite the limited contribution which they may be able to make to the corporate life.

There is a growing consciousness that in judging the degree of guilt of any person one must reckon not only with the deed but with the intention. That is to say, accidental manslaughter is not first-degree murder. No longer is it such a general practice to execute innocent relatives along with guilty offenders. Except in the now famous "Peoples' Courts" guilt is determined on the basis of laws which are not subject to the whims and passions of the moment, but are defined on the basis of what people regard as eternally valid principles of equity. Moreover, justice and equity are supposed to embrace all mankind, not just one's own tribe or nation. These advances in human justice have been substantial, even though in some quarters they may be threatened, and in others they are only poorly developed or little appreciated.

Religious practices emphasize less and less the purely physical aspects of the body. Clitorectomy, mummification, head-hunting, ritual prostitution, cannibalism, burial of widows, and scarification all figure less in the religions of the world.

Technology, despite its threat of total destruction, has nevertheless eased a multitude of human burdens, relieved an immeasurable amount of suffering, and made possible (though not actual) an enrichment of life unparalleled in history.

These positive cultural gains must not be overlooked, even though they do not signify that the egocentric nature of man has appreciably changed. Perhaps it is only more socially refined. Man's incredible capacity for self-deception and self-centered activity leaves the Biblical appraisal of man as true as it ever was.

10

NEW SOLUTIONS TO OLD PROBLEMS

As the result of only about fifteen years of missionary work in one tribe of Latin America there are more than 3,000 Indians who are no longer the victims of drunken debauchery, paralyzing fear of black magic, and the meaningless jumble of pagan and semi-Christian beliefs. Despite a very limited missionary staff (or perhaps because of it) these Indians have shown a remarkable sense of responsibility for the church and the community. In another tribe not far from this region, missionary work has been undertaken by equally devout persons for more than twice this period but with meager to negligible results. The latter missionaries have had more money to spend, more personnel to invest, and a generally more sympathetic environment. Nevertheless, instead of the dynamic, contagious Christian spirit which characterizes the first group of Christians, the latter are jealous of one another, suspicious of missionary leadership, and indifferent to the church.

We must not assume that the results of missionary work can always be easily predicted by the application of neat formulae, for the work of the Spirit of God is not controlled by or directly proportionate to our formulations of proper missionary principles and practices. However, a close examination of successful missionary work inevitably reveals the correspondingly effective manner in which the missionaries were able to identify themselves with the people—"to be all things to all men"—and to communicate their message in terms which have meaning for the lives of the people. Conversely, where missionary work has been singularly unsuccessful, one will always find a failure to resolve the missionary's two great problems: identification and communication. Successful missionary work should not be judged simply as a question of the number of converts, but of an integrated, self-propagating church, adjusted to the problems and needs of the surrounding culture.

A Pagan Looks at Missionary Work

To the average "pagan" the Christian message is both puzzling and disconcerting. The insistence upon uniting religion and morality often seems weird. How can spirits, who are themselves unpredictably mischievous, be concerned with ethical behavior? To the Quechua Indian who declared, "Our gods are all drunkards and so are we," the missionary's talk about sobriety as a part of religion seems foolishness. Furthermore, most people argue, "Religion is a specialty —a job for priests, shamen, sorcerers, and seers. It is not for me, and certainly can have no claim upon all of life." Many Navajos abhor the idea of worshiping a dead man who rose again and who offers to live in their hearts by means of His Spirit (i.e. his ghost—as they understand it). Their almost pathological fear of the spirits of the dead makes the preaching of the resurrection more than simply "a stumbling block" or "foolishness." In the eyes of many Africans the God of Christianity is either cheap or stupid, for he requires no continual sacrifices. How can one establish an advantage in bargaining without putting God under obligation by the requisite offerings of meal and blood and the careful recital of secret words? A missionary's denunciations against smoking tobacco seem almost blasphemous to the man who thinks that the acrid smell of dense tobacco smoke induces more perfect communion with his god.

Nevertheless, it is not primarily the message but the messenger of Christianity that provides the greatest problems for the average non-Christian. Fortunately, the missionary who shouts at "natives" as he would at a dog and who by threatening corporal punishment forces the people to build chapels and to till the soil is the exception to the rule; but those well-intentioned victims of a superiority complex who exude a holier-than-thou condescension full of paternalistic piety still delude themselves into thinking that their task is to work *for* people rather than *with* them. Their unsuspected self-righteousness and their identification of Western culture with Christianity keeps them from spiritual comradeship. They remain foreign, not only in the outward phases of race and culture, but also in the inward emotional responses. Gross insensitiveness in one mission resulted in a program for the training of "native leadership" which requires the young preachers to be separated from their families for almost eleven out of twelve months over a period of nearly eight years, during which time they are to prove their spirituality by abject submission to authority as evidenced in their doing drudge work.

A missionary's failure to identify himself with the people, not in sympathy, but in empathy, is sometimes made more acute by reluctance, inability, or callousness to the proper use of the people's language. Communication is essentially a two-way experience; one must understand before he can talk, one must learn before he can teach. The proper use of language is not only the key to open the hearts of non-Christians, but it can also help to open the culture-closed heart of a missionary to the unsuspected needs and aspirations of the people.

The same type of mentality which complains, "These people can never form an indigenous church, for there is not one of them who can set a table correctly!" is also likely to favor the mission-barrel psychology, which appeals to the opportunist hanger-on and parasite who exists in any community but rarely impresses the thoughtful non-Christian as being anything other than cheap propaganda. "Can't these missionaries make a living at home? Is that why they have come here?" a bright young African asked in all sincerity, for he had suspected that the inferior qualities which he had noted in some would make them quite unacceptable as government officials or businessmen. Insult was added to injury when an enterprising Argentinian evangelist saw an article written by a missionary for United States consumption. The missionary, who had been a self-invited, nonpaying guest on an evangelistic tour, arranged to have his own picture taken as though he were preaching but with a caption identifying the musically talented evangelist "Native playing the organ."

The competitive spirit which exists between some missions (an unhappy reflection of back-home bitterness) has prompted many non-Christians to ask with puzzled scorn, "Why are there so many different churches, but only one Christ?"

Not a few students in mission schools have suspected that they were being educated for merely second-class jobs and that no matter how gifted they might be, their color of skin, protruding lips, or slanted eyes would somehow prevent them from advancing from a state of perpetual tutelage. Such suspicions are often well founded, as was evidenced by the complete shock and utter consternation which a missionary expressed at the very suggestion that further education of a particularly gifted Filipino might "qualify him to direct the mission some day." Nevertheless, another mission (the Presbyterian U. S. A.) has taken just such a step in appointing a Filipino as director for their work in the Philippines, Thailand, and Indonesia. It is high time that we rid ourselves of the "Foreign Mission" complex, in which there is special virtue in being foreign.

In Defense of Missionaries

"These men who have turned the world upside down have come here also!" cried the rabble in Thessalonica as they denounced Paul and Silas before the local authorities. From that day to this missionaries have been committed to the task of turning the world upside down, and in large measure they have done a constructive piece of work. Trial by ordeal of poison, haunting fears of black magic, cruel mutilations in the name of religion, pathetic squalor resulting from caste disabilities, widespread ignorance, legal and social disabilities of women, and unrelieved suffering of body and spirit have all been combated with the most selfless devotion that the world has ever found in any group of people. The British government was quite helpless to deal with the "Criminal Tribes" of Central India, and no indigenous group or institution would raise a hand to change such an age-old social plague. However, the Salvation Army missionaries were willing to enter this area, learn the language of the people, establish industrial and agricultural schools, minister to their bodily needs, and instruct them in the Christian faith. The transformation of the individuals and of the society was such that the official designation of "Criminal Tribes" was rightly dropped. Of course, missionaries have made mistakes, but we are not justified in blaming them for not having had the knowledge which is available only today as the result of long research by anthropologists, who have themselves made abundant use of missionaries' experience, research, and publications.

Some missionaries have been so "conscience-stricken" about past failures, have so dreaded any semblance of a superiority complex, and have so sincerely sought vital contacts with people, that they have not fully appreciated the revolutionary character of their ministry. Their desire to share with others has kept them from perceiving clearly the significance of Jesus' words, "I have not come to bring peace, but a sword. For I have come to set a man against his father, and a daughter against her mother, and a daughter-in-law against her mother-in-law. . . . He who loves father or mother more than me is not worthy of me . . ." (Matthew 10:34–37a, R.S.V.). One missionary was so appalled by the social consequences of a decision for Jesus Christ in the Mohammedan world that he said quite frankly that if a young lady in his school declared her intention to become a Christian he would plead with her not to do so. But missionary work is not truly Christian unless it implies a radical change, both for the individual and the society. Valenciano, a Guambiano Indian of southern Colombia, evidenced the redeeming love of God in the midst of a society in ferment by saying, "Before I became a true believer no one hated me, but now there is no one who wants to see me, for they claim that I am bad because I follow Jesus Christ, who I know will never fail me. Nevertheless, I shall not let my heart feel hatred for anyone."

It is little wonder that many missionaries have been unsympathetic with some anthropologists, who were perfectly willing to study the tensions and serious maladjustments in primitive societies but who would not raise a finger to change such situations—all in the name of supposed neutrality and objectivity. Many of the mistakes made by missionaries have been the result of wrong leads given by early anthropologists who grievously oversimplified the structure of aboriginal cultures by describing the various phases of culture as

quite isolated compartments and by failing to take into account the
constant interaction of the material, social, religious, linguistic, and
esthetic aspects. Some missionaries have been slow to profit from the
findings of present-day anthropology, but many are increasingly
aware of their basic task, namely, to place God (in terms of His will
and plan) at the center of each cultural institution and to make
Jesus Christ the absolute Lord of life. Some mistakes have arisen out
of a false time perspective, for missionaries did not realize that it
took some four centuries to evangelize the Belgians, three centuries
for the Frisians, and at least an equally long time for Germany, despite the great prestige of Christianity as a political and religious
force in Western Europe.[1] However, present-day theological developments are being reinforced by sound anthropological findings,
and we are becoming increasingly aware that salvation is not just
for the "soul" but for the whole man, and that the church is the
"salt" and the "light" of the earth, not a temporal or spiritual
policeman.

Christendom Is Not Christianity

How else was a young Liberian preacher to indicate the prestige
which came from his new appointment as an "ordained preacher" if
he did not insist on speaking in English and using an interpreter
(even though talking to his own tribesmen)? This was in his mind
an inseparable part of his new position. His reactions were no different from those other Liberians who consider a Prince Albert worn
in a stifling hot, tin-roofed church as being a necessary part of the
religious equipment of Christian worship. Bathing frequently,
brushing one's teeth, abstaining from beer, tobacco, and betel nut,
and refusing to eat clams or oysters have all been preached by various missionaries as symbols of the "new life in Christ Jesus."

The missionary's confusion of Christendom with Christianity, of
Western culture with the gospel of Jesus Christ, has been the basis
of tragic misunderstanding and frustrating endeavor. White supremacy and superiority have been assumed by many and even
defended as Biblical. It has been hard for some to see why their
own culture should not be carted bag and baggage to every part of

the world and there imitated by devoted adherents of *the* way of life. We are little prepared to appreciate the cultural sensitivity of the Cherente chief who wished to visit some relatives living among the Chavantes, a tribe which had sworn perpetual vengeance on the white man and anyone who associated with him. He lived alone in the jungles of Brazil for one year in order to rid himself of any body odor acquired through association with the white man or his way of life.

It has been hard for some missionaries to understand why Roman Catholics in Latin America have not responded with exuberant enthusiasm to some of the religious "boogie-woogie" and cheap slapstick promotion advanced as new techniques in mass evangelism. Is it really necessary to have a ring and a veil to solemnize a Christian wedding in Southeast Asia? Is a corpse in a stretched-out position any more spiritual or better prepared for the trump of God than one buried in a hunched-over, fetal position? Are churches more orthodox because the buildings resemble New England chapels or Gothic cathedrals?

However, the confusion of Western culture and Christianity is not primarily in the realm of Mother Hubbard clothing, the hymn-collection-sermon order of worship, or our classification of sins (with sex near the top). Our more serious mistakes are subtle and less easily eradicated. Our incurably individualistic temperaments make us half blind to people as a part of a society. Collectivism in any form becomes for some a mark of Satan. Though we may deny it in theory, yet we show by word and act that we are convinced that material possessions mark the successful man—even the spiritual Christian. Some missionaries even judge the devotion and spirituality of their colleagues by the degree to which "God blesses their work by sending in funds," and some preach tithing on the basis of the greater prosperity which it will bring the tither.

Pragmatism is so much the watchword of truth that we offer to prove the validity of our religion purely by its social and personal values, rather than proclaim the uniqueness of its message with a realism characteristic of the Bible. Relativism has had a healthy effect in blasting into bits our unwholesome ethnocentric pride, but it is also responsible in large measure for much of the cultural fatigue in Western Europe. Rightly suspicious that their formulations of theological truth were not absolute, many have tended to deny the absoluteness of God and of His design in the world. The resultant pathetic longing for absolute moorings in a cultural storm has prompted many to embrace the absolutism of statism in any one of its various forms. But the missionary's message must not be formulated as "Since this is good for you, it must be true," but rather, "This is true, and therefore it is good."

The debilitating departmentalization of Western culture insidiously threatens to make some missionaries satisfied with producing emotional Christians who are intellectually still pagans. This type of cultural hybrid is not only reproductively sterile, but what is worse, has become one of the principal (though rarely acknowledged) reasons for mounting suspicion among foreign peoples, who resolutely reject imperialism, whether political, economic, or socioreligious.

The fact that missionaries frequently live in what to the foreigner's eyes is nothing less than a mansion, wear clothes incomparably superior to what those around them can afford, and eat not only strange but expensive, imported food might seem to constitute a major obstacle to the missionaries' contact with the people; yet the gulf of material possessions seems to be relatively unimportant unless, as is too often the case, it only symbolizes or reinforces a spiritual separation, often described as a "mission compound psychology." There are the relatively rich and the poor in all societies, and people do not hate the rich solely because of their riches, but because of the real or imagined contempt of the rich for the poor. Identification with the people is not attained by wearing a breechcloth, eating manioc and termites, or dwelling in a grass hut; what really counts is having a mind which can understand, hands which join with others in common tasks, and a heart which responds to others' joys and sorrows.

Wood, Hay, and Stubble

Failure to appreciate fully the anthropological problems in any cultural situation can result in consecrated endeavor being dissipated in fruitless undertakings. Church membership is an important concern of any missionary, but when it is magnified out of proper proportion and when in the people's minds it becomes the equivalent of initiation into some secret society, then church membership becomes an end in itself and is no longer the beginning of ever-increasing Christian fellowship and service. Baptism is too often viewed as simply a reward for keeping a certain number of taboos during a prescribed period, after which the new member may be less concerned with sin and righteousness than with keeping his name on the church roll, as a guarantee of mission benefits on earth and eternal rewards after death.

The missionary who becomes embroiled in settling the multitude of village quarrels and church-member controversies will soon discover that his commission to "sow the seed" has degenerated into "judging the would-be saints." Furthermore, failure to commit such problems to local elders and deacons robs the church of the very experience which it must have if it is to grow in spiritual strength and understanding.

Elaborate institutions demanding heavy financial commitments, rigid systems of priority in personnel (which tend to prejudge the movement of the Spirit of God for years to come), and the vested interests which many times grow up around missionaries' own pet projects or which reflect arbitrary regional divisions of responsibility, have resulted in startling lack of mobility in the missionary enterprise.[2] In the present stage of unprecedented historical and cultural fluidity and change, such immobility may result in the complete ossification of a dying institution, spelling doom to the present system of Christian missions.

The well-intentioned but needless destruction of valid constructive features of some cultures has undermined the very society which missionaries have sought to aid. Missionaries are not solely responsible, but they have had a share in such developments as the breakdown of clan loyalties (by denouncing respect for ancestors), lessening of community responsibility (by substituting mission authority for that of the tribal elders), personality disintegration (by detribalizing young people, that is, by weaning them away from old loyalties without giving them a corresponding sense of belonging to something else), and diminution of artistic skills and esthetic tastes of the people (by apparent wholesale condemnation of all sculpture, music, and folk dancing as "bad," "immoral," or "debased").

The Mission and the Indigenous Church

The more than 800 "native denominations" in South Africa are a soul-searching evidence of widespread failures, which cannot be attributed merely to the South Africans' instinct for demagoguery and propensity for beer drinking and adultery. These denominations, with bizarre rites, gaudy costumes, and outlandish names (such as the Holy Castor Oil Church), reflect not only the outgrowth of a desire for leadership opportunities and the welter of local, tribal, and clan loyalties, but most important of all a longing for close fellowship and comradeship, for which Africans have a remarkable capacity. In much of African religious life the clan is in a sense more important than God, so it is little wonder that purely theological concepts have been relatively powerless to hold people together. A measure of unity could only have been achieved by racially sympathetic white churches and by a missionary leadership with an extraordinary gift for genuine friendship.

Equally disastrous for church-mission relationships is the lack of a constructive program, whereby new converts, whose consciences have been rendered sensitive to social and economic injustices, can find vital ways in which to express their deep spiritual convictions. Not a few of the Christian leaders of China embraced Communism because it seemed to offer them a practical means of putting into action what they believed in theory. The same is true of many young people in South India. Foreign missionaries are prevented by their immigrant status from taking an active part in colonial or national politics, but they are not prevented from helping Christians put into practice on a local level a program of social and economic transformation (for example, recreational halls, nurseries, reclaimed land, and improved water supply) as an outworking of an inner change of heart and life.

The tendency for new converts to look constantly to the mission (from which come benefits of education, employment, and prestige) rather than to the indigenous church poses a whole series of unfortunate developments, in which not the least is the tendency for politically adroit persons to play the mission off against the indigenous church. This situation is further aggravated by the false idea (strongly nurtured in some quarters) that the receipt of foreign funds is an inevitable sign of inferior status. There are many people who find it hard to adjust to a concept of "fraternal aid" without strings attached. However, within the world-wide ministry of the church it should not be necessary to maintain that "he who pays the piper must call the tunes." The missionary who claims that "the natives don't want leadership" is badly disillusioned by clever people who have played on egoistic interests to obtain their own ends. It is true, however, that many people refuse leadership if it is only nominal and not real. Nevertheless, people cannot be trained in leadership without making decisions (even wrong ones) and having to take the full consequences of such decisions.

None Righteous

The person who imagines that all "native" believers are true Christians will be as much disillusioned as the one who regards all missionaries as "saints." Realistic accounting of the people and problems in our own home churches should prevent romanticizing upon the virtues of primitives. The Marshallese churches have an enviable record of faithfulness and an official standard which is exceptionally high and puritanical, but this does not prevent many from openly condemning immorality while secretly condoning it—a not unfamiliar tendency in American church life as well. In some regions jealousy and competition for prestige and position may be as intense as the morals are loose, and tithing may be simply an opportunity of displaying the biggest heap of peanuts, corn, or sweet potatoes. Those who denounce racial prejudice in missionaries may be equally guilty themselves. Not infrequently Hindus have lashed out unmercifully against social disabilities imposed on them by whites, but they in turn have manifested smug contempt for Negroes, whose rights they may paternalistically defend. People are people; and skin color, flat noses, or high cheekbones make them inherently no worse and no better.

Bridges and Chasms

Shall the missionary build an intellectual or spiritual bridge so that the prospective convert may more easily cross, or should he be equally concerned with describing the chasm which divides Christianity from other religions? The so-called "common ground" is fundamentally an illusion. To our Western way of thinking the personality endowed with dynamic power and realism is a perfectly understandable ideal, but the Buddhists' starting point is the non-existence of personality and the need for obliterating the deceptive appearances of what we call personal human life. In 1 John 2:17 "the world passeth away, and the lust thereof," one may find a parallel to the Buddhist belief in the transiency of all matter, but the latter part of the same verse ("but he that doeth the will of God abideth for ever") separates one from Buddhism by ideological light years. Anyone who has discussed Christianity with a Mohammedan has discovered many initial points of contact, but nothing on which one can build a Christian structure; for regardless of the theme (whether the sovereignty of God, the historicity of Jesus, or the method of revelation) fifteen minutes of sincere discussion results in opinions being poles apart. The fact that the Chinese believe in a "high god" does not inevitably lead to belief in a God who has personal qualities. However, despite the failure to find "common ground," the introductory use of points of contact is essential and valuable, even as Paul found it meaningful to refer to "the Unknown God" of the Athenians (Acts 17:23). The Mohammedans' interest in the Gospel of Matthew (since it begins with Abraham), the Valiente Indians' vague memories about *Ngöbö* (the benevolent Creator), the Tzeltal Indians' love for religious instruction in the form of songs, the Hindu intellectuals' insatiable interest in philosophy, and the Africans' love of proverbs can all be points of contact useful in winning a sympathetic hearing for the gospel of Jesus Christ. However, the valid common starting points ("points of contact" in contrast with "common ground") are the human needs shared by all: mental and physical health, fulfillment of hopes and aspirations, satisfactory training of one's children, security for the future, relief from family tensions, personal conflicts and moral failures, and a faith as to the ultimate meaning of life. In these matters all mankind finds a common starting point, even though the cultural expressions may vary. But it is here, at the heart of human need, that one becomes more fully aware of the real significance of the divine plan which calls not only for a message but also for a Man, the inevitable corollary of an incarnational religion.

New Solutions

Present-day missionaries are for the most part quite aware of the fact that cultural traits do not all have the same value. While customs such as idol worship, caste, color bar, and child marriage must be rejected, others, such as frequent bathing, proper exercise, and good dietary practices, should be encouraged, even though they may be sanctioned by the non-Christian religion. As regards many customs a missionary can and should be completely neutral, e.g. posture in prayer, vegetarianism, social etiquette, and style of dress. If some custom is rapidly dying out, as is excision in some parts of Central Africa, there is no special need of making a great fuss about such a practice. However, the cultural decay may be hastened by judicious discussions of the physical and psychological harm of such an operation, but "a victory over a dying lion is no triumph."

The most successful anthropological and missionary methods of approach to non-Christian peoples have resulted not from theoretical formulations dreamed up in the isolation of one's study but from on-the-spot dealing with the complex, living situations. Anthropology may point out the nature of the problems and the possibilities of various solutions, but only the man at grips with the human factors involved can be expected to be successful in finding an adequate solution. The genuine sensitiveness to human needs has prepared many missionaries to be "shockless" and objective in dealing with strange and personally abhorrent customs. By continued intimate association, careful inquiries, and diaries of anthropologically significant events, they have learned to understand something of the people's way of thinking. When they discover that people are loath to tell what actually took place or what they really think, these missionaries many times are clever enough to describe similar circumstances in order to elicit a response to a hypothetical situation and thus obtain the needed answers.[3] For the most part they have avoided the pitfall of trying to keep the "natives" as tourist exhibits or thinking that they should arbitrarily encourage native crafts just as symbols of bygone days. However, the converted idol carver need not throw away his skill when it can be usefully employed in beautifying the church, the school, and the home with esthetically meaningful renditions of new themes in old styles.

Missionaries for the most part are no longer thinking in terms of building huge foreign-looking churches with foreign funds in areas which cannot be expected to maintain them in the foreseeable future. Dependence upon a highly paid foreign pastor, expensive imported literature, and the impersonal direction of a distant mission board have given way to more realistic programs of indigenous church growth relying more on local resources.

Medical missions are increasingly concentrating their attention on preventive medicine, the training of thoroughly qualified assistants, and work in village dispensaries, where they are less hindered than in the impersonal atmosphere of a hospital organized along foreign lines. In the village they can more effectively reach the people in a context in which the missionary can be something more than just a white-skinned witch doctor. Complicated operations requiring elaborate hospital facilities may be more professionally intriguing to the missionary doctor, but the time invested in the village dispensary brings the physician closer to those for whom the Great Physician died.

Kroeber's analysis, "It is chiefly when the missionary succeeds in controlling secular education of the young that he becomes really influential," [4] has been repeatedly confirmed. The village school is still the principal source of lasting converts. However, alert educational missionaries are no longer content to adopt in wholesale fashion curricula from the United States or European countries. They are determined to train people for life situations, despite the conservatism of some few colonial educators, who still insist on Latin, classical history, and English literature while almost totally neglecting a study of the peoples' own traditions. Teachers of the

Bible are endeavoring to make the message of Scripture a contemporary reality as well as an historical revelation.

Culturally sensitive missionaries have seen the need for a new attitude on initiation rites. Some have suggested that circumcision be done by hospital doctors who can prevent infection; others have provided effective functional substitutes for the female initiation rites by reproducing what was good about previous practices but discarding what was harmful. Among the Cewa [5] the Christian puberty rite has a private and public aspect. A mature Christian woman of good character and with capacity to teach is appointed as an *alangizi* ("instructress"). It is her task to instruct the young girls as to body hygiene, sex, procreation, and child care; and not infrequently a doctor or a nurse may assist. The public part of the puberty rite consists of a formal reception of the young girls by the older women in a special religious service held once or twice a year. On this occasion they are further admonished as to good behavior, self-control, and respect for authority. They are then received by their elders with handshaking and singing and are allowed to take their place as members of the adult group. In its formal outline this rite does not bear much resemblance to the former practices including seclusion in a hut for six days, abstaining from salt, enforced sexual intercourse (with a fiance, a relative, or a man hired for the purpose) and instruction in sex taboos. However, despite the lack of formal correspondence with previous rites, the new Christian ritual provides the essential features which make it a culturally acceptable functional substitute. Some anthropology-conscious missionaries have insisted on retaining too many features of old patterns, not realizing that "new wine bursts old wineskins." [6] It is not the cultural form but the valuable cultural functions which should be preserved.

Polygamy is generally no longer treated by informed missionaries with shocked denunciations, but with an appreciative understanding of the numerous problems. More and more missions are sympathetic to permitting polygamists to become church members (but not to hold office) if such persons became polygamists before becoming acquainted with the gospel. Rather than have unwanted widows turned out to prostitution, churches have acted as sponsors of such women in arranging marriages. An awakened consciousness as to the need of educating women is changing the prevailing practice of concentrating some 90 per cent of the educational budget on training boys and men.

Rather than oppose harmless but "strange" customs approved by the people, missionaries are learning to wait and work with cultural developments. Missionaries among the San Blas have not made an issue of the gold rings which the women wear in their noses. Gradually the Christian girls are no longer wearing them, simply because they seem strange in a modern world and not because of any artificial attempts to give religious sanction to the mores of the Western world. Similarly, these Christians have abandoned the three-day bathing for girls' puberty rites, but have retained the associated feast, at which, however, they serve Coca Cola and hot chocolate rather than the mildly intoxicating *chicha*. The girls have also taken to wearing clothes purchased in Colon or Panama City, not because they are any more modest or attractive than the indigenous costume, but largely because they are cheaper and less conspicuous if one makes a trip away from the islands. The true missionary is entirely too much occupied with the vital aspects of his ministry to take sides in matters of mores which are religiously nonsignificant. On the other hand, he can make excellent use of indigenous proverbs and fables which teach valuable moral lessons. He can use well-known ancient legends to inculcate a pride in his students' own cultural heritage. Missionaries have also used retreats and conferences (which are often the functional substitute for former powwows and festivals), have introduced folk games (which may take the place of undesirable community dances), have made abundant use of songs (either composed or spontaneous) to tell the Good News, and have employed indigenous drama to provide a creative outlet and a wholesome means of expression.

Missions are increasingly more aware of the value of intelligent judgment as to the possible receptivity of people. Old towns controlled by long-ruling families are a veritable network of unseen cultural strands which largely impede any break with the socio-religious pattern. But young cities, recent subdivisions, and new housing units provide opportunities for entrance of the gospel message before life crystallizes into fixed habits and pressures.

Fuller appreciation of linguistic and anthropological problems has convinced the competent present-day Bible translator that the Scriptures must make sense. Such phrases as "it came to pass" are either translated as "it happened that," or they are simply omitted if there is no equivalent introductory expression in the language in question. The ultimate purpose is that the translation may convey the message to living men, not reproduce dead idioms in a meaningless form of speech.

The far-sighted missionary is alert to the possibilities of subordinating the mission to the church. As part of this program religious conferences dealing with the spiritual life or church organization are held away from the mission station so that people will not look constantly to the mission as the central and indispensable force. People are discouraged from starting villages to grow up around mission stations. Candidates for baptism are accepted by the elders of the church, with advice and counsel from the missionary when he is asked for it. Young candidates for further training and ordination are chosen and at least partially supported by the church.

All of these new solutions to old problems (though in many instances only "new" because of new and awakened awareness of their importance) point to the development of the church as the real goal of the missionary enterprise, the divinely appointed task "to teach all nations" and "to entrust to faithful men who will be able to teach others also." However, what is even more important than revised programs and new strategies is an all-embracing consciousness of the reality of God, the saving grace of Jesus Christ, the transforming work of the Spirit of God, and our own cultural inadequacy. The power of Jesus Christ working through His consecrated and teachable servants can sanctify all of life to the glory of God.

PRACTICAL SUGGESTIONS CONCERNING WAYS IN WHICH
MISSIONARIES MAY ACQUIRE HELPFUL ANTHROPOLOGICAL
BACKGROUND AND FIELD DATA

Customs and Cultures has presented primarily the needs for, and the viewpoints of, a proper anthropological orientation. Students and missionaries may very well ask, "What can one do about acquiring a background in anthropology? How can a person obtain the significant data concerning the tribe in which he is working? How can one apply such information in solving field problems?" These questions imply the need of a missionaries' handbook on cultural anthropology. But before such a volume is available (it is now being planned), the following suggestions may prove helpful:

A. *Reading*

There is a vast literature on anthropology, and one should never be satisfied with reading a single book or the works of a single author. On the other hand, one must be somewhat selective, at least at first, and then gradually branch out along lines corresponding to one's own interests and needs. The following list of books, if read in the order given, will provide one with a graded approach to cultural anthropology (see the Bibliography for complete bibliographical details):

1. Clyde Kluckhohn, *Mirror for Man*
2. Ruth Benedict, *Patterns of Culture*
3. George Peter Murdock, *Our Primitive Contemporaries*
4. A. L. Kroeber, *Anthropology*
5. Melville J. Herskovits, *Man and His Works*
6. Robert Redfield, *The Primitive World and Its Transformations*

Anyone who wishes to keep abreast of developments in anthropology should by all means subscribe to *American Anthropologist*, published six times a year by the American Anthropological Association (Menasha, Wis.). There is rarely a number which does not have some article which would be of keen interest to anthropologically alert missionaries. The book reviews are also extremely valuable in keeping one informed as to important contributions being made to anthropological literature.

Other journals, of regional as well as general interest, include: *Africa*, published for the International African Institute by the Oxford University Press; *Equatoria*, published by the *Mission du Sacre Coeur*, Coquelhatville, Belgian Congo; *African Studies*, published by Witwatersrand University Press, Johannesburg, South Africa; *Oceania* (a journal devoted to the study of the indigenous peoples of Australia, New Guinea, and the Islands of the Pacific Ocean), published by the Australian National Research Council, Sydney, Australia; *Anthropos*, published by the Anthropos Institute, Freiburg, Switzerland; and *Practical Anthropology*, modestly published (beginning in 1953) by Robert B. Taylor (Wheaton College, Wheaton, Ill.) with the express purpose of helping missionaries better to understand the anthropological problems of their fields.

Missionaries should be well acquainted with Hendrick Kraemer's book *The Christian Message in a Non-Christian World* and should keep up with the many valuable articles on anthropological phases of missionary work which appear from time to time in *The International Review of Missions* (Edinburgh House, Eaton Gate, Sloane Square, London S. W. 1, and 156 Fifth Avenue, New York City). The Bibliography lists a number of other books which deal specifically with problems of missions and anthropology. Of these perhaps the most important and practical are Arthur Phillips (ed.), *Survey of African Marriage and Family Life*; J. H. Bavinck, *The Impact of Christianity on the Non-Christian World*, and J. Merle Davis, *New Buildings on Old Foundations*. Dr. Davis has written a number of other books which treat mission and anthropological problems, of which some of the most helpful are *The Economic and Social Environment of the Younger Churches* (1939), *The Church in the New Jamaica* (1942), *The Cuban Church in a Sugar Economy* (1942), and *How the Church Grows in Brazil* (1947). The first of these was published by the International Missionary Council in London, and the rest by the same council in New York.

B. *Visiting Museums*

Museums are objects of curiosity for tourists, but "laboratories" for students. One should not miss any opportunity to visit museums which have anthropologically significant exhibits. Perhaps the most important anthropological museums are Musée de l'Homme in Paris, Natural History Museum in New York City, Smithsonian Institution in Washington, D.C., and the Field Museum in Chicago. Many colleges and universities also have interesting exhibits, which enable one to study the material culture of many areas of the world. It is not enough, however, to get a general impression of life in distant parts of the world. One should make careful observations as to the construction of artifacts, similarities and diversities between related regions, and relationship of the artifacts to the over-all pattern of life. A careful study of museum exhibits can help make books on anthropology come to life.

C. *Gathering Data on the Field*

A person can learn a great deal about the life of foreign peoples by just being alert as to what is constantly going on. However, one can acquire much more information by systematic observation and recording of data. The following suggestions may be of help:

1. *Taking nothing for granted*

   If people are hesitant about giving their names to strangers, this fact may be an important clue to a number of cultural features, including attitudes toward strangers, use of names for magical purposes, or the existence of multiple names (it is not always clear to the people what name is being sought). One cannot find all the answers to this problem at first, but the fact of hesitance about giving names should be noted in one's diary.

   Someday all the men may without apparent reason leave the village for several hours. They may give very evasive answers for having left, but the fact should be noted, for this departure may be part of a larger ceremonial rite.

   A man may come and sit in the doorway for several hours without attempting to explain his presence or without doing anything, except to pick up a little trash swept out of the house and off the back porch. Who is he? What did he want? Where did he come from? Will he ever come back? Later on this person may be identified as the leader of a secret society of witch doctors. He was undoubtedly intent upon obtaining some nail cuttings, hair, or scrap of cloth by which he could feel that he had a measure of control upon the newcomer.

One should not, however, begin life in a new area with a suspicious air of cultural touchiness, but rather with eyes open to different customs and a mind alert to appreciate different motivations and purposes.

2. *Keeping a diary*

We are hopelessly incapable of remembering all the numerous events which happen each day and which can only be understood or explained when we see them in their entirety and in retrospect. For this reason a diary is an inevitable "tool" for investigation. Some of the recorded data may prove very trivial and unimportant, but other facts will help us to weave together the otherwise inexplicable sequences of events. The data of one's diary become invaluable information for an ethnological file.

3. *Participating in indigenous life*

There is no way to acquire an adequate understanding of indigenous life without a large measure of participation. One's presence at a "pagan" funeral ceremony does not mean belief in local spirits, nor does witnessing a puberty rite imply full agreement with such practices. Whether it be healing by incantation, a rain ceremony, village courts, or a hunting expedition, one can often be a welcomed guest (and in some instances a participant) if one has established the right rapport with the people. This does not imply that a person should compromise his beliefs or convictions, but a genuine empathy with the people will help to remove any suspicion of morbid curiosity and will make it possible to convince others of one's deep personal interest in and concern for all phases of life.

An essential aspect of participation is living in as close contact with the people as possible. Some missionaries have complained of the constant noise, the ever-present dirt, the continuous "snooping" by curious neighbors, and the incessant demand upon one's time as justifiable reasons for not living in a "native village." However, in avoiding village life missionaries often rob themselves of the most valuable contacts which they could possibly have with the people.

One cannot learn a language without constantly hearing it; one cannot become acquainted with a culture without effective participation in it.

4. *Making inquiries of informants*

Much of one's information about a culture must come from informants who are members of the indigenous culture, but who can communicate to others something of the forms and meaning of their culture. There are a number of cautions and suggestions which one should bear in mind when selecting informants and when working with them:

a. An informant must be fully acquainted with his own culture. He should not be a person who has spent most of his life away at a boarding school or in the employment of foreigners.

b. Wherever possible, all questioning of the informant should be in the indigenous language. The use of a foreign language places serious barriers to proper identification of traits, and understanding of their cultural function.

c. Data from one informant should always be checked with information given by others. One must, of course, avoid the impression of "checking up" on a rival informant's statements. Where there are different accounts given by various informants or by the same informant in subsequent sessions, all this may be very significant for obtaining clues as to alternative patterns of behavior and to the differences between ideal and real behavior.

d. Data may be elicited by telling the informant about customs and beliefs of other tribes of people and by asking him if anything similar or different is done or believed by the people in question. This technique of "swapping" information develops a climate of sharing which is helpful in establishing the right rapport.

e. One should attempt to make a comprehensive investigation of the various phases of the culture by following some such guide as *Outline of Cultural Materials* by Murdock or *Notes and Queries*, published by the Royal Anthropological Institute.

f. One may guide the areas of conversation, but should not attempt to switch the informant's order of giving data, since the order itself may provide important clues as to the relationship between the traits of a culture.

g. One should avoid all arguing with informants about the data or their evaluations of the actions described. One's primary duty is to understand the culture before attempting to evaluate.

5. *Audiovisual recording*

Recording machines can be a great advantage to a missionary, not only in learning a foreign language, but in studying many aspects of the indigenous cultures, e.g. music, poetry, folklore, prayers, incantations, myths, and legends. Recordings have been made surreptitiously by some missionaries, but on the whole this practice is unwise, for sooner or later it creates suspicion. If a missionary has made extensive use of recordings during the language-learning process and if during this process he has taken occasion to let the people listen to the recordings of their own voices and those of others, he can usually establish the kind of friendly relationship with the people which will enable him to obtain all kinds of recordings without arousing suspicions.

Photographs can be excellent devices for recording numerous details for further study. However, people must be convinced that such pictures are not magical means of "catching their souls," making a great deal of money or publicizing the more "shocking" aspects of their culture. As in the case of recordings, one should make it a practice of showing the developed pictures to the people, so that they may understand what is involved.

D. *Filing Data*

In order for ethnological data to be fully useful, it must be systematically arranged. The data may come from one's diary, scattered notes made from conversations with informants, descriptions of religious ceremonies, and analyses of various problems, e.g. drunkenness, barter system, or percentage of leprosy cases. The information should be filed under appropriate headings, following Murdock's *Outline of Cultural Materials* or some other helpful systematization of cultural data. As the file grows and is carefully studied it increases in value as a working tool for the study of cultural problems which are relevant to the missionaries' work.

E. *Application of Anthropological Data to the Solving of Missionary Problems*

Someone asks the question, "Are they really married?" In our culture that can be answered quite easily by inquiring for the legal proof. But in the Quechua culture of Llano Grande, Ecuador, Dr. and Mrs. William Reyburn, who made an anthropological and linguistic study of the region for the Brethren Mission in that area, found that there are four different wedding ceremonies: (1) an initial ceremony (no doubt of pre-Columbian origin) which is recognized by the people as sanctioning the cohabitation of a man and woman, (2) the civil registration of the marriage with the government authorities, (3) the registration of the marriage by the church, and (4) a wedding fiesta, lasting for about a week, beginning with a religious ceremony but consisting mostly of heavy drinking for the entire period. Between the first and the last of the wedding rites two or three years may elapse, and one or two children may be born. Accordingly, the precise time of marriage is not so easily decided, and the attitude of the mission as to what position to maintain relative to the "native marriage" cannot be determined without a full understanding of the elaborate process and the relationship of these events to the total social structure.

A careful study of a culture may reveal, as it did in the investigations of Dr. and Mrs. Reyburn, cited above, that a number of recommendations can be made in order to adapt a mission program to the needs of the people. For example, it was found that the people understand relatively little standard Spanish. Accordingly, a program for missionaries' use of "peon Spanish" and the Quechua language was undertaken. Because of the Quechuas' suspicion of what the missionaries might be saying in English, it was recommended that English never be used when any Quechua-speaking person was within listening distance. Since the young people are rapidly being drawn away to the urban culture of Quito and hence are not growing up to form the nucleus of a church in the area, emphasis has been shifted to reaching the adults. The people are very suspicious of the mission-built chapel, and accordingly arrangements have been made for some groups to worship in individual homes. It was noted that the Quechuas get up very early in the morning, so that for them a church service by six or seven in the morning is much better than one at ten o'clock. Since fiestas have constituted the central social feature of the culture, a functional substitute is required which will provide for all the socially valuable features of such gatherings without the intoxicating *chicha* (a cokes-for-chicha development). Because of the fact that women do most of the agricultural work, it has been decided that any instruction in better farming methods should be given primarily to the women, not to the men. There is a popular superstition that the missionaries write down in blood the names of newly baptized converts and hand the names to the devil. To dispel this idea certificates of baptism are printed, with names written clearly in ink and given to each new believer.

A careful and systematic study of any culture can reveal numerous ways in which any mission program can be more effectively oriented to meet the needs of the people and to bring to them in a more meaningful way the life-transforming significance of the Good News in Jesus Christ.

BIBLIOGRAPHY

BAVINCK, J. H. *The Impact of Christianity on the Non-Christian World*. Grand Rapids, Mich.: Eerdmans, 1948.

BEALS, RALPH L. and HOIJER, HARRY. *An Introduction to Anthropology*. New York: The Macmillan Company, 1953.

BENEDICT, RUTH. *Patterns of Culture*. New York: Penguin Books, by arrangement with Houghton Mifflin Company, 1946.

BIRKET-SMITH, K. *The Eskimos*. New York: E. P. Dutton and Company, 1936.

BLOOMFIELD, LEONARD. *Language*. New York: Henry Holt and Company, 1933.

BOAS, FRANZ. *The Mind of Primitive Man*. New York: The Macmillan Company, 1938.

BOAS, FRANZ, and others. *General Anthropology*. Boston: D. C. Heath and Company, 1938.

BOYD, WILLIAM C. *Genetics and the Races of Man*. Boston: Little, Brown and Company, 1950.

BUCK, PETER H. *Anthropology and Religion*. New Haven: Yale University Press, 1939.

BURNS, SIR ALAN. *Colour Prejudice*. London: George Allen and Unwin Ltd., 1948.

DAVIS, J. MERLE. *New Buildings on Old Foundations*. New York: International Missionary Council, 1947.

DE PEDRALS, D. P. *La Vie Sexuelle en Afrique Noire*. Paris: Payot, 1950.

DVORIN, EUGENE P. *Racial Separation in South Africa*. Chicago: The University of Chicago Press, 1952.

FORDE, C. DARYLL. *Habitat, Society and Economy*. New York: E. P. Dutton and Company, 1950.

FORTES, M. and EVANS-PRITCHARD, E. E. (eds.) *African Political Systems*. London: Oxford University Press, 1940.

FRAZER, SIR JAMES G. *The Golden Bough*. One vol. Abridged Ed. New York: The Macmillan Company, 1928.

HALL, ROBERT A., JR. *Leave Your Language Alone*. Ithaca, N. Y.: Linguistica, 1950.

HERSKOVITS, MELVILLE J. *Acculturation, the Study of Culture Contact*. New York: J. J. Augustin, 1938.

———. *Man and His Works*. New York: Alfred A. Knopf, 1948.

———. *Economic Anthropology*. New York: Alfred A. Knopf, 1952.

HOLLIS, A. C. *The Masai*. Oxford: The Clarendon Press, 1905.

HOOTON, EARNEST ALBERT. *Up from the Ape*. New York: The Macmillan Company, 1946.

HOWELLS, W. W. *The Heathens, Primitive Man and His Religions*. New York: Doubleday & Company, 1948.

KARDINER, ABRAM. *The Individual and His Society*. New York: Columbia University Press, 1939.

KLUCKHOHN, CLYDE. *Mirror for Man*. New York: McGraw-Hill Book Company, 1949.

KLUCKHOHN, CLYDE, and LEIGHTEN, DOROTHEA. *The Navaho*. Cambridge: Harvard University Press, 1946.

KRAEMER, HENDRICK. *The Christian Message in a Non-Christian World*. New York and London: International Missionary Council, reprinted 1947.

KROEBER, A. L. *Anthropology*. New York: Harcourt, Brace and Company, 1948 (rev. ed.).

LARA, JESÚS. *La Poesía Quechua*. Mexico: Fondo de Cultura Economica, 1947.

LEENHARDT, MAURICE. *Do Kamo: La Personne et le Mythe dans le Monde Mélanésien*. Paris: Gallimard, 1947.

LINTON, RALPH. *Ethnology of Polynesia and Micronesia*. Chicago: Field Museum of Natural History, 1926.

———. *The Study of Man*. New York and London: Appleton-Century-Crofts, 1936.

———. *The Cultural Background of Personality*. New York: Appleton-Century-Crofts, 1945.

——— (ed.). *The Science of Man in the World Crisis*. New York: Columbia University Press, 1945.

LOWIE, ROBERT H. *Primitive Society*. New York: Liveright Publishing Corporation, 1947 (rev. ed.).

———. *Primitive Religion*. New York: Liveright Publishing Corporation, 1948 (rev. ed.).

MALINOWSKI, B. *Argonauts of the Western Pacific*. New York: E. P. Dutton and Company, 1922.

———. *Sex and Repression in Savage Society*. New York: Harcourt, Brace and Company, 1937.

———. *The Dynamics of Culture Change*. New Haven: Yale University Press, 1945.

MEAD, MARGARET. *Coming of Age in Samoa*. New York: William Morrow and Company, 1928.

MEANS, PHILIP A. *Ancient Civilizations of the Andes*. New York: Charles Scribner's Sons, 1931.

MURDOCK, GEORGE PETER. *Our Primitive Contemporaries*. New York: The Macmillan Company, 1934.

———. *Social Structure*. New York: The Macmillan Company, 1948.

MURDOCK, GEORGE P., and others. *Outline of Cultural Materials*. New Haven: Human Relations Area Files, Behavior Science Outline, Vol. 1, 1950.

NIDA, EUGENE A. *Bible Translating*. New York: American Bible Society, 1947.

———. *Learning a Foreign Language*. New York: National Council of the Churches of Christ in the U.S.A., 1950.

———. *God's Word in Man's Language*. New York: Harper & Brothers, 1952.

OPLER, MORRIS E. "Themes As Dynamic Forces in Culture," *American Journal of Sociology*, Vol. 51, No. 3, 198–206, 1945.

PHILLIPS, ARTHUR (ed.). *Survey of African Marriage and Family Life*. London: Oxford University Press, 1953.

RADIN, PAUL. *Social Anthropology*. New York: McGraw-Hill Book Company, 1932.

———. *Primitive Religion, Its Nature and Origin*. New York: The Viking Press, 1937.

REDFIELD, ROBERT. *The Folk Culture of Yucatan*. Chicago: University of Chicago Press, 1941.

———. *The Primitive World and Its Transformations*. Ithaca, N. Y.: Cornell University Press, 1953.

RYCROFT, W. STANLEY. *Indians of the High Andes.* New York: Committee on Cooperation in Latin America, 1946.

SAPIR, EDWARD. *Language.* New York: Harcourt, Brace and Company, 1939.

SCHMIDT, WILHELM. *The Culture Historical Method of Anthropology.* (Trans. by S. A. Sieber.) New York: Fortuny's, 1939.

SHROPSHIRE, DENYS W. T. *The Church and Primitive Peoples; The Religious Institutions and Beliefs of the Southern Bantu and their Bearing on the Problems of the Christian Missionary.* London: Society for the Propagation of Christian Knowledge, and New York: The Macmillan Company, 1938.

SMALLEY, WILLIAM A., and MARIE FETZER. "A Christian View of Anthropology," in *Modern Science and Christian Faith,* pp. 98–195. Wheaton: Van Kampen Press, 1950.

SMITH, EDWIN W. (ed.). *African Ideas of God.* London: Edinburgh House Press, 1950.

SPIER, LESLIE, A. IRVING HALLOWELL, and STANLEY S. NEWMAN (eds.). *Language, Culture, and Personality.* Menasha, Wis.: Sapir Memorial Publication Fund, 1941.

TAX, SOL (ed.). *Acculturation in the Americas.* Chicago: University of Chicago Press, 1952.

THOMPSON, LAURA. *Culture in Crisis: A Study of the Hopi Indians.* New York: Harper & Brothers, 1950.

THOMPSON, STITH. *The Folktale.* New York: Dryden Press, 1947.

THURNWALD, RICHARD. *Economics in Primitive Communities.* London: Oxford University Press, 1932.

VAILLANT, GEORGE C. *Aztecs of Mexico.* Garden City, N. Y.: Doubleday-Doran Company, 1944.

WALLIS, WILSON D. *Religion in Primitive Society.* New York: F. S. Crofts and Company, 1939.

WHITE, LESLIE A. *The Science of Culture.* New York: Farrar, Straus and Company, 1949.

WISSLER, CLARK. *The American Indian.* New York: Oxford University Press, 1938.

CHAPTER 1   SHOCKS AND SURPRISES

1   The reader is warned against assuming that in this and succeeding chapters the writer is attempting to condone or justify various "shocking and surprising" practices (the Christian point of view is extensively treated in the last chapter). However unless we can see customs in the light of the indigenous setting and attitudes, we are largely incapable of appreciating either the problems or the solutions which are posssible for Christian missions.

2   Maurice Leenhardt, *Do Kamo, La Personne et le Mythe dans le Monde Mélanésien* (Paris, Librarie Gallimard, 1947), p. 156.

3   Burying people alive was also of frequent occurrence in Polynesia.

4   The highly arbitrary character of all such attempts to legislate on matters of pious conduct is well illustrated by conclusions reached by a mission on the problem of whether or not to permit tobacco smoking, betelnut chewing, and opium smoking on the Bible School grounds. Tobacco smoking was taken off the list of forbidden practices because some colonists or foreign government officials might conceivably come onto the grounds smoking a pipe or cigarette, and it would be embarrassing to ask them to stop. However, betelnut chewing and opium smoking were not so likely to be practiced by visiting white men, especially those whom the missionaries did not wish to offend, and accordingly these two practices were forbidden on Bible School property on the basis that it was "holy ground." However, the servants' quarters, about three yards away from the dormitory and classrooms and on the same compound, were not felt to be "holy," and hence no regulation was made about them.

5   The Marshallese have elaborate sea charts constructed of slender sticks skillfully tied together with fiber, but the actual determination of one's location on the open sea is accomplished by observation of wind and wave movements.

6   The San Blas are of course not the only primitive people with high morality. However, one should not assume that high morality is

necessarily a characteristic of the more primitive groups of people, or as some contend, "of the oldest culture strata."

7 *Time*, Vol. 62, July 6, 1953, pp. 24–26.

8 J. H. Bavinck, *The Impact of Christianity on the Non-Christian World* (Grand Rapids, Mich.: Eerdmans, 1948), p. 46.

9 Leenhardt, *op. cit.*, p. 16.

10 We are not including here such Christianizing efforts as were conducted by Roman Catholic missionaries in the Western Hemisphere and in the Philippines during the time of Spanish and Portuguese colonialism, for in too many instances (though not in all) conversions were dictated more by political and military power than by religious persuasion.

11 *Op. cit.*, p. 212.

12 The meaning of the New Caledonian word includes both the spirit of man as well as the spirits of ancestors, and by extension was used by Leenhardt in the meaning of Spirit of God.

13 It is possible that such reports are slightly exaggerated, but there is substantial evidence that there were heavy penalties for adultery after marriage, which was, however, preceded by a period of several years of "trial marriages," during which time there was considerable sexual freedom.

14 Of course, government and missions are doing what they can to correct this situation, but there is no easy solution to this problem.

15 The anthropologist is obliged to study missions as simply one aspect of culture change. As an impartial, professedly neutral descriptive science, anthropology aims at an analysis of the cultural facts and is not primarily concerned with the vindication or condemnation of historical developments.

CHAPTER 2   RHYME AND REASON

1 A. L. Kroeber, *Anthropology*, rev. ed. (New York: Harcourt, Brace and Company, 1948), p. 1.

2 By the use of the word "primitive" we do not imply any depreciatory judgment as to the cultures so designated. The term "nonliterate" is sometimes employed as a more noncommittal synonym, but it is not wholly adequate, for it is readily confused with "illiterate," and during the last few decades quite a number of so-called primitive groups of people have become literate, largely due to the activities of Christian missionaries.

3 In the broad comparative analysis of cultures there is a further set of historically significant questions: What is the history of the cultural institutions? What regularities and parallels can be found in cultural history?

4 Culture may also be defined as "all learned and shared human behavior."

5 Culture should not be confused with the acts of behavior or the material artifacts. That is to say, culture is manifest in acts and artifacts but does not consist of them. In its broadest sense, culture (as used by anthropologists) includes the ways of life or "designs for living" employed at any time by all mankind. However, one can speak of a culture as being the ways of life characteristic of a single society or of a group of closely related societies. One can also use the term "culture" in referring to the particular patterns of behavior of a distinctive segment in some highly complex society, in which case we often speak of a subculture. One exception to the above usage occurs in the phrase "material culture," which includes the material artifacts as well as the skills employed in making and using them.

6 It is very easy to assume too much homogeneity on the part of primtive societies. There are often marked differences of behavior and outlook. Such societies can be spoken of as homogeneous only in contrast with the decidedly more complex and heterogeneous societies of "civilized" peoples.

7 Further evidence along such racial lines will be treated in the following chapter.

8 Presumed aversion to intermarriage is primarily only a relatively late development and exists principally among some Caucasians as a result of socio-economic developments.

9 "Unnatural" is used here purely in its common meaning, without any consideration of theological implications.

10 Wife-lending among the Eskimos is an important technique for gaining prestige.

11 This, of course, does not deal with the problems of beginnings, but since there are no living cultures which have not had antecedent cultures, the problem is more theoretical than practical.

12 We may also distinguish between (1) basic and (2) acquired drives. These latter are "taught" by the culture and include such drives as fame, power, and attractive appearance.

13 These two psychological drives could be subsumed under "desire for response from others."

14 There are a number of other ways in which anthropological data may be organized and profitably discussed. Some of these are (1) Linton's items, traits, and activities, (2) patterns (including the items and their "constellations") and processes of modification, (3) Opler's themes, e.g. respect for old age, desire for power, reverence for the supernatural, and (4) Herskovits' foci, e.g. technology (in the United States) and religion (in West Africa). No one perspective or system for the organization of data is adequate, but each has its own validity

since it makes possible a valid, and often fresh, view of significant facts.

15   It is sometimes difficult to decide what aspect of any cultural feature represents an esthetic contribution and what is strictly utilitarian. The two are so often combined. However, if a particular feature of a religious rite is obligatory in order to "compel" the deity to respond, this would not be classified strictly as an esthetic feature. But beautifying of a rite beyond such a point does represent an esthetic purpose. Of course, during the history of a rite, that which is at one time strictly esthetic, may later be regarded as obligatory and utilitarian since only by such means is one assured of a proper response from the deity. An illustration from the Christian rite of communion will illustrate the point in question. Without doubt the original manner of celebration was quite simple, and necessary features very restricted. However, at the present time even in the "low churches" the use of expensive silver dishes, candles, beautiful linen, immaculately dressed ushers, a rhetorically elaborate ritual, and specially robed clergymen reflects essentially an esthetic interest. In some Christian churches, however, the communion is not regarded as fully efficacious unless some of these "added" features are present.

16   This feature of African marriage is discussed further in Chap. 5.

17   By "imaginary" we mean that which does not rest on a scientifically proven biological fact. We must not doubt the fact that as far as the young parents are concerned the couvade corresponds to a very "real" subjective need.

18   Robert Redfield, *The Primitive World and Its Transformations* (Ithaca, N. Y.: Cornell University Press, 1953), p. 144.

19   *Ibid.*, p. 145.

20   *Ibid.*, p. 157.

21   *Ibid.*, pp. 160–62.

22   The only absolute in Christianity is the triune God. Anything which involves man, who is finite and limited, must of necessity be limited, and hence relative. Biblical cultural relativism is an obligatory feature of our incarnational religion, for without it we would either absolutize human institutions or relativize God.

CHAPTER 3   RACE AND RANTING

1   We are not attempting to go into the numerous problems of classification of races. For full discussions of such problems students are referred to such books as Kroeber, *op cit.*; Ralph L. Beals and Harry Hoijer, *An Introduction to Anthropology* (New York: The Macmillan Company, 1953); Earnest Albert Hooton, *Up from the Ape* (New York: The Macmillan Company, 1946); and William C. Boyd,

Genetics and the Races of Man (Boston: Little, Brown and Company, 1950).

2 In accord with the newer genetic approach races may also be classified in a somewhat different manner (see Beals and Hoijer, *op. cit.*, pp. 161–78:

    1. Caucasoid

      A. Archaic Caucasoid Races: Ainu, Australoid, Dravidian, and Vedda.

      B. Primary Caucasoid Races: Alpine (central and southeastern Europe), Armenoid (Armenia and southeastern Europe), Mediterranean, and Nordic.

      C. Secondary or Derived Caucasoid Races: Dinaric (said to result from intermixture of Armenoid and Nordic types and found in eastern Alps), East Baltic (said to result from intermixture of Alpine, Nordic, and Asiatic Mongoloid types, and found in Finland, northern Russia, the Baltic states, and parts of north Germany), and Polynesian (said to result from intermixture between Mediterranean, Asiatic Mongoloid and Oceanic Negro types and found scattered throughout Micronesia and Polynesia).

    2. Mongoloid

      A. Asiatic Mongoloid.

      B. Indonesian-Malay.

      C. American Indian.

    3. Negroid

      A. Primary Negroid Races: Forest Negro (West Africa and the Congo basin) and Negrito (pygmies in the Congo basin, Andaman Islands, several portions of Indonesia, Philippines, and the highlands of New Guinea).

      B. Secondary or Derived Negroid Races: Bushman-Hottentot (thought perhaps to be the result of intermixture of Negrito and some Mongoloidlike race), Nilotic Negro (said to result from an intermixture of early Mediterranean type with a Negroid race), and Oceanic Negro (a relatively archaic Negro variety plus a number of Mongoloid traits and found chiefly in New Guinea and Melanesia).

The entire problem of racial classification is very much in dispute at the present time. There is the tendency to eliminate all such terms as Nordic, Alpine, dolichocephalic, etc., and to attempt classifications based upon criteria, e.g. blood types, of which the manner of inheritance is more fully understood.

3 Kroeber, *op. cit.*, p. 126

4 Anthropologists' rejection of the use of skin color as an important criterion of racial classification is largely based upon ignorance as to precisely how it is inherited.

5   Attempts to relate criteria of racial classification to the popularly accepted scheme of the direct evolution of the human races from contemporary species of apes have broken down completely. For example, the texture and quantity of hair, which are two of the most reliable criteria for racial classification, would result in the Negro being the most advanced type, since no monkeys have kinky hair and Negroes have much less body hair than Caucasians. Even in the matter of the form of lips, the Negro is the furthest separated from modern apes.

6   Franz Boas, *The Mind of Primitive Man* (New York: The Macmillan Company, 1938), pp. 93 ff.

7   Kroeber, *op. cit.*, p. 144.

8   For the most part these cultural features are recognizable only where there has been social isolation for considerable periods of time, as in the ghettos of Europe and the Jewish communities of the United States.

9   Clyde Kluckhohn, *Mirror for Man* (New York: McGraw-Hill Book Company, 1949), p. 197.

10 Laura Thompson, *Culture in Crisis: A Study of the Hopi Indians* (New York: Harper & Brothers, 1950), p. 92.

11 *Ibid.*, pp. 92–96.

12 The Negroes of Africa and the Negroid people of Melanesia are only very distantly related, but they have been generally subsumed under one of the three or more major divisions of mankind.

13 The red herring of most discussions about race is the subject of intermarriage. Just because there are no biological reasons against interbreeding does not mean that such mixed marriages will be lacking in severe social problems and that the children are not going to suffer social ostracism in some societies. In any event, arguments for or against intermarriage should be based upon the cultural and not the biological factors. The rapid increase in transportation and the increased intermingling of populations, which is characteristic of our present world, will certainly lead to more and more intermarriages and eventually diminishing racial tensions, especially in view of the shifting of world power from its concentration in the West. The Biblical view on racial intermarriage is interestingly illustrated in God's judgment on Aaron and Miriam for having complained about Moses' marriage with an Ethiopian (Numbers 12).

14 In Brazil there is a considerable amount of class prejudice and consciousness, and there are some correlations with color. However, a person's dress and education are more important than the color of his skin.

15 It is very easy to denounce the Malan government for its obvious failures and abuses. However, the situation has been far more complicated in South Africa than appears at first glance. The reaction of the Boers is not solely an antinative hostility, but the festering of

long-nursed wounds inflicted by British aggression preceding and during the Boer War.

16   Missionaries are the product of the church and the society which sends them out, and they cannot be expected to be appreciably different in their attitudes just because of a trip to a foreign country.

17   At a conference on African statesmanship held at the Hartford Seminary Foundation, Hartford, Conn., May, 1953.

18   An interesting exception to this general situation is the fact that European Jews, though usually a "lower group," have had a much lower rate of violent crimes than any Gentile group of Europe. Probably their religious beliefs and strong in-group consciousness have in large measure been responsible for this fact.

19   There are no adequate statistics on the growth of religious groups in Africa, but these statements do indicate something of the trend.

20   This includes several schools in Africa.

21   Kluckhohn, *op. cit.*, p. 127.

22   See p. 10.

CHAPTER 4   HOES AND HEADACHES

1   In some instances the soil is more thoroughly worked by hoes than by plows.

2   It is not without interest that such an empire, though it was already beginning to show signs of disintegration, collapsed quickly, once its leadership was destroyed. On the other hand, the very individualistic self-reliant Araucanians in Chile vigorously resisted the Spanish for many years.

3   The high correlation between material culture and other aspects can be well understood from some of the names which may be given to certain cultural areas. The bamboo-rice area (reaching from Indonesia to Japan) contrasts with the coconut-breadfruit area (including Micronesia and parts of Polynesia). The Kaffir-corn and cattle regions of East and South Africa are in constrast with the plantain-manioc area of Central Africa. These typical possessions not only mark geographical areas but have come to symbolize whole bundles of cultural traits which are associated with the material environment of the regions.

4   Statistics cited in Arthur Phillips (ed.), *Survey of African Marriage and Family Life* (London: Oxford University Press, 1953), give some idea of the extent of such social problems. In the Bechuanaland Protectorate between 1930–40 the number of men who went away to work in the mines trebled. About 40 per cent of the married men under forty-four are away at one time and it is unlikely that about 6 per cent will ever return. Of the number of registered births (many are not registered) between June and December of 1940 in a

Johannesburg township of Negro population 65 per cent were illegitimate. Of 890 Negro children brought before a probation officer in Johannesburg in 1937–38, only 36 per cent were living with parents, 35 per cent were with relatives and friends, and 29 per cent could give no place of residence.

5   There is a real danger when Christian "charity" is used as a bait to catch prospective converts. The true motivation for Christian service is based on the fact that the God whom the Christian serves is the one who was in Christ, who took on the form of a servant, humbled himself, and went about doing good.

CHAPTER 5   FRIENDS AND FRUSTRATIONS

1   We are not attempting by this statement to show the reasons for the origin of human institutions, but rather to indicate the function of such relationships in any given society.

2   We are speaking here in general philosophical terms, for in many aboriginal societies individuals have fewer problems in social adjustments, since there are relatively few alternatives. Such societies have most of the rules well established by custom. Nevertheless, even in such societies there are some individuals who are not satisfied and hence rebel, especially in contemporary times where the possibilities for alternative behavior are so much more widely known and recognized.

3   The numerous and complex phases of social structure cannot be adequately treated within the brief limitations of this book, and hence in this chapter we have selected for primary consideration the family (including such subjects as marriage, family life, sex, and divorce), since the family unit (1) is basic to all other aspects of social culture, (2) reveals many of the fundamental problems of human relationships, and (3) is of great importance to Christian missions. Other features of social structure, e.g. caste, government, law, and war, are only briefly considered.

4   In conformance with an increasing number of works on anthropology, "clan" is used in this book in connection with both patrilineal and matrilineal descent. Some anthropologists, however, use "clan" when speaking of matrilineally related persons and "gens" of patrilineally related ones. The word "sib" indicates unilateral descent, whether matrilineal or patrilineal.

5   Any association which requires marriage within the group in question is called "endogamous."

6   It is a serious mistake to assume that a matrilineal society is a matriarchal one. Inheritance may be through the mother, but she may have relatively little direct influence in the decisions made by the society. Some missionaries have made the mistake of excluding women from

all church responsibilities, thinking that in so doing they were adhering strictly to the rules (though not the principles) laid down by the Apostle Paul. Other missionaries have thrust entirely too much authority upon women, assuming that the role of women in the indigenous culture was roughly equivalent to that which they possess in our own culture. Both extremes are ill-advised, for it is the genius of the Good News of God that by the action of the Holy Spirit it may enter in and sanctify all forms of human institutions.

7   This does not mean that such sex relationships are morally justified simply because a high percentage of the people in the world so regard them. This is pushing the democratic principle of majorities too far.

8   Phillips, *op. cit.*, p. 12.

9   *Ibid.*, p. 118.

10   See p. 21.

11   As regards sex the principal contrast between Western civilization and primitive societies is in large measure the difference between sexual promiscuity and socially channeled sexual activity, the latter being more characteristic of primitive peoples.

12   Phillips, *op. cit.*, p. 12.

13   Such cross-cousin marriages are quite widespread, occurring as they do in Australia, Melanesia, India, Assam, South America, British Columbia, and South Africa. See Robert H. Lowie, *Primitive Society*, rev. ed. (New York: Liveright Publishing Corporation, 1947), p. 27.

14   Very frequently the romantic element is quite different and it would be entirely wrong to suggest that it is generally lacking. Romanticism appears in many forms which we often fail to recognize.

15   Phillips, *op. cit.*, p. 27.

16   There are, of course, serious problems in such marriages, for the widow may become an unwanted wife in a polygamous household and may suffer serious injustices

17   Lowie, *op. cit.*, p. 26.

18   Polygamy (i.e. multiple mates) includes both polyandry and polygyny.

19   Phillips, *op. cit.*, p. 90.

20   In any analysis of polygyny it is important to distinguish three different types of societies: (1) one in which polygyny is regarded as the ideal type of marriage, (2) a transitional society, in which polygynous tendencies are losing out in the face of urbanization or other disruptive factors, and (3) a society in which there are irregular polygynous unions, but the majority of the people do not desire or condone such practices. Polygyny is quite a distinct "moral" problem in these three types of societies.

21   *Ibid.*, p. 59.

22 This depends somewhat upon the beliefs regarding sex and pro-creation; see following section.

23 It may be of interest to know that in some instances missionaries who have children in rapid succession are regarded by the indigenous peoples as being much worse than adulterers, since they naturally interpret the missionaries' actions in the light of their mores, even as the missionaries interpret the people's behavior by quite alien standards.

24 The reader is cautioned against drawing any conclusions as to moral rightness or wrongness from such statements. These are only attempts to present the data in terms of the indigenous culture and involve no evaluations based upon moral judgments. Such problems are treated in the last chapter.

25 Leenhardt, *op. cit.*, p. 86,

26 B. Malinowski, *Sex and Repression in Savage Society* (New York: Harcourt, Brace and Company, 1937), pp. 9–10.

27 D. P. de Pedrals, *La Vie Sexuelle en Afrique Noire* (Paris: Payot, 1950), p. 34.

28 Ruth Benedict, *Patterns of Culture* (New York: Penguin Books, by arrangement with Houghton Mifflin Company, 1946), p. 155.

29 De Pedrals, *op. cit.*, p. 138.

30 *Ibid.*, p. 139.

31 *Ibid.*, p. 33.

32 In the study of family life in most cultures other than our own we need to pay proportionately more attention to the relationship between parents and children. In our culture we tend to think of the family primarily in terms of the sexual relationship of husband and wife, while in most other cultures the more significant point of view is the relationship of parents to children.

33 Phillips, *op. cit.*, p. 94.

34 Infanticide is quite uncommon, but the practice of inducing abortion is rather widespread.

35 Phillips, *op. cit.*, p. 19.

36 We should not assume that it is impossible for Christianity to develop properly in societies in which married men and women live in sepa-rate houses, e.g. the Mae of New Guinea. The Christian "home" must not be identified exclusively with the single-house, nuclear family. The Good News is not a fixed pattern of society, but the power of God to sanctify all the forms of human existence.

37 For the most part missionaries have looked upon puberty rites almost entirely as religious features of a society, and for that reason we treat them under religion. Actually, they are far more educational than religious, though from the indigenous point of view any such

distinction between "education" and "religion" is largely irrelevant. These rites are extremely important techniques for inculcating concepts of group loyalty, social responsibility, and individual maturity. Strong opposition to such rites by missionaries and failure to create satisfactory functional substitutes have been major factors in producing the "detribalization" which is so characteristic of many mission converts.

38 It is in a sense an "anachronism" to classify governments in this way, since church organizations have historically reflected the particular social structure, but for the sake of comparison with the problems of church government it is valuable to make these types of distinctions.

39 Missionaries have not infrequently asserted that they could predict the outcome of a church election if they knew the clan membership of the participants.

40 Leenhardt, *op. cit.*, p. 188.

41 In the technical sense "law" does not necessarily mean written codes, but it does imply the existence of constituted legal tribunals vested with power to enforce their judgments by means of organized sanctions. Accordingly, what we find in many primitive societies is not law in the strict sense, but a more informal treatment of abuses by headmen or elders on the basis of traditional attitudes toward equity.

42 Lowie, *op. cit.*, p. 413.

43 Leenhardt, *op. cit.*, p. 53.

44 *Ibid.*, p. 141.

45 Phillips, *op. cit.*, p. 456.

46 *Ibid.*, p. 414.

47 For a full treatment of the many complex problems involved in polygamy, see *Ibid.*

48 There are a number of minor problems which are mentioned earlier in the chapter, and others are treated in the last chapter of the book.

49 Many democratic concepts taught by American schools during the period in which the United States had control have been enthusiastically received by the Filipinos.

50 In this section we have only considered two problems involving the conflict between indigenous social structure and Christian missions. There are a number of others, e.g. secret societies, tendency for group decisions (resulting in "mass movements"), strong family loyalties which are deterrents to individual decisions, hereditary or honorary designations to lead or pay for indigenous festivals having religious significance, inherited obligations to take revenge on traditional enemies, and the normal desire for social expression and acceptance, which in too many instances is inadequately provided for by the mission program. However, the two problems which have been treated, namely polygyny and church government, indicate the basic

factors and the principles which must be employed in resolving the difficulties.

51 If missionaries wish to transplant alien church structures, they must be much more thorough than they have been in most instances in the past. Some of the more effective techniques are considered in Chap. 9.

CHAPTER 6   DEVILS AND DOUBTS

1 However, for a number of years the Hawaiians had been acquainted with certain aspects of Western culture through frequent visits by crews of whaling vessels. No doubt these contacts played an important part in their rejection of the traditional religious system.

2 There are, of course, other forms of nontheism which are not animistic, e.g. some of the philosophical forms of Hinduism.

3 Strictly speaking, we should distinguish between (1) animism, which is the belief in the spirits or souls of humans (and in some instances animals) and (2) animatism, the belief in spirits living in inanimate objects. However, for the practical purposes of this type of book, we do not need to distinguish constantly between animism and animatism, since they are generally closely associated.

Animism and animatism are distinguishable from belief in *mana*, the impersonal supernatural power, which is not only characteristic of Melanesian and Polynesian religions but which underlies many Western ideas of good-luck charms. The prize fighter who attributes special "power" to an old pair of shoes and the pilot who insists on wearing a certain jacket when on combat flights believes in some impersonal, supernatural force which is associated with the objects in question.

We need to recognize the fact that an object such as a stone, glass bead, or metal ring may be regarded as the "abode" of either a spirit (animatism) or of impersonal power (mana). The subjective reaction of the "believer" will in the first instance be more readily characterized as "religious," while in the second his point of view is more closely related to our understanding of "scientific." (See footnotes 15 and 19 of this chapter.)

4 The word "fetish" is used to cover many distinct types of objects. There are so many different ways in which this term is used, that for the most part we avoid its use in this book. When, however, it is used, it implies the widest possible range of objects which are regarded as having or being indwelt by some sacred power.

5 "Theistic" is here used in a sense quite different from its conventional use in Christian theology.

6 Final judgment is, of course, only one aspect of the ethical nature of Christianity.

7 The later and more philosophically refined developments of Hinduism

see Brahman as somewhat more than a force. It is the first cause, the only reality, and the essence of being and bliss. Nevertheless, it is indeterminate, for any distinct definable qualities would, according to Hindu thought, limit and thus destroy its infinite character.

8 Hendrick Kraemer, *The Christian Message in a Non-Christian World* (New York and London: International Missionary Council, reprinted 1947), p. 178.

9 The use of the terms "revelational" and "nonrevelational" in this context does not imply any judgment as to whether or not such religions are true divine revelations. The terms are used here only as means of describing what the religions claim for themselves.

10 Perhaps it should be noted that we are not referring here to social exclusivism, but only to the theological aspects, though it is no doubt true that the theological exclusivism has had considerable influence upon the tendency toward social exclusivism.

11 This does not imply a relativity of belief. The Christian does and should regard his beliefs as true doctrines. It is only for the sake of scientific investigation and a sympathetic approach to other peoples that we should attempt not to stop inquiry by prejudicial vocabulary.

12 Edwin W. Smith (ed.), *African Ideas of God* (London: Edinburgh House Press, 1950). It is essential to distinguish between *henotheism* (the belief in one god, but without denying the existence of others) and *monotheism* (the belief that only one God exists).

13 Sacrifices may serve a number of purposes, e.g. provide food and animal companionship for the dead, nourishment for the gods, substances (such as blood, fat, and certain glands) which are necessary for additional rites, and meat for the people. In fact, in some cultures meat is rarely consumed except on such religious occasions.

14 W. R. Bascom, "The Focus of Cuban Santeria," *Southwest Journal of Anthropology*, Vol. 6, No. 1 (1950), pp. 64–68.

15 In the technical sense of the term it is inaccurate to speak of the religious beliefs and practices of nonliterate peoples as simply "animism" or of the people as being just "animists." Animism is actually not a religion, but a kind of religious belief. Such belief in spirit beings exists not only in the religions of nonliterate peoples, but in such highly organized religions as Hinduism, Mohammedanism, Judaism, and Christianity. Nevertheless, when we are dealing with religions in which animistic beliefs are predominant, we may use the terms "animism" and "animist," bearing in mind, however, the wide diversity of beliefs and practices which are present in such religious systems.

16 Leenhardt, *op. cit.*, p. 85.

17 Melville J. Herskovits, *Man and His Works* (New York: Alfred A. Knopf, 1948), p. 352.

18   Leenhardt, *op. cit.*, pp. 40 ff.

19   This does not mean that animism is an historical outgrowth of magic, but that magic forms the core around which animistic ritual is developed or functions. Magic is employed not only to control impersonal supernatural forces but to influence and coerce personal spirit beings. However, for a proper understanding of primitive religions it is important that one attempt to distinguish in so far as possible between the belief in spirit beings (animism) and the confidence in magic. Both magic powers and spirits are in a sense supernatural, but the emotional attitudes of the people toward these two features of the religious life may be rather distinct. Magic tends to create an awe similar to modern man's attitude toward the exploits of science. Magic may produce fear, but it does not challenge personal obedience. The belief in personal spirit beings does, however, touch the vital point of personal relationship and loyalty. To this extent, animism is more competitive with and antagonistic to Christian teaching, but magic is no less deeply rooted in people's consciousness, and is generally more persistent.

20   George Peter Murdock, *Our Primitive Contemporaries* (New York: The Macmillan Company, 1934), p. 217.

21   *Ibid.*, p. 128.

22   *Ibid.*, pp. 103–4.

23   Smith, *op. cit.*, pp. 268–69.

24   *Ibid.*, pp. 149–50.

25   Leenhardt, *op. cit.*, pp. 82–85.

26   In the skull rack on one of the large temples of Mexico City, Cortez' men found 136,000 skulls.

27   Nobody thought out in advance the rites which cluster about this cannon, they just "grew"—even in the Mohammedan city of Djakarta. However, the patterns conform closely to the whole system of animistic beliefs which pervade the thinking of the masses.

28   Analogic magic, which may be regarded as a subtype of imitative, is also rather widely used. For example, a person may put a large stone in his field so that his yams will be large.

29   No doubt some of these demonstrations, which are most common in India, are explainable in terms of sleight of hand, but others have never been satisfactorily explained on any known scientific basis.

30   This is reflected in the pointing, which the later Masoretes gave to the consonantal text.

31   Some anthropologists restrict the word "priest" to designate professional, full-time religious functionaries who are regarded as in some measure distinct from the common people by virtue of some rites of consecration. The word *shaman* also designates one who may

represent the people before deities, but in a somewhat less elaborate and formalized manner.

32 It is unquestionably true that from a medical standpoint much of primitive medicine has high psychotherapeutic value. Whether the treatment be sucking, piercing, or incantation, it is seldom confined to the act of a single individual, but rather of an entire group, including one's family, clan, or friends, all of whom work in favor of the sick person. In view of the fact that at least 50 per cent of medical patients in our society suffer from some psychosomatic ailment, it is unfortunate that our medical system does little to offer what primitive medicine provides in the way of psychotherapeutic help.

33 "Myth" is here used in its technical sense. One could also describe such figures of speech as based on prescientific assumptions.

34 By "construct" we refer to the total historical process.

35 Thompson, *op. cit.*, p. 123.

36 Whenever one particular image is credited with some special powers in contrast with another image of the same person, then the object is no longer an image but an idol, since the object possesses special powers of its own. That is to say, if the Virgin of one town is supposed to heal stomach trouble and the Virgin of another town is credited with miraculous powers for rheumatism, or if one Virgin is supposed to have more power than others, then the power is no longer residing in the Virgin as a person, but in the images, which have by this process become idols.

37 Shintoism had its origin in tribal animism, but it does not now teach certain animist practices, which are nevertheless maintained by the people.

38 It is accordingly not surprising that a relatively high number of students in Christian institutions in Japan adopt at least some of the more obvious forms and beliefs of Christianity without realizing the exclusiveness of the demands which orthodox Christianity has traditionally made. This is in no way a reflection upon the sincerity of the students. It is simply an indication of the fact that Japanese are not accustomed to thinking in terms of the exclusive demands of any set of religious beliefs.

39 Such religions as Zoroastrianism, Mithraism, some of the Greco-Roman mystery religions, and Sihkism are often included among the world religions, but we are limiting ourselves in this brief survey to only the more common and widespread religions.

40 Adherents of world religions are to some extent more self-conscious about their religious beliefs than are animists. A typical reaction of animistic people is, "We have no religion, just spirits." Even some missionaries have been inclined to minimize the indigenous religion because it had no elaborate forms or well-defined and easily describable concepts. For many animists religion is so automatic that it does

not seem to be a separate cultural feature. However, the automaticity and tendency for religious beliefs to be implicit rather than explicit are also true of many Confucianists and Hinduists, and hence such qualities cannot be taken as primarily characteristic of animistic beliefs.

41   Kraemer, *op. cit.*, p. 217.

42   *Ibid.*, pp. 164–66.

43   The same can also be said of many professing Christians.

44   Of course, the wax does not move at all; but if the worshiper is really convinced that he will receive the answer to his prayer, he is "physically" unable to stretch his arms as far as he did the first time. The psychological strength of his wishes and hopes are such as to condition his reach.

45   Howard F. Cline, *The United States and Mexico* (Cambridge: Harvard University Press, 1953), p. 20.

46   This must not be intrepreted to mean that qualifications for church membership should be drastically reduced or abolished, but it does mean that emphasis should be directed toward the work of the church, not the privilege of membership; and discipline should be largely handled by the congregation, not the missionary.

47   This does not mean that the missionary needs to express approval of all that the medicine man does, but it does mean that what is valuable and helpful to people should not be discarded or despised.

CHAPTER 7   DRUMS AND DRAMA

1   Murdock, *op. cit.*, p. 429.

2   Individuals differ greatly as to personal likes and dislikes, but in general the culture provides the broad patterns which channel personal responses.

3   Kroeber, *op. cit.*, pp. 331–36.

4   The flat side of the stone follows a line from near the chin to the crown of the head.

5   Herskovits, *op. cit.*, pp. 385–98.

6   That is to say, everything should be thoroughly tested.

7   Jesús Lara, *La Poesía Quechua* (Mexico: Fondo de Cultura Economica, 1947), pp. 159–60.

8   The numerous parallels with fertility cult dramas of the ancient world are quite evident. However, the Last Supper has its cultural and historical basis in the Hebrew "covenant meal."

9   Though the Pentecostal churches of Chile have been entirely independent of outside help and almost entirely free from missionary

influence, they have more than four times as many members as all the other evangelical churches combined.

10   One interesting contrast between these churches and others is that any empty seats in such Pentecostal churches are at the rear, while the front seats are crowded with those who are intent on participating as fully as possible in this folk drama.

11   See John V. Taylor's excellent article on "The Development of African Drama for Education and Evangelism" in *Africa*, Vol. 39 (1950), pp. 292–301.

12   *Ibid.*, p. 300.

CHAPTER 8   QUEER SOUNDS, STRANGE GRAMMARS, AND UNEXPECTED MEANINGS

1   Kroeber, *op. cit.*, p. 231.

2   *Ibid.*, p. 239.

3   Eugene A. Nida, *Learning a Foreign Language* (New York: National Council of the Churches of Christ in America, 1950), p. 17. The colon in the Ilamba data indicates length of vowel, but the distinctive tones of the syllables are not indicated.

4   *Ibid.*, p. 128.

5   Of course, individuals may differ widely as to speed of utterance, but the over-all averages of pronunciation are substantially equal.

6   For an introduction to the principles of phonemics see Kenneth L. Pike, *Phonemics* (Ann Arbor, Mich.: University of Michigan Press, 1947), and Nida, *op. cit.*, pp. 141–44.

7   The lists of membership in the various branches of the Indo-European languages do not include some of the smaller and less-known languages.

8   A family of languages includes all those languages which can be related in such a way as to indicate that they have come from a single source. Some groups of languages which are described as constituting separate families may have been related historically, but there is no available linguistic evidence of such.

9   So far as is known, the languages of Papua (New Guinea), Australia, and Tasmania are not related to Malayo-Polynesian.

10   There are some theories about the relationship of Basque to some of the languages of the Caucasus.

11   The apostrophes represent glottal catches, and the word is pronounced on a low tone.

12   Compare Greek *opisthe* which may refer to the future, but also means "behind." In this instance, however, the derivational development is somewhat different from what has occurred in Quechua.

13   Technically we should speak of the sounds which comprise the mor-
     phemes, the smallest units which have meaning, and then the con-
     structions consisting of the combinations of these morphemes in
     words, phrases, and sentences.

14   Many words were not borrowed direct, but came by way of other
     languages, e.g. *chocolate* and *tomato* came into English by way of
     Spanish.

15   This has happened not infrequently in some countries in Latin
     America.

16   There is fortunately a growing realization on the part of missionaries
     that proficiency in language is a "must." However, one cannot assume
     that there is a one-to-one correlation between language proficiency
     and the number of converts which will be won. The response of
     people to the message of the Gospel is dependent upon numerous
     cultural factors, as well as upon the work of the Holy Spirit.

17   Leenhardt, *op. cit.*, pp. 22–24.

18   Meaning "conception," "resurrection," and "circumcision" respec-
     tively.

19   Kroeber, *op. cit.*, p. 536.

20   The latest figures give approximately 65,000 Navajos, of whom not
     more than 25 per cent at the most can be regarded as being able to
     communicate effectively in English.

21   The traditional arguments about "translation" as legitimate and
     "paraphrase" as forbidden are really quite beside the point. It is not
     a matter of how many words are necessary to reproduce the meaning
     of the original, but the degree of fidelity with which the thought of
     the original is expressed in another language. It is not infrequent that
     a so-called paraphrase is far closer to the meaning of the original than
     a more tight-laced translation.

22   For a popular treatment of this subject, see Nida, *op. cit.*

CHAPTER 9   OLD CUSTOMS AND NEW WAYS

1   In using the phrase "moral order" we do not imply that the standards
    of any culture are "moral" in the ideal sense of the term. We are only
    contrasting this phase of culture from the technological one.

2   Redfield, *op. cit.*, pp. 23 ff.

3   Many of these concepts are found in the Bible, which itself clearly
    reflects some of the great cultural conflicts between the ancient civi-
    lizations and the moral orders of that day. However, this fact in no
    way invalidates the divine nature of the revelation.

4   Kluckhohn, *op. cit.*, p. 201.

5   Kroeber, *op. cit.*, p. 589.

6   Benedict, *op. cit.*, p. 237, *passim.*

7   Rather than describing cultures in terms of a single dominant and integrating drive, it is generally more satisfactory to treat a culture in terms of its "themes," those explicit or implicit factors which tend to control behavior and to stimulate activity. Such themes may include such complex "traits" as personal prestige, respect for old age, emphasis on physical prowess, high valuation of personal bravery, stoic disregard for suffering, and indifference as to material possessions. In some instances there may be contradictory and opposing themes operative within a single culture, sometimes producing sharply contrasting alternative possibilities of behavior and resultant frustration, and in other cases distinct patterns of behavior for different subcultures within the same society. The degree of integration of a single society depends largely upon the balancing and reciprocal interplay of its themes, which may reinforce, limit, or oppose each other. See Beals and Hoijer, *op. cit.*, pp. 216–18, and Morris E. Opler, "Themes As Dynamic Forces in Culture," *American Journal of Sociology*, Vol. 51, No. 3, pp. 198–206, 1945.

8   Kluckhohn, *op. cit.*, pp. 229 ff.

9   So-called "palace revolutions" which occur rather frequently in Thailand and in some countries in Latin America are primarily shifts of political power from one person or clique to another, but they do not entail any appreciable changes in social, political, or economic policy.

10 De Pedrals, *op. cit.*, p. 166.

11 Kraemer, *op. cit.*, p. 264.

12 There are so many social, political, economic, and geographical reasons for the differences between the Japanese and the Filipino attitudes. However, the ultimate basis of selectivity is essentially cultural.

   No foreign cultural trait will be accepted by people unless it appears to have some meaning or value to them. This principle is equally applicable to the Christian missionary or the sewing-machine salesman. This does not mean that the ultimate validity of Christianity is to be reckoned in terms of its pragmatic values, but certainly its presentation must be in the framework of its value to the person whom the missionary wishes to reach. Truth unrelated to life is neither appealing nor Biblical.

13 There is, however, a tendency to use the word "acculturation" to cover all types of cross-cultural change.

14 See p. 144.

15 See pp. 173–74.

16 This type of construction, however, is not the only type. In some instances the pyramids consisted only of hills, the sides of which were properly shaped and then covered with stone.

17   Leenhardt, *op. cit.*, pp. 106–7.

18   Robert H. Lowie, *Primitive Religion* (New York: Liveright Publishing Corporation, 1948, rev. ed.), p.80.

19   Herskovits, *op. cit.*, p. 553–54.

20   Kroeber, *op. cit.*, 468–71.

21   See pp. 13, 16–17, 20, 21, 90–91, 127–33, 177–80.

22   Kluckhohn, *op. cit.*, p. 172.

23   In a sense, however, the concept of progress stems from the Christian teaching of the Kingdom of God and the meaningful quality of life.

CHAPTER 10   NEW SOLUTIONS TO OLD PROBLEMS

1   Kraemer, *op. cit.*, p. 50.

2   In retrospect the failure of missions to meet more effectively the challenge posed by the Harris movement in West Africa is nothing less than tragic. Harris left Liberia toward the end of 1913 and was proclaimed a great prophet by the people of the Ivory Coast. He had remarkable powers to cure the sick and to heal people afflicted with various psychoneurotic troubles. He baptized well over 100,000 people and made much use of an English Bible, which he put on the head of each candidate, as he admonished him to have nothing to do with any religious teacher who did not have such a book. However, except for some rather limited efforts in restricted areas the great potential of this movement was lost since missions failed to follow up the work of Harris with constructive teaching and organization of believers.

3   The use of the "hypothetical situation" in order to obtain culturally pertinent reactions is very valuable in circumstances in which people are reticent to speak of or describe actual events. However, in all eliciting of information one must beware of the tendency for an informant to answer what he thinks the missionary wants or should hear rather than what is true to the cultural context. Furthermore, answers to "hypothetical situations" are likely to reflect ideal, not real behavior.

4   Kroeber, *op. cit.*, p. 412.

5   Similar programs have been developed by the late Bishop Lucas of Masasi, Tanganyika, and by Miss Mabel Shaw at Mbereshi, Northern Rhodesia. For a description of the Cewa program see Pauline Pretorius, M.D., "An Attempt at Christian Initiation in Nyasaland," *International Review of Missions,* Vol. 39 (1950), pp. 284–91.

6   The artificial retention of some older patterns may explain in part the opposition to and only partial success of Gutmann's experiments in Tanganyika. See Phillips, *op. cit.*, pp. 386–88.

INDEX